Good parents or good
 workers?

DATE DUE

MAY 6 9 2006			

Demco, Inc.' 38-293

Good Parents or Good Workers?

Good Parents or Good Workers?

How Policy Shapes Families' Daily Lives

Edited by

Jill Duerr Berrick

and

Bruce Fuller

GOOD PARENTS OR GOOD WORKERS?
© Jill Duerr Berrick and Bruce Fuller, 2005.

First published in 2005 by
PALGRAVE MACMILLAN™
175 Fifth Avenue, New York, N.Y. 10010 and
Houndmills, Basingstoke, Hampshire, England RG21 6XS
Companies and representatives throughout the world.

PALGRAVE MACMILLAN is the global academic imprint of the Palgrave Macmillan division of St. Martin's Press, LLC and of Palgrave Macmillan Ltd. Macmillan® is a registered trademark in the United States, United Kingdom and other countries. Palgrave is a registered trademark in the European Union and other countries.

ISBN 1–4039–6964–7

Library of Congress Cataloging-in-Publication Data

Good parents or good workers? : how policy shapes families' daily lives / Jill Duerr Berrick, Bruce Fuller, editors.
     p. cm.
Papers originally presented at a national conference sponsored by the Hass Jr. Fund of San Francisco in 2001.
Includes bibliographical references and index.
ISBN 1–4039–6964–7
1. Poor families—Government policy—United States. 2. Family policy—United States. 3. Public welfare—United States. I. Berrick, Jill Duerr.
II. Fuller, Bruce.

HV699.G66 2005
306.85'0973—dc22   2004060232

A catalogue record for this book is available from the British Library.

Design by Newgen Imaging Systems (P) Ltd., Chennai, India.

First edition: September 2005

10 9 8 7 6 5 4 3 2 1

Printed in the United States of America.

CONTENTS

ACKNOWLEDGMENTS

The original seed for this collection sprouted with a conference that illuminated the daily lives of poor families, sponsored by the Haas Jr. Fund of San Francisco. This convening of activists, policy analysts, scholars, journalists, and several women experiencing welfare reform first-hand offered the chance to corral the best qualitative research being conducted with low-income families across the nation, five years after the dramatic 1996 reforms. Special thanks are due Hedy Chang for supporting this initial idea of pulling together such a wide range of citizens and policy leaders, and to Jennifer Foulkes Coakley for her help in organizing the national conference and pulling together the authors whose work appear in this volume.

Bob Hass carefully aided the process of editing the chapters with his sharp pencil and equally sharp wit. Ken Eisinger and Cynthia King at the Berkeley Center for Child and Youth Policy handled the many tasks associated with crafting an edited volume. The Center is funded by the University of California and offers an opportunity for rich interdisciplinary exchange between faculty involved in children's research. Work on children's issues and welfare reform by the collaborating institute—Policy Analysis for California Education—was funded by the David and Lucile Packard Foundation and the Walter and Elise Haas Fund. The Haas families have consistently enhanced Berkeley's capacity to illuminate the problems facing low-income families, and to advance policy remedies. Thanks to Amanda Feinstein and Marie Young for their steady backing.

Jill Duerr Berrick
Bruce Fuller
Berkeley, California

ABOUT THE CONTRIBUTORS

Jill Duerr Berrick is codirector of the Center for Child and Youth Policy at the University of California, Berkeley, and a professor at the School of Social Welfare. She conducts research on various topics concerning poor children and families, and has authored or coauthored seven books on child abuse, foster care, and family poverty. Her book *Faces of Poverty: Portraits of Women and Children on Welfare* (Oxford University Press) focuses on welfare issues prior to the reforms of 1996. Another book, *The Tender Years* [with Barbara Needell, Richard Barth, and Melissa Jonson-Reid (Oxford University Press)], examines child-welfare policy for young children.

Laura Frame is a mental health worker and coordinator of the Therapeutic guidance for Infants and Families program at Children's Hospital and Research Center at Oakland. Her research interests include policy and practice reforms to the welfare and child welfare systems; poverty, parenting, and child neglect; and mental health and developmental interventions for very young children in the foster-care system. She is the author of several publications and reports on child welfare and welfare reform.

Karie Frasch is a senior research analyst at the Center for Child and Youth Policy at U.C. Berkeley where she studies work-family policies. Her research interests include the effectiveness of child welfare policies on permanency, the well-being of children in out-of-home care, normative development in transracial adoptive families, and child well-being in the context of family poverty.

Desiree French is a doctoral candidate in social and cultural studies at the University of California, Berkeley, and currently teaches courses in women studies at San Jose State University. As a research associate at Policy Analysis for California Education (PACE), she codirected the qualitative substudy of the Growing Up in Poverty Project. Her research and teaching interests include the impact of state policy on institutional change, how policy affects the daily lives of teachers and students, and the intersection of class, race, and gender in education.

Bruce Fuller is a professor of education and public policy at Berkeley. His work explores the decentralization of public policies and institutions, including schools, child care, and family support organizations. Fuller's most recent books include, with Susan Holloway, *Through My Own Eyes: Single Mothers and The Cultures of Poverty* and *Inside Charter Schools: The Paradox of Radical Decentralization* (both by Harvard University Press). He has codirected the Growing Up in Poverty Project with Susanna Loeb and Sharon Lynn Kagan since 1997.

Laura Lein is a professor at the School of Social Work and Department of Anthropology, The University of Texas at Austin. As a social anthropologist, her work has concentrated on the interface between families in poverty and the institutions that serve them. She is the author, with Kathryn Edin, of *Making Ends Meet: How Single Mothers Survive Welfare and Low-Wage Work* (The Russell Sage Foundation). Her most recent work focuses on low-income, nonresidential fathers, and on welfare reform and the experience of poverty among Texas families.

Andrew S. London is an associate professor of sociology at the Center for Policy Research at Syracuse University. His research focuses on the health, well-being, and care of stigmatized and vulnerable populations. He has contributed to studies on: The health of poor, urban women; the intersections of domestic violence and welfare reform; carework for children with chronic health problems in the context of welfare reform; and the effects on maternal welfare-to-work transitions on adolescent well-being.

James Mensing, a lawyer and developmental psychologist, is a senior research analyst at California's Center for Families, Children and the Courts, a research arm of the state court in San Francisco. Dr. Mensing also worked as a postdoctoral scholar at the University of California, Berkeley, studying the effects of welfare reform on mothers and young children.

Pamela A. Morris is a senior research associate at MDRC and a William T. Grant Foundation scholar. Her work focuses on the effects of welfare and antipoverty policies on children. Dr. Morris leads MDRC's effort to examine the effects of social policies on children's development. She has published numerous articles, including several that use cutting-edge analytic techniques to advance knowledge about the effects of income-based social policies on child development. Her newest work examines how changes in parents' depression affect the development of children and adolescents in low-income families.

David J. Pate, Jr. is a postdoctoral research fellow at the Institute for Research on Poverty at the University of Wisconsin, Madison, and director of the Center for Family Policy and Practice. Dr. Pate is a longtime practitioner and public policy advocate working on behalf of low-income adolescents, adult males, fathers, and families. He is a frequent presenter and the author of several articles regarding social services to minority males.

Anu Rangarajan is a senior economist and associate director of Research at Mathematica Policy Research, Inc. in Princeton, New Jersey. Her research expertise includes welfare policy and related issues, and she is the project director of the Evaluation of the Work First New Jersey Program.

Ellen K. Scott is an associate professor of sociology at the University of Oregon. Her research focuses on the intersections of gender, race, and class inequality. For the past several years, she has been involved in two large-scale studies of the impact of welfare reform on low-income women and their children. Scott has coauthored numerous articles and reports on a range of topics concerning single mothers, their children, and transitions brought about by welfare reform.

Allison Zippay is an associate professor in the School of Social Work at Rutgers University. Her research includes work in the areas of poverty, employment policy, and community development, and her qualitative and ethnographic studies encompass poor and low-income groups including teen mothers, welfare recipients, and working poor men.

FOREWORD

Policy makers and scholars have engaged in heated debates ever since the nation's welfare system was dramatically recast in 1996, especially on the question of how these reforms are touching the lives of parents and children. Too often these debates have simply reflected prior conceptions about the nature of poverty. Some look at the lives of the poor and say, "there but for the grace of God (or good luck), go I." Others look at the same reality and say, "I made it. Why can't they?" For those interested in a deeper understanding of poverty, we sorely need up-close studies of how the poor actually live, and how they cope with a lack of resources each and every day.

This book offers a wide, clear window into the lives of low-income families and shows how their pathways have been altered by welfare reform. The new requirement that mothers work in exchange for public assistance has produced new stresses in their lives, resulting in less time with their children and creating new work-related expenses for child care, transportation, and clothes. But the news is not all bad. As documented in this volume, these stresses are balanced, in many cases, by enhanced self-respect felt by women, serving to mitigate the possible negative effects of work on their children. Where both employment and family income have increased when mothers are able to find stable jobs or receive wage supplements from government the children appear to benefit as well.

What makes this volume especially valuable is the way it combines quantitative and qualitative data. We hear about the lives of these families from the parents themselves, through their own eyes. And their voices are compelling. Most of the mothers are simply exhausted from trying to juggle work and family. Moreover they tend to value their role as parents more than their role as workers. This produces enormous anxiety when they cannot find adequate and trustworthy child care or when their absence from home is extensive due to the need to work long hours, sometimes at more than one job. To improve the lives of these families will require not just a focus on work but on other supports: First and foremost good child care for their children. It also will require solid health care, shorter or more flexible hours, a higher minimum wage, or a more generous earned income tax credit. Although children are better off when they grow up with two married parents, promoting healthy marriage may not be as important as encouraging good parenting by fathers and mothers alike.

Another striking fact is the extent to which the more things change, the more they stay the same. Welfare reform has not altered the lives of these families as much as its proponents would like to believe. They still have extremely limited resources and a multitude of social problems, from drug abuse to depression, which complicate their lives. Their children do poorly in school and still display limited life chances. When researchers randomly assigned one group of families to a work program and the rest to a control group, what is striking is how little difference interventions focused on encouraging or requiring employment made.

As this book goes to press, the Congress is still debating what to do about the welfare bill that was enacted in 1996 and which now needs to be reauthorized. The big debates are about how much funding to provide for child care, how many hours single mothers should be required to work, and the extent to which encouraging marriage should be a priority. Those interested in learning more about how such measures would affect the way low-income families actually live and their ability to cope with their daily realities will find much valuable material in this volume.

Isabel V. Sawhill
Senior Fellow, The Brookings Institution
Washington, D.C.

Introduction

New Family Policy:
How the State Shapes Parents' Lives

JILL DUERR BERRICK AND BRUCE FULLER

Parents in America, until quite recently, crafted their daily lives according to their own moral commitments and economic interests, free of government intrusion. Yet these lives, especially those led by poor and working-class mothers and fathers, have become the subject of sharp public debate over the past generation. Following closely behind, increasingly aggressive policies have been enacted aimed at improving how parents lead their lives at home or work, even where and by whom their children are raised. Americans have rarely been so divided over the government's proper role in "fixing" the practices of families that don't seem to fit the mainstream.

Contradictions abound. While most Americans continue to worship the classically liberal motto, "Don't tread on me," when it comes to government meddling in their own private lives, they are equally ready to reshape the employment or parenting practices of those who are impoverished or somehow different. In this opening chapter, we examine the suddenly public engineering of parents' lives, assessing its causes and detailing its policy manifestations.

Few question that powerful economic and social forces are at work. The starting question is how policy makers interpret these forces and mobilize public institutions to support or tinker with the lives of parents and children. Take, for instance, the resurgent feminist movement in the 1970s, prompting the question of whether women should focus on being mothers or also pursue careers. European states have long shared the responsibility and cost of child care, paid family leave, and have provided help for single mothers. But the private aspirations of women and the public sector's role continue to be debated in America.

Still the revolution in women's roles contributed to the government's ability to turn family welfare policy upside down. In 1996, for instance, President Clinton and the Republican Congress eliminated low-income mothers' entitlement of minimal cash assistance, guaranteed for some since the Civil War. Being a good mother is no longer the moral imperative. The publicly sanctioned goal now is to turn mothers into workers. Raising one's infant or preschooler at home might be best for well-heeled families in the leafy suburbs. But for poor families, children should be moved into child care as their mothers search for a job. And the regulation of poor women's lives continues to intensify. As we finish this book, the Congress is debating a proposal, from a conservative president, under which the government would determine if taking one's child to the library or volunteering at the preschool is an allowable "work activity" to meet escalating employment requirements.

Certainly the steady incursion into parents' and children's lives is not explained by the victories of feminists, ironic as these dynamics have become. A growing public perception that millions of single mothers had grown dependent on welfare lent popular support to presidential candidate Bill Clinton's campaign slogan in 1992, "To end welfare as we know it." The wider push by New Democrats to move the party toward the center through "tough love" and "personal responsibility" proved enormously popular (DeParle, 2004). Indeed it was the political left that pioneered the supposition, back in the 1930s and then in the 1960s, that government "intervention" could improve the lives of poor families. And the booming economy of the 1990s provided necessary tax revenues to fund dramatic expansion of child care programs and allied work supports which contributed to shrinking welfare rolls and helped to legitimize more intrusive regulation of poor women's work and marital and child care behaviors.

Equally important, political conservatives have exhibited a new willingness to take the culture wars to Washington, shaking their Jeffersonian roots and crafting centralized policies that aim to right a society they believe is lurching toward moral decay. The domestic policy revolution—including welfare reform, child care legislation, child support enforcement, and new initiatives to encourage marriage—is as much about symbolic messages as it is about real economic and social support for families. Looking across these policy shifts, detailed later, the messages for women have become clear: Leave home, go to work, marry, and limit your child bearing. For men, the messages are a bit different. Men are urged, and now receive government incentives, to stay or head back home, get married, and exert themselves as responsible fathers.

These are obviously virtuous social goals. Few citizens or policy makers feel good about the dismal conditions confronting poor families in America. The starting questions are: How will policy makers frame the problem and how can government act efficaciously? The growing political will to engineer parents' moral beliefs and daily behavior implies a particular conception of the problem. Siding with President George W. Bush by voting for an even tougher set of work rules for mothers and against additional child care support in 2003, Senator Rick Santorum (R-Pennsylvania) said, "Making people struggle a little bit is not necessarily the worst thing" (Shogren, 2003). What he failed to mention is that the economy has only been creating minimum wage jobs for most women who leave the welfare rolls, and that three successive years of massive tax cuts, disproportionately benefiting wealthy families, have forced states to cut the child care supports these mothers need to go to work. Instead the plight of poor families is still simplistically blamed by some on the weakening of parents' moral fiber.

We begin this story by detailing how new family policy is attempting to change the daily lives of mothers and fathers. Then the original research reported in subsequent chapters illuminates how these policy interventions are or are not felt by parents and children. We also describe how broader economic and institutional forces that constrain the lives of poor families often eclipse the moral symbols and mechanical incentives now emanating from Washington, DC.

Work and the Good Mother

Public policy has long played a role in fashioning various supports for certain families. Over a half-century ago, the Social Security Act was established, in part, to provide cash to indigent women and children who had no other means of support. The fathers, absent due to death or abandonment, could no longer provide the economic support upon which families typically rely. So government aid was made available as an economic substitute. The government's message at that time was clear:

> [Aid to Dependent Children is] . . . designed to release from the wage-earning role the person whose *natural* function is to give her children the physical and affectionate guardianship necessary not alone to keep them from falling into social misfortune, but more affirmatively to make them citizens capable of contributing to society (Report of the Committee on Economic Security, 1935: 5–6, italics added).

Indeed lawmakers at the time referred to a woman's role in the home as her "highest duty" (see Berrick, 1996). In short, the good mother was the stay-at-home mother. That message has been recast over the past 60 years. Efforts in the 1960s encouraged women to join the labor market; efforts in the 1980s offered supports to women with school-age children who went to work and began to sanction those who did not. By the 1990s, the government's message was turned totally upside down. The good mother was no longer the stay-at-home mom; good motherhood was equated with the out-of-home worker who relied on others to raise her children. Wage labor was to bring stronger material and moral rewards than simply raising children.

Among the several political and cultural shifts that led to this new message for low-income mothers (for a review, see Abramovitz, 1988; Gordon, 1994), one powerful change stood out: The shift in the normative work behavior of middle-class American women. In 1950, just under a third of all women with school-age children were working full time; by the end of the century, more than three-quarters were engaged in the labor market. For women with young children, the change was equally dramatic. About one-tenth of women with children under age six were working full time in 1950, rising to almost 65 percent five decades later (U.S. Department of Health and Human Services, 2000; U.S. Department of Labor, 1999). Whether married or single, wage employment among mothers became the norm.

The 1996 welfare reform law, the Personal Responsibility and Work Opportunity Reconciliation Act (PRWORA), put real teeth into the government's message about the moral value of work outside the home. This law compelled low-income women to work in exchange for cash benefits, and for that work to be substantial—30 hours per week of paid employment. Moving from the previous generation's notion of dependence on a husband to the next generation's perceived dependence on the government, the shifting message of reform was truly about depending on work for moral and economic sustenance.

Legislators at the time equated work with independence, largely unaware or uninterested in data showing the instability of the low-wage labor market (Pavetti, 1997). Congressional debates presumed that work participation among low-income mothers would promote various benefits for children. They claimed that motherhood and family life would be strengthened through work, and that by encouraging mothers to work, they were counteracting the previous government policy that they perceived as "anti-family." For example, according to Congressman Sanford Bishop (R-Georgia):

> Our country is at a crossroads. We can go to the left and return to an irresponsible nonsense agenda that is anti-work, anti-opportunity, anti-family, and that breeds insecurity, dependency, and despair . . . I believe that not to go forward (with welfare reform) would cause us to aimlessly drift farther away from the core American values of work, personal responsibility, opportunity, stronger families, and communities (Congressional hearings, July 31, 1996).

Welfare recipients across the nation have heard the new call to work. In 1994, over five million families collected public cash assistance. A decade later, that number stands at about two million (Blank and Haskins, 2002; Weil and Finegold, 2002)—an astounding 50 percent drop in the welfare caseload nationwide. Some women may choose to avoid the new welfare system, finding alternative strategies to support their children; but among women who leave it, research from a variety of sources suggests that the vast majority are moving into jobs (Loprest, 2002).

Whereas the data suggest that men and women are actively responding to the new policy messages when it comes to work, less is known about how these changes are more deeply affecting their personal and family lives. How are daily relationships altered? How has the care of children shifted to kin or others? And how are men's and women's social bonds refashioned as parents take on new roles and responsibilities vis-à-vis the workplace and the family?

The new policy message that views mothers as workers also has strained their role as parents, often in already fragile families. Moving from welfare to work means less time to parent one's children and heavier psychological burdens as women juggle the needs of family with government work requirements (Loeb et al., 2004). We are not denying the *potential* rewards, economic and psychological, of maternal employment. But managing the demands of multiple roles, termed *role strain* by some analysts, can suppress women's satisfaction with their parental role and raise levels of depression (Tiedje et al., 1990).

Burris (1991) notes that many women identify more with their role as a mother than as a worker. And other researchers (Pleck, 1977) find that women, more than men, allow family issues to intrude upon their working lives. One of the primary forces moderating role strain is the fulfillment that women derive from their jobs: The more personally satisfying, and engaging the work, the less women experience their divergent roles as contradictory (Bielby and Bielby, 1989; Jones and Butler, 1980).

Not surprisingly, single mothers are most challenged by their dual roles. According to one study, these parents experienced more time pressure, stress, and anxiety than any other group (Burris, 1991). They also saw their family and their jobs as equally important. The challenges they faced may be explained, in part, by the fact that both roles held great meaning. The consequences of reducing one's responsibility for either of the roles would have serious and deleterious effects for them and for their children. Some suggest that many low-income women may favor traditional images of women as homemakers, in spite of their work outside the home, especially when faced with low-wage, unstable job prospects (Burris, 1991). Although ideologically drawn to one image, the practical realities of single parenthood often require an equal commitment of time and energy to the home and the workplace, and under welfare reform these dual commitments become all the more real.

New research, using qualitative methods, has begun to uncover the challenges women face and the strategies they devise to manage the competing demands of the workplace and the family. These studies—including those detailed in this volume—uncover variable webs of social supports, economic arrangements, and psychological coping mechanisms, which are used in order to maintain what many low-income women see as their priority: To be a parent first, a worker second.

When Mom Goes to Work, Where are the Kids?

As more low-income women move into the world of work, others must step in to care for their young children. Creation of the first national child care program in 1990 was an historic moment, two years after the Children's Defense Fund pushed both presidential candidates—George H. W. Bush and Michael Dukakis—to address women's child care needs. Both put forward significant proposals to expand child care and preschool programs to support a wider range of families than only half-day Head Start preschools for the poor. Since 1990, when the first President Bush signed into law the new child care program, total federal spending on early care and education has grown to $18 billion per year, attempting to accommodate women's new work roles and evolving conceptions of family.

Here too, the federal government encourages certain forms of child care, again shaped by certain moral beliefs that result in particular policy mechanisms. As central government alters the balance between parent and worker, public institutions must then step in and engineer where, how, and by whom young children are raised. The 1990 deal between the Bush White House and the Democratic Congress included a mandate on states that new child care dollars (including states' own matching funds) would be allocated to parents as portable vouchers. This was a major departure from the centralized focus on expanding quality preschools under Head Start and state early education initiatives. Vouchers are pro-choice in principle. Washington trusted that low-income parents would express demand for optimal forms of child care, even though such trust doesn't apply to reproductive or employment behaviors. Policy makers have more effectively encouraged the use of low-cost care by kin members and babysitters, who many mothers trust. In effect, the voucher policy mechanism also diverts dollars from efforts to strengthen center-based child care (Fuller et al., 2002). And ironically, this policy incursion also monetizes kin care—settings and relationships previously deemed as private.

Fifteen years after his father's child care legislation, George W. Bush's White House is pushing for aggressive regulation of how mothers spend time with their children. Under new welfare legislation proposed by Mr. Bush, and already approved by the House, mothers drawing cash aid would be required to engage in "allowable activities" for 40 hours each week. Since 1996, this has meant work and some training activities. But under the Bush bill, 16 hours per week could be spent by mothers engaged with their children in activities such as trips to museums, time together at child care, or meeting doctors' appointments—and Washington would dictate which activities were permissible, and which were not.

Governing Reproduction

Beyond the sphere of work, the "good mother" also must engage in certain reproductive behaviors. In previous decades, the government issued warnings to adolescents to carefully manage their fertility and reproduction (Lawson and Rhode, 1993). Today that message has been expanded to include all low-income women, regardless of age. Public policy on reproduction is now governed first by affordability considerations and only second by emotional or social gratification in pregnancy and parenting decisions (Zelizer, 1985); signifying policy makers' distaste for supporting large families at public expense.

The 1996 welfare reform encouraged states to implement "family caps." Under such provision, women who bear another child while on aid cannot collect additional funds for that child, effectively capping the monthly cash grant. Almost half the states have elected to implement a family cap. Congressional debate on this issue at the time proved to be ill informed, if not intentionally misleading. For instance, Congresswoman Marge Roukema (R-New Jersey) stated at the time:

> This bill keeps the family cap in place, which means that mothers on welfare don't get extra cash benefits for having babies. In other words, the United States will no longer be the only nation in the western world that pays young girls to have babies (Congressional hearings, July 17, 1996).

In fact the United States is one of only a handful of western nations that does *not* provide a cash allowance for each child born into a family (Kamerman and Kahn, 1997). Further the average age of women receiving aid is 31 years; only 7 percent of adult welfare recipients were adolescents in 2003 (Office of Family Assistance, 2003)—hardly the "young girls" to which the congresswoman refers.

Regardless of the rhetoric at the time, the family cap policy may be exerting effects on poor women's behavior. Some studies suggest that its imposition modestly dampens the likelihood of a future birth while increasing the likelihood of abortion (O'Neill, 1994; Camasso, 1998; Rutgers University, 1998). Other studies suggest that in some states, where the family cap has been in effect for several years, almost half of single-mother welfare recipients are unaware of the policy (Reardon et al., 2002).

While the family cap may be targeted at women, its effects are absorbed by the youngest children in the welfare system. And since an accumulation of research evidence suggests that poverty experienced in the early years of life can be especially hazardous to children's long-term well-being (Duncan and Brooks-Gunn, 1997), the family cap may be one of the most risky family policies arising out of the 1990s. For women who do not hear or heed the government's message on childbearing, the cap is a rather blunt instrument of public policy and likely to have deleterious effects on vulnerable infants who will, by explicit design, become more deeply impoverished.

Women, Men, and Marriage

The new policy incentives that discourage childbirth have been coupled with government efforts to encourage marriage—which would seemingly boost fertility rates. The emphasis on marriage derives from particular moral values and a conceptual framework that links healthy marriages to better child outcomes (Dion and Devaney, 2003). The policy thrust also stems from a narrow interpretation of well-established research findings.

The data are clear: Rates of poverty for children raised in single-parent families are very high. Of all children residing in single-parent households in 2000, 40 percent lived at or below the official poverty line. Poverty rates were highest for families with children under age five (U.S. Census Bureau, 2001). The income gap between single versus two-parent families is also significant. The poverty rate for children raised in single-parent households is five times greater than that for children raised in two-parent families (Cancian and Meyer, 2002). And the effects of poverty are greatest for younger children, for the most impoverished families, and when bouts with poverty are long-lasting (for a review, see Duncan and Brooks-Gunn, 1997).

Some researchers have advanced the notion that marriage alone will reduce poverty by up to 25 percent among unwed mothers (Lerman, 2001; Thomas and Sawhill, 2001). Lerman's research (2001), in particular, suggests that material hardship, including food scarcity and housing security, could be notably improved if poor women simply married. So in an effort to persuade low-income parents to marry, the most recent Bush Administration has forwarded the "marriage initiative" (The White House, 2002) as part of a strategy to further reform welfare.

Under the Bush Administration's proposal, federal funding would be available to offer training, education, advertising, and mentoring to promote healthy marriages. In addition, funding would be provided to test demonstration projects aimed at encouraging healthy unions (Fremstad and Neuberger, 2002). The President's initiative is based upon demonstration projects already underway in several states. In Oklahoma, for example, federal TANF[1] (i.e., welfare) monies are used to support marriage promotion rallies and forums organized by "marriage ambassadors" (Oklahoma Marriage Initiative, 2002). The state of Utah has developed a video promoting marriage, sponsors a Commission on Marriage, and has set aside a "marriage week" (Washington Post, 2001). Arizona's state government has used TANF funds to develop a "marriage handbook" (Ganow, 2001), and Arkansas has declared a "marriage emergency" (Washington Post, 2001).

While identification of the poverty problem for children living in single-parent households is clear, a solution depending largely on marriage may not be sufficient. European nations similarly assess the problem of child poverty, yet in most of these countries, the policy solution revolves around wage increases, income transfers, and family support (Gornick and Meyers, 2003; Kamerman and Kahn, 1997). Of course it remains unclear whether marriage per se advances the quality of women's and children's lives (Scott et al., 2002). Still, intensifying policies designed to shape "family formation" are another indication of how aggressive government has become in recasting women's basic roles and daily lives.

Fathers as Breadwinners and Parents

While much of the 1996 welfare reforms centered on women—their role vis-à-vis the workplace, the unborn, and the men in their lives—government incursion into family life did not stop there. Through the child support and paternity establishment provisions, men were singled out as pieces of the family-formation puzzle. The precedent for government involvement in crafting fathers' roles arose first within states during the Progressive Era, then again in the 1950s with legislation enabling the collection of financial support for dissolved marriages (Gordon, 1994; Mason, 1994). Fundamental reform occurred in 1975 with the founding of the Child Support Enforcement Program, strengthened in the mid-1980s and again under the Family Support Act of 1988 (Sonenstein et al., 1993). Each policy initiative aimed to strengthen child support collection and fully disclose the identity of children's fathers.

The 1996 welfare reform initiative attempted to further strengthen these policies. Now rather than encouraging low-income mothers to disclose a father's identity, women are required to do so as a condition of aid. Further child support collection strategies have been emboldened with the implementation of automated systems, new-hire directories, and state allowances to withhold professional licenses, passports, and other legal documents as a means of pushing absent fathers to make good on their financial obligations.

The premise behind these efforts is on the one hand economic; indeed, the financial side of the equation is pivotal. According to official estimates, $23 billion was owed in child support payments in 2000, only $13 billion of which was collected (U.S. Department of Health and Human Services, 2001). Sorenson (1997) suggests that these numbers underestimate the potential for child support collection, as they only include those families already in the child support system. Instead she suggests that over $20 billion additional dollars might have been collected annually if all absent parents had paid their child support obligations.

Whether child support payments make a substantial difference in the financial lives of otherwise poor families is debatable, however. Some studies suggest that child support collection moves 5–7 percent of low-income women above the poverty threshold (Sorensen and Zibman, 2000). Nevertheless it appears that early results from PRWORA show that low-income, never-married mothers are seeing increases in child support establishment and payment by absent fathers (Sorensen and Oliver, 2002).

Overall, the fatherhood components embedded in the 1996 welfare law are grounded in a deep philosophical belief that "deadbeat dads" should play a more active role in their children's lives. The work of Blankenhorn (1995), Popenoe (1996), and others may have influenced congressional debates on the role of fathers in families' lives, as these authors contend that father absence may be the precursor to other social problems, including teen pregnancy, high school dropouts, and poverty. The political left also has embraced the notion that fathers are able to, and morally should, play a renewed role in the lives of their children (Ehrenreich, 1983). Taken together, these similar themes represent a "centrist discourse" on fatherhood (Curran, 1999, p. 5), which is more similar than dissimilar in its call for active involvement of fathers in childrearing. The empirical question remains; What policies are being felt by fathers and with what sustained effect?

Although uniformly heralded as beneficial for children, the assumptions underlying father involvement may neither accurately reflect diverse fathers' interests or capacities, nor actual effects on children's well-being. Some research suggests that extremely involved fathers may strengthen children's academic and social–emotional development, although the number of these heavily invested fathers in American society remains quite small (Pleck, 1997).

Some researchers (Amato and Booth, 1997; Furstenberg and Cherlin, 1991) argue instead that fathers' presence may have little if any impact at all on children, beyond the influence of the mother. One perspective suggests that the effects of father presence can be muted or absent under many conditions. According to this work, father presence appears to make the greatest positive difference for children when fathers "have supportive and nurturant relationships with (their children) . . . when they are competent and fulfilled breadwinners, when they are successful and supportive partners" (Lamb, 1997, p. 13).

But to what extent do these properties characterize the vast majority of low-income men owing child support? And does more intense regulation of fatherhood lead to behavioral change that aids mothers and children? Clearly the "fulfilled breadwinner" category may be compromised for many. According to one study, in 1999, 40 percent of low-income nonresident fathers had not completed high school, over 40 percent had been jobless for over a year, and 25 percent had a health condition limiting their employment (Sorenson, 2002). The capacity of noncustodial fathers to pay child support is likely greater, on average, than the amount they actually pay, nationwide, but there is great variability in terms of poverty status, marital status, and ethnicity. Low-income men are especially challenged to pay a great deal toward supporting their children (Miller et al., 1997).

We know very little about fathers' experiences and capacities vis-à-vis their affective relationships with their children and their former partners. The recent policy reforms were designed to convey a strong message to fathers regarding their obligations to children. How men are responding to these public affirmations of fatherhood, however, is not well understood; and how women regard these forced familial arrangements has largely been ignored in policy debates. Here again, new ethnographic research is illuminating how mothers and fathers alike are experiencing these dramatic policy shifts.

Through Parents' Own Eyes:
Which Policies Really Matter?

Longitudinal evidence continues to emerge on the effects of welfare reform and allied policies that shape the daily lives of families. As described earlier, employment rates are up, receipt of cash aid is down, and child support payments are on the rise. But these phenomena, informed by large-scale surveys, only dimly illuminate the daily lives, perceptions, and reasoning of low-income parents. As child care, welfare, and family policies evolve over time, researchers are beginning to uncover the lived experiences of mothers and fathers as they struggle to integrate or adapt to the demands of the market and of government regulators. And as Congress, state governors, and legislatures again take up a range of family policy proposals, the new work detailed in this volume brings to light parents' own words and insights into how these policy thrusts actually touch their lives.

This new qualitative research is typically embedded in multi-method studies of low-income families, welfare reform, and the growth of child care initiatives in the wake of the 1996 reforms. The qualitative studies included in this volume come from two national and three state studies of policy reforms, typically done in tandem with quantitative analyses. This book focuses on how women and men are reading the policy signals, rules, and incentives as they attempt to raise their children and earn sufficient income to hold their families together. In short, this volume places the panoply of family policies in the context of the daily demands faced by these parents.

The book is divided into three themes centered around *women's roles as workers and mothers, policy effects on children*, and the *evolving role of fathers* vis-à-vis their families. By amplifying parents' voices and perspectives, we brightly illuminate the human-scale experience and feelings of those parents on the receiving end of welfare reforms.

In Section 1, we examine the changing role of women vis-à-vis the workplace and their newly adjusted roles as parents. Laura Lein draws upon 14 years of related ethnographic studies to uncover the principal features that characterize family life among the poor. First as women struggle to parent with scarce material resources, the rich complexity of daily life is revealed. Women manage an array of public and private agency demands and expectations in order to qualify for a patchwork of cash and in-kind assistance. As they move into the labor market, their reliance on outside aid may shift, but it rarely diminishes. Consequently these now *working* low-income women are challenged even more intensively to meet the demands of parenthood. Working women spend less time with their children, work more, yet still negotiate a complex set of agencies in order to make ends meet.

Desiree French, Bruce Fuller, and Jim Mensing help us see the central role children play in mothers' lives as women attempt to meet children's needs first, and then turn to the world of work. Whether decisions revolve around child care options, educational support, or neighborhood safety, women regularly return to the needs of their children in assessing their current circumstances or their future opportunities for work.

Laura Frame explores those families who struggle most with the demands of parenting in an environment of economic deprivation. Her sample of families includes parents who are receiving or have received TANF, some who are involved in the child welfare system for reasons of child maltreatment.

Frame attempts to uncover the unique role poverty may play in parenting capacity and suggests that in some families, poverty's influence may be so handicapping that it interferes with parenting abilities.

Section 2 offers two chapters that delve into the effects on children as women attempt to parent in an environment in which they are pressed for time and money. Pamela Morris, Ellen Scott, and Andrew London use qualitative data to complement their quantitative findings on the effects of welfare reform on children. They examine both the role of increased income and that of increased work effort on elementary school-age children and tease out the distinct consequences as parents reduce their time with children during the transition.

Karie Frasch investigates the paths that lead children toward positive or negative well-being in the new policy environment. Examining factors that contribute to children's well-being, Frasch focuses on how women experience highly variable social supports, psychological health, and personal finances, all exerting sometimes subtle and at other times overt influences on their parenting practices.

In the third section, we explore the role of fathers in low-income families' lives. Allison Zippay's and Anu Rangarajan's work speaks of mothers' perspectives on the new policies that encourage or enforce fathers' participation in the lives of their children. In some instances, their participation in family life and in the household economy is most welcome. These authors show how fathers and mothers negotiate time with children, parenting responsibilities, and mutual financial obligations, using systematic or haphazard strategies. For other families, however, fathers' involvement—spurred on by the state—can create additional complications for which the family may be unprepared.

The final chapter in Section 3 includes the voices of men who are attempting to respond to the new policy messages about responsible fatherhood. These men struggle daily with an interest in supporting their children both economically and emotionally, yet do so—in many cases—against the odds. David Pate lays out the complicated set of issues men face as they battle against societal representations of the "bad father" and attempt to live out the role of the "good father" for their children.

As low-income women and men attempt to balance their evolving roles as parents and providers, they must simultaneously meet multiple challenges and adapt to changing circumstances and government policies. Some families are indeed benefiting from the family policy reforms of the 1990s; others still struggle mightily. Parenting in the context of poverty, including dismal neighborhoods, poor schools, and the panoply of other challenges associated with persistent poverty raises daunting problems for even the most resourceful of families. How these overburdened parents fare with a new overlay of work and family responsibilities can be instructive as new iterations of reform are considered for the next generation. Let's turn to their stories, as seen through their own eyes.

Note

1. TANF stands for Temporary Assistance to Needy Families. The name change, from AFDC (Aid to Families with Dependent Children), is a result of the 1996 federal welfare reform law, the Personal Responsibility and Work Opportunity Reconciliation Act. A number of changes in welfare policy resulted from the Act. For more information, see Weil and Finegold (2002).

References

Abramovitz, M. (1988). *Regulating the lives of women: Social welfare policy from colonial times to the present.* Boston: South End Press.

Amato, P. R. and Booth, A. (1997). *A generation at risk: Growing up in an era of family upheaval.* Cambridge, MA: Harvard University Press.

Berrick, J. D. (1996). From mother's duty to personal responsibility: The evolution of AFDC. *Hastings Women's Law Review Journal, 7*(2), 257–273.

Bielby, W. T. and Bielby, D. D. (1989). Family ties: Balancing commitments to work and family in dual earner households. *American Sociological Review, 54,* 776–789.

Blank, R. and Haskins, R. (eds.) (2002). *The new world of welfare.* Washington, DC: The Brookings Institute.

Blankenhorn, D. (1995). *Fatherless America: Confronting our most urgent social problem.* New York: Harper Collins Publications.

Burris, B. H. (March, 1991). Employed mothers: The impact of class and marital status on the prioritizing of family and work. *Social Science Quarterly, 72*(1), 50–66.

Camasso, M. J. (1998). *A final report on the impact of New Jersey's family development program: results from a pre–post analysis of the AFDC case heads from 1990–1996.* Unpublished document. New Jersey: Rutgers University School of Social Work.

Cancian, M. and Meyers, D. R. (2002). Responding to changing family organization. *Focus, 22*(1), 87–92.

Curran, L. (1999). *Deadbeat dads and down-and-out daddies: Contemporary social welfare interventions into men's fathering.* Unpublished manuscript. Berkeley, CA: University of California at Berkeley, School of Social Welfare.

DeParle, J. (2004). *American dream.* New York, NY: Viking.

Dion, R. and Devaney, B. (2003). *Strengthening relationships and supporting healthy marriage among unwed parents.* Princeton, NJ: Mathematica Policy Research, Inc.

Duncan, G. J. and Brooks-Gunn, J. (eds.) (1997). *Consequences of growing up poor.* New York: Russell Sage Foundation.

Ehrenreich, B. (1983). *The hearts of men: American dreams and the flight from commitment.* New York: Russell Sage Foundation.

Fremstad, S. and Neuberger, Z. (June 6, 2002). *Side by side comparison of family formation provisions in TANF reauthorization legislation.* Washington, DC: Center on Budget and Policy Priorities.

Fuller, B., Kagan, S. L., Caspary, G. L. and Gauthier, C. A. (2002). Welfare reform and child care otions for low-income families. *Future of Children, 12*(1), 97–119.

Furstenberg, F. F. and Cherlin, A. J. (1991). *Divided families: What happens to children when parents part.* Cambridge, MA: Harvard University Press.

Ganow, M. (August, 2001). Family formation resources for welfare decisions. Welfare Information Network. www.welfareinfo.org/familyformation.htm.

Gordon, L. (1994). *Pitied but not entitled: Single mothers and the history of welfare.* Cambridge, MA: Harvard University Press.

Gornick, J. C. and Meyers, M. K. (2003). *Families that work: Policies for reconciling parenthood and employment.* New York: The Russell Sage Foundation.

Jones, A. P. and Butler, M. C. (1980). A role transition approach to the stress of organizationally induced family role disruption. *Journal of Marriage and the Family, 42,* 367–376.

Kamerman, S. and Kahn, A. (eds.) (1997). *Family change and family policies in the West.* New York: Oxford University Press.

Lamb, M. E. (1997). Fathers and child development: An introductory overview and guide. In M. E. Lamb (ed.), *The role of the father in child development.* New York: John Wiley & Sons, Inc.

Lawson, A. and Rhode, D. L. (eds.) (1993). *The politics of pregnancy: Adolescent sexuality and public policy.* New Haven: Yale University Press.

Lerman, R. (2001). *Marriage as a protective force against economic hardship.* Paper presented at the 23rd Annual Research Conference of the Association for Public Policy Analysis and Management, Washington, DC, November 1–3.

Loeb, S., Fuller, B., Kagan, S. and Carrol, B. (2004). Child care in poor communities. *Child Development, 75,* 47–65.

Loprest, P. (2002). Making the transition from welfare to work: Successes but continuing concerns. In A. Weil and K. Finegold (eds.), *Welfare reform: The next act.* Washington, DC: The Urban Institute. pp. 17–32

Mason, M. (1994). *From father's property to children's rights: The history of child custody in the United States.* New York: Columbia University Press.

Miller, C., Garfikel, I., and McLanahan, S. (1997). Child support in the U.S.: Can fathers afford to pay more? *Review of Income and Wealth, 43*(3), 261–281.

Office of Family Assistance. (2003). *Temporary assistance for needy families: Fifth annual report to Congress.* Washington, DC: Administration for Children and Families.

Oklahoma Marriage Initiative. (July 15, 2002). www.governor.state.ok.us/policy.htm.

O'Neill, J. (1994). *Report concerning New Jersey's Family Development program.* Unpublished paper. New York, NY: CUNY, Baruch College, Department of Economics.

Pavetti, L. (July, 1997). *How much more can they work? Setting realistic expectations for welfare mothers.* Washington, DC: The Urban Institute.

Pleck, J. G. (1977). The work–family role system. *Social Problems, 24,* 417–427.

Pleck, J. G. (1997). Paternal involvement levels, sources, and consequences. In M. E. Lamb (ed.), *The role of the father in child development.* New York: John Wiley & Sons, Inc.

Popenoe, D. (1996). *Life without father: Compelling new evidence that fatherhood and marriage are indispensable for the good of children and society.* Cambridge, MA: Harvard University Press.

Reardon, E., DeMartini, C., and Klerman, J. A. (2002). *Statewide CalWORKs evaluation: Results from the California Health and Social Services survey.* Unpublished document. Santa Monica, CA: Rand Corporation.

Report of the Committee on Economic Security. (1985). Reprinted in *50th Anniversary issue, the Report of the Committee on Economic Security of 1935 and other basic documents relating to the Social Security Act.* Washington, DC: National Conference on Social Welfare.

Rutgers University. (1998). *A final report on the impact of New Jersey's Family Development program: Results from a pre-post analysis of AFDC Case Heads, 1990–1996.* New Brunswick, NJ: Rutgers University.

Scott, E. K., Edin, K., London, A. S., and Mazelis, J. M. (2002). My children come first: Welfare-reliant women's post-TANF views of work-family trade-offs and marriage. *For better and for worse.* New York: Russell Sage Foundation.

Sorenson, E. (1997). A national profile of nonresident fathers and their ability to pay child support. *Journal of Marriage and the Family, 59*(4), 785–797.

Sorenson, E. (2002). Helping poor nonresident dads do more. Assessing the New Federalism. Short Takes on Welfare Policy, (3). Washington, DC: Urban Institute.

Sorensen, E. and Oliver, H. (2002). Child support reforms in PRWORA: Initial impacts. Assessing the new federalism. Discussion Paper 02–02. Washington, DC: The Urban Institute.

Sorensen, E. and Zibman, C. (2000). To what extent to children benefit from child support? Assessing the new federalism. Discussion Paper 99–19. Washington, DC: The Urban Institute.

Sonenstein, E., Halcomb, P., and Seefldt, K. (1993). What works best in improving paternity rates? *Public Welfare, 51*(4), 26–33.

Thomas, A. and Sawhill, I. (2001). *For richer or for poorer: Marriage as an antipoverty strategy.* Brookings Institution Working Paper. Washington, DC: Brookings Institution.

Tiedje, L. B., Wortman, C. B., Downey, G., Emmons, C., Biernat, M., and Lang, E. (1990). Women with multiple roles: Role-compatibility perceptions, satisfaction, and mental health. *Journal of Marriage and the Family, 52,* 63–72.

U.S. Census Bureau. (2001). *Age, sex, household relationship, race and Hispanic origin—poverty status of people by selected characteristics in 2000.* www.ferret.bls.census.gov.

U.S. Department of Health and Human Services. Office of the Assistant Secretary for Planning and Evaluation. (2000). *Trends in the well-being of America's children and youth.* Washington, DC: Government Printing Office.

U.S. Department of Health and Human Services. Office of Child Support Enforcement. (2001). http://www.acf.dhhs.gov/programs/cse.

U.S. Department of Labor, Bureau of Labor Statistics. (February 3, 1999). *Labor force participation of fathers and mothers varies with children's ages.* http://www.bls.gov/opub/ted/1999/Jun/wk1/art03.htm.

Washington Post. (2001). Help before the honeymoon. February 25, C1.

Weil, A. and Finegold, K. (2002). *Welfare reform: The next act.* Washington, DC: The Urban Institute.

The White House. (February 2002). *Working toward independence.* Washington, DC: Author.

Zelizer, V. A. (1985). *Pricing the priceless child: The changing social value of children.* New York: Basic Books.

SECTION I

The Good Worker/The Good Mother

CHAPTER ONE

Barriers to Self-Sufficiency: Are Wages and Welfare Enough?

Laura Lein

Low-income mothers are caught in a conundrum: Neither the income from the jobs they get, nor welfare—when they are eligible and can receive it—is sufficient to support their households. The pressures of their situation are exacerbated by at least three aspects of their lives: The need to deal with multiple agencies and complex bureaucracies in order to gain the goods and services they need for their families; the combination of their own and their children's heightened probability of medical conditions coupled with irregular access to medical insurance; and the frequent household and community crises that sap their personal and financial resources.

The last few years of welfare reform have been based on the assumption that the mother's employment can go a long way to raise an impoverished single-parent family out of poverty and stabilize it. Programs in many states (Nathan and Gais, 2002), such as Texas' "Work First" program (Schexnayder et al., 1998), are aimed to move mothers off welfare and into the labor force, in an effort to move them to economic self-sufficiency and out of poverty. However recent large-scale studies of welfare leavers both nationwide (Acs and Loprest 2001; Isaacs and Lyon, 2000; Joyce Foundation, 2002) and in Texas (Schexnayder et al., 2002) indicate that although welfare reform has changed women's and children's lives, in particular by reducing the welfare roles substantially, it has not lifted them out of poverty.

Nor, according to other ethnographic studies (Newman, 1999, 2001) as well as the work discussed here, has it led to independence from public and private assistance. Both mothers who have recently left welfare and mothers in low-income jobs with little welfare history find it nearly impossible to raise their children without some use of Food Stamps, Medicaid, WIC, and other federal-state programs, the occasional assistance of local programs, and support from relatives and close friends. Thus although policy makers have tended to focus on low-income mothers as earners, these mothers can rarely, if ever, support themselves and their children solely on the income provided either by low-wage work or by welfare cash transfers (Edin and Lein, 1997, 1998).

Furthermore much of our poverty policy is based on a somewhat unidimensional picture of low-income mothers as family breadwinners. Mothers themselves are much more focused on their mothering than on their economic self-sufficiency. Rather than make decisions about their children and family life based on employment possibilities, they are more likely to make decisions on employment based on what is best for their children (Garey, 1999; Henly and Lyons, 2000). This concentration on parenting leads mothers simultaneously to seek from many sources what they need for their children in order to parent effectively while poor. When the income from the available jobs cannot support their households, or when the exigencies of family responsibilities make regular employment difficult to sustain, they seek out other sources for what their families need.

The Studies

In this chapter, I draw on ethnographic data from several studies based in San Antonio, Texas, over the last 14 years. Each of them involved participant observation and interviews with impoverished single-parent families and a team of researchers with whom I collaborated. Also each was concerned, at least in part, with the strategies that single mothers used to draw together the goods and services their families required. These studies illustrate some of the continuing realities faced by mother-headed families in poverty.

While some of the examples are as much as 14 years old, more recent work indicates that many elements of life for poor families have not changed markedly, even though the work and welfare options available to them have undergone considerable change. Low-income single-parent families in San Antonio continue to maintain their households through their efforts at putting together resources from their informal employment, assistance from agencies and organizations, and support from friends and relatives (Edin and Lein, 1996, 1997). In few cases can these families remain economically viable and independent of assistance from these sources, whether they are welfare-dependent or include someone with a formal sector job.

The earliest study was conducted in San Antonio. It included initial fieldwork[1] and the detailed, ethnographically oriented interviews[2] that contributed to the volume *Making Ends Meet* (Edin and Lein, 1997). This work started with participant observation in 1989, and continued during the early 1990s with intensive interviews with single mothers in four cities, one of which was San Antonio. Although there were distinctive differences among the cities (Edin and Lein, 1996), we also discovered core similarities in how impoverished mothers supported their families. In this chapter, I draw most heavily on my record of participant observation during the first summer of my fieldwork in San Antonio.

In 1999, the second study[3] included detailed ethnographically oriented interviews with families in six Texas cities, who had recently left welfare or had been diverted from welfare during the application process. One of the six cities was San Antonio. During the course of this work (Schexnayder et al., 2002), we found that the constraints under which poor Texas families operated were such that changes in the TANF program appeared to have little long-term impact on their economic status, or on the kinds of strategies they brought to bear on the problems they faced. In this chapter, I draw on interviews with the San Antonio families, which were structured in ways very similar to those used in *Making Ends Meet*.

In 1998, we undertook a third investigation, a series of ethnographic interviews with families in San Antonio,[4] as part of the larger study, *Welfare, Children, and Families: A Three-City Study*. My work, with a team of ethnographers in San Antonio, was part of a much larger effort to track the impact of welfare reform among low-income families in three cities. Ethnographic work was combined with a larger two-wave survey, a neighborhood ethnography, and studies focused on the development of young children, and on families including a member with a disability (Johns Hopkins University, 2002; Winston, 1999). I draw here on the interviews with San Antonio families, through which we tracked households with monthly visits over an 18-month period to understand in detail the ways in which welfare reform affected household strategies. We looked particularly at how families negotiated the welfare–work transition (Lein et al., 2002), and the impact of those strategies on family life.

One role of ethnographic research is to debunk single-issue images of poor families and provide greater insight into the more complex picture that is the reality of their lives (Henly and Danziger, 1996). To the extent that public policy is formed in response to a limited set of over-simplified myths about the poor, it can fail to address the multiple issues, double-binds, and crises that are endemic to living in poverty in the United States. Ethnographic research can show us the ways in which the complex problems faced by low-income families evoke complicated responses from them, and require more thoughtful policy responses.

Although the strategies that low-income single mothers bring to bear in support of their families may do the job for a period, families are left fragile and vulnerable to the impact of even minor crises. Here we will explore several kinds of experiences that occur frequently in the lives of low-income single parents: Experiences dealing with multiple agencies; experiences dealing with health problems in the context of the U.S. medical care system; and the aftermaths of household emergencies. Although the work described here is San-Antonio-based, it has considerable applicability to life issues in most parts of the United States, as shown later.

San Antonio: The Field Site

Texas and San Antonio are certainly no different than the rest of the country in terms of the core economic difficulties facing low-income single mothers. Both before and after welfare reform, women have found it difficult, if not impossible, to make ends meet for their family with either the resources offered by a low-wage job, or the benefits offered by welfare (Edin and Lein, 1997). In the state of Texas, with welfare benefits being among the lowest in the nation (Texas Department of Human Services, 2003), and its own state minimum wage (until it adopted the federal guidelines in 2001) being considerably less than the federal minimum wage, the pressures remain heavy for single mothers trying to sustain a household.

On researching several cities (San Antonio among them), we discovered what low-income mothers have known all along—that they could not make it on either paid employment available to them or on welfare. They engaged in a range of activities that included elements of both work and welfare, combined with the assistance offered by small community-based organizations and their informal networks. Putting these resource nets together took considerable time, energy, and creativity. Furthermore the networks were fragile— they often depended on the good health, good will, and resources of small underfunded organizations and relatives who themselves were impoverished.

I first learned about the details and complexities of these packages, as experienced by families in Texas, 14 years ago when I began fieldwork in a San Antonio public housing project. At that time, the average annual household income in the area dominated by the housing project was under $7,000 (U.S. Census, 1990). The area was heavily Mexican American, and inhabited primarily by families, many of them single parents, with young children (U.S. Census, 1990).

My goal in that initial fieldwork was to discover how families sustained themselves in their environment of overstretched human services, low-wage jobs, and poor health. During that first summer, even before I focused on jobs and employment, I discovered that families had to patch together strategies that usually combined public welfare services, such earnings as they could garner in the jobs available to them, and assistance from both public and private agencies as well as from other family members.

In order to discover the details of family sustenance activities, I moved, with my family (husband and children, ages four, eight, and twelve), next to a public housing project in San Antonio, volunteering and living at a local community center, and meeting and talking to mothers both at the center and in walks around the neighborhood. In the course of that first summer and the following year, I met hundreds of mothers and their children. I also shopped, visited many agencies, needed medical care for my own children, and so learned the ins and the outs of family life in public housing. I began to discover the many ways in which mothers caring for their children bring resources into their households.

This activity laid the groundwork, in a sense, for the two later studies. As a Texas version of welfare was implemented in 1995, followed by the federal version in 1996, I returned with research teams for two more recent studies to examine the ways in which families were responding to welfare reform and its impact on their lives. Although welfare reform changed the access that mothers had to cash transfers and some associated benefits, it did not appear to markedly change the overall approach and strategies that low-income mothers brought to bear on the problem of supporting their households.

Agencies, Health, and Crises

Many mothers worked hard to get and keep jobs. There is a growing literature on the nature of the labor force as experienced by low-income mothers (Lambert, 1999; Lambert et al., 2002), and the reasons why they have so much difficulty rising out of poverty on the basis of paid employment. There is also an extensive literature, encompassing the last several decades, that examines the degree to which low-income single mothers, whether employed or on welfare, draw on the resources of their own informal support networks of family and close friends (Jarrett, 1994; Stack, 1974).

This chapter, however, concentrates on other factors in the lives of low-income single mothers and their families that simultaneously make it difficult for these mothers to keep their jobs and increase the pressures on them. There are, as might be expected, a great many factors that affect the lives of impoverished mothers and their children. Here, I delineate three of these pressures, which were illuminated by that first summer's fieldwork and confirmed in later work, and which can lead to new analyses of the impact of welfare policy. These pressures are:

- Families face the necessity of dealing with multiple agencies, and it is hard and time-consuming work.
- The health conditions experienced by impoverished families are both quantitatively and qualitatively different from those of other families.
- Life in poor families is full of crises and these crises exacerbate and magnify the problems low-income families face.

Each of these areas is described in some detail below.

Dealing with Multiple Agencies

Every strategy that low-income mothers use to support their families carries with it pressures and demands that complicate their lives. Mothers' use of both state and local agencies exemplifies this aspect of their lives. The women I met and interviewed that first summer were involved with as many as 25 agencies (or different programs in agencies) in order to meet the needs of their families. They did not describe many institutions or helping agencies of which I was unaware; however they explained the necessity for approaching many of them simultaneously.

The Example of Medical Care

As mothers in each study described their situation, the need to approach so many agencies arose in three ways. First aside from the cash transfer benefits of welfare itself, most agencies had programs that specialized in specific needs. For instance, Medicaid provided health insurance, which covered most medical needs for children (although not necessarily for adults in the same household). However for at least some of the years I worked in San Antonio, a different local program, funded by a Texas grocery store chain, provided extra coverage for some pharmaceuticals not covered by Medicaid. A school-based program provided regular screening for some health conditions and assisted with some necessary over-the-counter products. Some local clinics provided services for particular groups (such as pregnant teenagers) or conditions (such as diabetes). In order to obtain what they needed, mothers usually used a combination of these and other programs.

Thus, even in one particular area of need, most agencies and programs could not meet all of a family's requirements, nor were they intended to. Although Medicaid is designed to cover most needs of the individuals it insures, it does not cover all of the individuals in a household. Furthermore it does not cover all prescriptions, over-the-counter drugs, and at-home care. Mothers of children with Medicaid coverage may still need additional care and services. Also mothers regularly need to demonstrate their own and their children's eligibility for any of these services.

Medicaid, the largest and most inclusive of the services, determines eligibility on an individual-by-individual basis, rather than by household. Therefore it often does not cover all members of a household. In order to acquire medical care for all of her children and for herself, a mother may need to seek multiple sources of service. And in order to receive these services, mothers have to make sure that their eligibility papers for Medicaid are kept current for each of their children and, if they are eligible, for themselves. They need to seek out other sources of assistance for what Medicaid does not cover, and they also need to keep their eligibility for those services up-to-date.

For instance, a mother not on welfare might need to acquire health care for herself through a hospital-based clinic if she was ineligible for Medicaid. She would also need to provide documentation of her eligibility for any available reduction in fees. Meanwhile, her children might well still be eligible for Medicaid, although she would have to apply for it for them and be prompt in dealing with the regular renewals also required. Most local clinics also demanded applications for any reduction in payments, and other services required applications to prove that the applicant matched their criteria for service. Meeting all of these requirements takes work and organization.

Somewhat more invisible, but very serious, in family lives were the ramifications of untreated health conditions. Under the pressures of the Medicaid system, and the health problems that permeated the neighborhood, mothers were likely to leave some health conditions untreated. Often they would leave unconsidered their own health conditions for a period, particularly if treatment would interfere with their commitments to their children. In all three studies, there were numerous accounts of mothers who would not stay overnight in the hospital for tests or minor surgery, since they could not leave their children unsupervised. Mothers who could arrange for their children's care might then be stymied by their inability to pay for all of the testing or treatment recommended. In the long run they, their children, and the community suffer if they become more seriously ill, particularly if they have contracted an infectious condition.

As earlier ethnographies have also documented (Howell, 1973), when mothers are faced with situations where their families would have to go into debt to acquire the treatment they need, or where their treatment would incapacitate their ability to tend to her children, mothers often delay treatment. Mothers I met had received diagnoses of hypertension, diabetes, bronchitis, and other conditions, but treatment was going to have to wait until the family had the necessary resources. In all three studies, bills relating to medical treatment were an important cause of family indebtedness.

Food and Nutrition

This same kind of multiplicity of service use occurred in other areas. Both the need to draw on multiple services and the demands of complex eligibility requirements applied to family use of food and nutrition agencies. Just as most families I met that first summer included children who were eligible for and were using Medicaid, most families I met were eligible for and were using Food Stamps. Although Food Stamps, unlike Medicaid, allocate benefits to households rather than to individuals, the composition of the household, as reported on the Food Stamp application, determines the amount of the Food Stamp grant.

Therefore the Food Stamp allowance rarely met all of the family's food needs. Several issues contributed to the inability of households to get the food they needed from Food Stamps alone. First efficient use of the Food Stamp allowance (as is the case for any food budget) is based on careful shopping. Depending on the neighborhood, it may not allow for the increased prices in some inner-city neighborhoods where impoverished families live, for the additional household members such families are trying to feed, and for the dietary requirements of any household members with special needs. Furthermore, as we will see later, families may face either household or neighborhood-wide food crises for which the Food Stamp allowance provides few resources.

Comparison shopping studies have demonstrated, over a number of years, the higher prices of many goods in impoverished communities. Often lacking in large, high-volume stores, the smaller stores available to them have higher rates (Weinberg, 2000). Even larger chain stores tend to charge higher rates in low-income neighborhoods (Kolodinsky and Cranwell, 2000). Impoverished single-parent families are less likely to have ready access to transportation that would enable them more easily to comparison shop and shop outside their home neighborhoods. The use of public transportation for grocery shopping may cost enough (for the round-trip for a mother and her children) to cancel out the financial benefits of lower prices elsewhere.

Many single mothers, as well as other types of families, often feed people who are not part of their regular household, which places additional pressure on them to stretch their food resources. Mothers may be housing people— such as adult children—who need emergency support. They may be feeding people, such as nieces or nephews who live elsewhere but come by for meals. They may have a partner who lives with them. Given the exigencies of public housing regulation, they may not be prepared to list such residents in a Food Stamp application. (Inviting someone to reside in a public housing unit who is not on the lease can lead to eviction.) Furthermore either members of the household or visitors may present dietary needs connected with health conditions, which require greater than usual food expenditures. Households in all three studies frequently fed people in addition to the family in the housing unit—often the children of close relatives, or older children who had moved out but returned frequently for meals.

Edin (1993) wrote in an early work, "There's a lot of month left at the end of the money," and the same problem applies to many families' Food Stamps: There's a lot of month left at the end of the Food Stamp allowance. In order to get all of the food they needed, mothers in low-income families often used multiple agencies to eke out the Food Stamp allowance. In the neighborhood of the San Antonio housing project where we gathered data, there was an Agricultural Surplus service, which provided families with cheese and other surplus food items on a semi-regular basis. Many mothers I talked with planned their meals around the plentiful cheese allotments that might be available from agricultural surplus. The days following cheese deliveries were full of enchiladas, beans with cheese, and other casseroles.

Most families also expected their school-age children to have lunch, and possibly breakfast too, at school when school was in session. In order for children to receive free or reduced price lunches and breakfast, parents had to submit an annual application to the school for each child. When school was not in session, families often registered their children in recreation and other local programs that provided free lunches.

The school lunch program, in particular, was a critical part of many families' food strategies throughout the three-year period when we conducted the San Antonio study. Summers and school vacations often placed considerable burdens on mothers, as they tried to find additional food resources to replace the lost benefits of that program. Mothers of eligible children or who were pregnant often registered for the WIC (Women, Infants, and Children) nutrition program. It provides allowances of selected foods to support the nutritional needs of impoverished children aged five and under, and of impoverished pregnant women.

Almost all of the families contacted were aware of alternative emergency food pantries and soup kitchens, which provided free meals in the neighborhood. Although soup kitchens—which usually served dinner several times a week—tended to have an open-door policy, many mothers only availed themselves of a soup kitchen when they had exhausted all other possibilities. Attending a soup kitchen, and particularly having to bring children there, they reported, was the final proof of poverty and demonstrated their inability to provide for their own children.

In San Antonio, in the early 1990s, most soup kitchens were attended almost totally by single men, so mothers often kept their families away. However many mothers used emergency food outlets where a person in need could get two or three days of groceries. Even these outlets, however, required an application and eligibility review. They also were not always dependable. For instance, pantries and kitchens might limit their services with little warning if their food donations unexpectedly declined.

This discussion of food programs explores just one of the many areas for which low-income families—whether on welfare or employed in low-wage jobs—often need to seek out services to eke out a livelihood when their cash income falls short. Families are likely, at the same time, to be using multiple health-care systems and multiple food and nutrition programs. They are also likely to seek out subsidies for housing and child care, assistance with utility payments, and special clothing programs. Each of these programs requires some combination of application, eligibility review, travel to reach the service, and other work. Attempting to orchestrate their households' relationships with the multiple services they used was a demanding, time-consuming task for mothers.

When women were on welfare in Texas, where the maximum cash allowance for a family of three was around $200, they used multiple-agency strategies like those mentioned earlier to "make ends meet." [In 2003, the average TANF recipient's household received less than $210, according to the Texas Department of Human Services (TDHS, 2003)]. When women moved from welfare to the low-wage jobs available to them, or had consistently avoided welfare throughout their employment, their wages still fell short of their expenses; hence, most continued the use of services from multiple agencies in order to acquire—with their limited income—the goods and services needed by their families. This negotiated relationship with so many agencies was time- and energy-consuming. Women who were employed talked, in particular, about the difficulties entailed in combining employment with its demands and the work required to maintain agency contributions to their families.

In the most recent studies, under welfare reform, many women reported that the requirements of the TANF system, with multiple time-consuming visits to agencies, often put their newfound jobs in jeopardy. Employers did not excuse absenteeism for such a cause. The pressures of appointments with the welfare office added to the pressures of employment, and to the continued necessity of dealing with agencies in other areas of family need.

Health Conditions among Low-Income Families

For some time we have known that impoverished families suffer more illness and different types of illness than families that are better off (Williams and Collins, 1995). We also know that, based on poverty, some neighborhoods—many of them impoverished inner-city areas—have different overall health profiles than do other better-off ones (Winkleby and Cubbin, 2003). In the area of our San Antonio study, one colleague suggested that the overall health conditions of families in the neighborhood more nearly resembled that of a developing country than of a mainstream U.S. community.

There certainly is information suggesting links between socioeconomic status and social support, on one side, and health on the other (Link and Phelan, 1995). In fact, many chronic conditions were widespread: Epidemiologists found that the incidence of diabetes, for instance, always high in San Antonio, tripled between 1987 and 1996, part of the period of our work there (Burke et al., 1999).

Among the chronic conditions that affected many of the children in the neighborhood where I worked were asthma, dental problems, ongoing ear infections, and vision problems requiring glasses. The low-income single mothers I met were often dealing with multiple conditions among the children in their household. In fact, as in many areas, asthma seemed to be increasingly prevalent, and a mother might well be caring for two or more young children who required regular monitoring for their asthma. Her life became increasingly complicated if she too became ill or was dealing with a chronic health condition. In our most recent study, we are just beginning analysis of what we call family "comorbidity" (Burton and Whitfield, 2003)—the occurrence of multiple health conditions among family members, which places even more pressure on the mother.

Resources for Health Care: Medical Insurance

Mothers faced financial as well as logistical problems in caring for ill children with chronic conditions. First of all, such care demanded time and energy, often in short supply. It usually involved negotiations with schools, child care centers, recreation programs, and any other program where the child spent time. It also required expenditures. Families were dependent on public health insurance programs; very few had access to health insurance through their jobs. However almost all of the children I met in my field site were eligible for Medicaid and enrolled in that program most of the time.

Medicaid covered medical visits and prescription pharmaceuticals, but it did not cover the over-the-counter remedies that were frequently part of the treatment for a chronic condition. The humidifiers and air cleaners and over-the-counter remedies that were often recommended had to be paid for by the mothers. Although mothers too were usually covered by Medicaid, there were ineligible mothers, who more often than not had no health insurance. While their income made them ineligible, the jobs they held rarely made health insurance available to them. Under welfare reform, there has been a decline in the number of children and adults covered by Medicaid (Zedlewski, 2002), and the San Antonio families in the most recent study were also showing incomplete medical insurance coverage (Angel et al., 2001).

Mothers also dealt with children with ongoing ear infections, dental problems, and the early stages of vision difficulties. In all these cases, while Medicaid covered a significant share of the costs of diagnosis and treatment, most mothers were left with expenses that were sudden and irregular, making substantial inroads on their budgets. Mothers could receive assistance with doctor's visits, prescription medications, and any emergency hospital care through their Medicaid coverage for their children. However they were likely to pay cash for baby aspirin, ear drops, and other related treatment expenses. Although none of these items, by itself, is usually very costly, a mother dealing with two children with different chronic conditions might well spend a substantial amount of money on their care.

Furthermore during many of the years of my work in San Antonio, the Medicaid program there had rationed prescription medication. Under ordinary circumstances, no individual on Medicaid was authorized to fill more than three prescriptions in a given month. For children in relatively good health, this presented little problem. However children dealing with chronic health conditions or undergoing the diagnosis for a new condition might well require more than three prescriptions. Mothers faced difficult choices: Pay money out of an already stretched budget for the prescription; go into the informal neighborhood trading system to see if someone else had some of the medication desired; or wait until the beginning of the next month.

There were a number of side effects to the restrictions on prescriptions. During one visit to an elementary school, it was reported that the school had joined with a local grocery store to provide low-cost prescription drugs to Medicaid children who had used up their prescription ration for the month. The school was responding to an attendance problem. They had noticed that attendance fell at the end of the month, and were concerned about that trend.

In order to understand its cause, they called on families with children absent at the end of the month. During these calls, they learned that mothers were keeping ill children home at the end of the month, waiting until they could receive a new prescription for their health problem at the beginning of the next month. In order to help deal with this problem, the grocery store agreed to provide free- or low-cost pharmaceuticals to families in this situation. Valuable as this service was to families, it also represented yet another program that required eligibility proceedings.

The neighborhood responded to the difficulties in accessing prescription drugs with an informal sharing and purchase network. Families held onto any unused prescription drugs. They were prepared to share these medicines with their own informal support network, or to sell or barter them with others. Some families had carefully kept boxes or drawers of such medications.

Health issues in low-income communities were ubiquitous. In poor neighborhoods of San Antonio, for instance, with its hot summers, most families did not have air-conditioning, making it hard to distinguish illness from the continuing fatigue and lassitude that working in such heat brought on. Moving in, in June, with three healthy children, we left three months later with a health picture that looked much more like that of other low-income families in the community.

My 12-year-old daughter was testing positive for exposure to tuberculosis and entered the required nine-month, state-mandated treatment program. My 4-year-old son had a systemic infection that results when very young children get large numbers of fire-ant bites. In our community, fire ants lived not just in the dirt and nests of yards, but in the walls of the buildings. Many children had episodes, like my son's, where they sat on the wrong piece of furniture or reached into the wrong box only to find themselves covered with biting fire ants. The resulting treatment was expensive and difficult, and left him with scars similar to those of many other preschoolers in the area.

In some cases, mothers found the struggle to deal with health needs nearly overwhelming. Maintaining eligibility for Medicaid, learning the ins and outs of getting what you and your children needed, and dealing with the supervision and support required by children with chronic conditions was hard. It was made more difficult by the conditions of the neighborhood and the likelihood that the mother herself was dealing with health problems. The effort to take care of family health was only one part of a challenging and complex job that also involved getting the food and nutrition children needed, dealing with the larger welfare organizations, and often trying to find and sustain employment.

Crises in Low-Income Families

Because families are so close to an economic precipice, and because their livelihoods come to them in such complicated ways, events that might seem transitory under other conditions can trigger a crisis that threatens family well-being, and particularly the well-being of children in those families. Not only was family life complicated, but it seldom fell into a regular rhythm for any length of time. Household regularity and stability was always at risk—due, in part, to the nature of the community and the pressures it put on families. The example below gives a sense of how local events interacted with family well-being. Electricity blackouts occurred several times during the summer we lived in San Antonio. In two cases, the electricity remained off for at least a day.

Neighborhood Blackouts

In a community where there is little air conditioning to begin with, a power outage does not lead to increased illnesses and problems due to loss of air conditioning, a phenomenon in better-off communities. However the loss of power for a day or more at a time turned out to have considerable impact on family food for the rest of the month. Families tended to buy food in weekly forays, and they stored their milk, meat, and other perishables in refrigerators. In the hot, humid San Antonio summer, in residences with no air conditioning and old refrigerators, a day without refrigeration often cost families much of their food. They had little budget with which to make up these lost resources.

Furthermore the community nature of this disaster had specific ramifications. In most family emergencies, mothers reported that they often had relatives or friends on whom they could depend. They could send their children to a mother's or an aunt's house for a meal, or borrow food. However when the whole neighborhood was affected, as occurred during these blackouts, the members of their network also usually lost power and their own food supplies. Under these conditions, women talked about going to one or two meals a day, or skipping meals themselves in order to conserve food for their children.

Always on the Edge of Disaster

It is difficult to summarize the problems, issues, and complicated responses that make up the approaches low-income mothers take to supporting their families. They are engaged in a constant struggle to combine the usually inadequate wages they earn, the low level of cash transfer payments available through welfare if they are receiving it (in Texas), and the goods and services available to them through agency support, as well as through their own informal and social networks. Even when mothers use all of these resources as effectively as they can, their families are still fragile in their vulnerability to any of a number of unanticipated problems.

In fact, a variety of factors mediate against the stability of family life in these mother-headed, low-income households. Mothers and their families often live in impoverished neighborhoods. Although there is continued debate about the impact of high-poverty urban neighborhoods on families, they are settings that pose different health risks, safety risks, standards of housing, and available community resources than those available to residents in better-off neighborhoods. The neighborhood where families live can expose them to health and other risks, while limiting their resources in meeting those challenges.

Because mothers live close to destitution even while deploying resources from a number of different sources, the loss of any one resource can create a family catastrophe. A mother counting on three or four different food resources may still be close enough to the margin that failure of one resource leads to days without food. And the nature of family resources changes in response to many factors. Public policies and agency regulations may change what an organizational resource makes available to families. The jobs mothers hold make rigid requirements but offer little guarantee of regularity or job tenure. Members of their own informal support systems may become impoverished or simply disenchanted with the prospect of helping out the mother.

In addition, the use of all resources comes at a cost. Mothers spend a great deal of time and energy locating and maintaining eligibility with helping organizations. Informal support networks make demands, as well as provide goods and services. Jobs, while being the major income source most women seek, have substantial costs also, particularly those offering few benefits, no access to health insurance, and no promise of long-range security.

Welfare reform positions mothers as breadwinners and wage-earners. It is based on the expectation that, through paid employment, mothers can earn enough to support their households in jobs that have benefits enough to secure health care, and in communities that will not hamper their efforts to keep themselves and their children healthy and safe. Accumulated evidence from these and other studies may be telling a different story of life for low-income mothers and their children. In many cases, income through employment still falls short most months, benefits are irregular or nonexistent, and community change is slow at best. These characteristics of welfare reform continue to leave many families living in conditions of poverty or near-poverty, which place children at risk, even while parenting them remains mothers' first priority.

Notes

1. This study was supported in part by the Rockefeller Foundation.
2. The ethnographic interviews were supported in part by the Russell Sage Foundation.
3. The second study was funded by the Texas Department of Human Resources.
4. For information relating to the funders and details on the larger study, see http://www.jhu.edu/~welfare.

References

Acs, G. and Loprest, P. with Roberts, T. (2001). *Final synthesis report of findings from ASPE "Leavers" grants.* Report submitted to Office of the Assistant Secretary for Planning and Evaluation, U.S. Department of Health and Human Services. Washington, DC: The Urban Institute. http://aspe.hhs.gov/hsp/leavers99/synthesis02/index.htm.

Angel, R., Lein, L., Henrici, J., and Leventhal, E. (2001). Health insurance coverage for children and their caregivers in low-income urban neighborhoods. Welfare, Children, and Families. Policy Brief 01–2. Baltimore, MD: Johns Hopkins University.

Burke, J. P., Williams, K., Gaskill, S. P., Hazuda, H. P., Haffner, S. M., and Stern, M. P. (1999). Rapid rise in the incidence of Type 2 diabetes from 1987 to 1996: Results from the San Antonio Heart Study. *Archives of Internal Medicine, 159*(13), 1450–1456.

Burton, L. M. and Whitfield, K. E. (2003). "Weathering" toward poor health in later life: Co-morbidity in low-income urban families, *Public Policy and Aging Report, 13*(3), 13–18.

Edin, K. (1993). *There's a lot of month left at the end of the money: How AFDC recipients make ends meet in Chicago.* New York: Garland Press.

Edin, K. and Lein, L. (1996). Work, welfare, and single mothers' economic survival strategies. *American Sociological Review, 61,* 253–266.

Edin, K. and Lein, L. (1997). *Making ends meet: How single mothers survive welfare and low wage work.* New York: The Russell Sage Foundation.

Edin, K. and Lein, L. (1998). The private safety net: The role of charitable organizations in the lives of the poor. *Housing Policy Debate, 9*(3), 541–573.

Garey, A. (1999). *Weaving work and motherhood.* Philadelphia: Temple University Press.

Henly, J. and Danziger, S. (1996). Confronting welfare stereotypes: Characteristics of general assistance recipients and postassistance employment. *Social Work Research, 20*(4), 217–227.

Henly, J. and Lyons, S. (2000). The negotiations of child care and employment demands among low-income parents. *Journal of Social Issues, 56*(4), 683–705.

Howell, J. (1973). *Hard living on clay street: Portraits of blue collar families.* Garden City, NY: Anchor Press.

Isaacs, J. B. and Lyon, M. R. (2000). *A cross-state examination of families leaving welfare: Findings from the ASPE-funded leavers studies.* Office of the Assistant Secretary for Planning and Evaluation. U.S. Department of Health and Human Services. Washington, DC.

Jarrett, R. L. (1994). Living Poor: Family life among single parent, African-American women. *Social Problems, 41*, 30–45.

Johns Hopkins University. (2002). Website: http://www.jhu.edu/~welfare

Joyce Foundation. (2002). *Welfare to work: What have we learned.* Chicago, IL: The Joyce Foundation.

Kolodinsky, J. and Cranwell, M. (2000). The poor pay more? Now they don't even have a store to choose from: bringing a supermarket back to the city. *Consumers Interests Annual, 46*, 101–106.

Lambert, S. (1999). Lower-wage workers and the new realities of work and family. *Annals of the American Academy of Political and Social Sciences, 562*, 174–190.

Lambert, S., Waxman, E., and Haley-Lock, A. (2002). *Against the odds: A study of instability in lower-skilled jobs.* Working paper. Project on the Public Economy of Work. Chicago: University of Chicago.

Lein, L., Benjamin, A. McManus, M., and Roy, K. (2002). Economic roulette: When is a job not a job? American Anthropological Association, August 17.

Link, B. G. and Phelan, J. C. (1996). Editorial: Understanding sociodemographic differences in health—The role of fundamental social causes. *American Journal of Public Health, 86*, 471–473.

Nathan, R. P. and Gais, T. L. (2002). Implementing the personal responsibility act of 1996: A first look. New York: Federalism Research Group, The Nelson A. Rockefeller Institute of Government. http://www.rockinst.org/publications/federalism/first_look/1st-chapter03.html

Newman, K. S. (1999). *No shame in my game: The working poor in the inner city.* New York: Alfred A. Knopf, Inc. and the Russell Sage Foundation.

Newman, K. S. (2001). "Hard times on 125th Street: Harlem's poor confront welfare reform." *American Anthropologist, 103*(3), 762–778.

Schexnayder, D., Lein, L. Douglas, K., Schroeder, D., Dominguez, D., and Richards, F. (2002). Surviving without TANF: An analysis of families diverted from or leaving TANF. The Texas Department of Human Resources. http://www.dhs.state.tx.us/publications/index.html

Schexnayder, D., Olson, J., Schroeder, D., Betsinger, A., and Shao-Chee Sim. (1998). *Achieving change for Texans evaluation: Net impacts through December 1997.* Austin: University of Texas, Lyndon B. Johnson School of Public Affairs.

Stack, C. (1974). *All our kin: Strategies for survival in a Black community.* New York: Basic Books.

Texas Department of Human Services. (2003). Website: http://www.dhs.state.tx.us/publications/refguide/2000/StateRankings.html; http://www.dhs.state.tx.us/programs/TexasWorks/TANF.html

U.S. Census, 1990, Economic Characteristics.

Weinberg, Z. (2000). No place to shop: Food access lacking in the inner city. *Race, Poverty & the Environment,* (no page).

Williams, D. R. and Collins, C. (1995). U. S. Socioeconomic and racial differences in health: Patterns and explanation. *Annual Review of Sociology, 29*, 349–386.

Winkleby, M. A. and Cubbin, C. (2003). Influence of individual and neighbourhood socioeconomic status on mortality among Black, Mexican-American, and White women and men in the United States. *Journal of Epidemiology and Community Health, 57*(6), 444–452.

Winston, P. (1999). Welfare, children and families: A three city study. overview and design. Working Paper. Johns Hopkins University.

Zedlewski, S. (2002). Are shrinking caseloads always a good thing? Short takes on welfare policy, Number 6. Washington, DC: The Urban Institute.

CHAPTER TWO

"The Long Road to Quality Day Care and Work": Women Define Pathways

DESIREE FRENCH, BRUCE FULLER,
AND JAMES MENSING

Can the State Shape Women's Pathways?

Government recurrently attempts to better poor women, either by changing their behavior or by improving their local surroundings. Washington's original aid to Civil War widows assumed that mothering came first. The settlement house movement, at the start of the twentieth century, aimed to advance women as individuals and address the miserable living conditions of many, and limited job possibilities. The Great Society's community action movement, replete with health clinics and Head Start, also tried to improve people's local environs, rather than their behavior. More recently, dramatic growth in tax expenditures, such as the $22 billion earned income tax credit, banks on incentives, not rules, "to make work pay" (Blank and Haskins, 2001; Katz, 1986).

The far-reaching welfare reforms of 1996—and stiffer work requirements for welfare recipients still debated by the Congress—advance a web of mechanisms and motivators through which mothers' behavior, or resources in their local settings, are supposed to change. These include new rules, such as the five-year lifetime limit on cash aid, incentives to encourage employment, and government's moral message aimed at altering the value that mothers—and their children—place on leaving home each day for paid work (Mead, 1992; Weaver, 2000).

Yet we still know little about how women themselves are making sense of these various policy strategies.[1] In 1998, our team designed and carried out a qualitative study to find out more. We became acquainted with 15 women, all of whom were single mothers and had entered California's new welfare-to-work initiative, CalWORKs.[2] As with earlier qualitative studies, we first got to know them, then began to gather information about the social and economic resources that sustained them each day. We did not assume that the linear pathway implied by the motto, "welfare to work," was viewed by these women as a straight line or an easy transition to make. Instead, over a three-year period, we discussed with them how well the pursuit of work fit with other aims and demands of their daily lives. We also examined how these women interpreted and responded to the rules, incentives, and moral signals coming at them from a variety of government agencies.

We begin this chapter with a brief review of how theorists and policy makers portray the state's capacity to alter the behavior and beliefs of low-income parents. These causal accounts illuminate the ways in which policy makers attempt to shape individual action and their efficacy in doing so. The fact that the number of poor parents on the welfare rolls has fallen from over five million in 1994 to under two million by 2002, suggests that public policy can make a difference (Haskins, 2001). It also leads to new policy challenges; such as, more than one million additional low-income parents are drawing public child care support today, compared to client levels in 1996 (Collins et al., 2000). Families benefiting from the earned income tax credit (EITC) rose steadily during the Clinton era as well. So sorting out the causal processes that operate between policy action and parents' everyday action holds pragmatic implications.

Next we highlight how our study moves beyond earlier research. We introduce the two women on whom this chapter focuses, and who we call Claudia and LaTasha. As we analyzed interview transcripts and field notes, we heard these women talk about their efforts to find jobs and supportive resources. Finding a job and securing welfare supports were linked to their parenting pathway. Yet we will hear how these mothers' first concern was their children's well-being—their immediate safety, the stability of child care, and finding better schools.

We conclude the chapter by asking whether the motivating power of raising children—the desire of mothers to be effective parents—might lead to more effective family policy.

How the State Tries to Change Poor Women

The Effective State and Its Policy Levers

One starting question is whether the state can act independently of the nature of labor or entrenched social norms, that structure the behavior and moral commitments held by low-income parents. Mainstream policy theorists assume the state can alter the behavior of poor individuals through regulatory rules, incentives, or moral signals.

Even rational-choice theorists, who might otherwise assume the supremacy of market forces, have argued that old welfare policies crafted by the state created distorted incentives for poor mothers to stay at home and avoid marriage (Murray, 1984). If government can get the incentives right, then low-income parents will pursue paid employment. Tandem assumptions are that poor people rationally try to optimize their economic returns, and thus government can act effectively to reward desired behavior (Michalopoulos and Berlin, 2001).

Others theorists, although confident of the state's ability to change behavior, disagree on the second-order question of *how* the state can be most effective. This line of thinking, which is based on Durkheim's work on social groups and institutions, suggests that the social environment in which many poor families are situated must change before the individual parent begins to make nontraditional choices (Durkheim, 1938; Giddens, 1986).

For example, poor women are less likely to pursue paid jobs if organized supports such as reliable child care remain unavailable, if public transportation can't move one across town to a job, or if community norms reward women for other roles such as full-time motherhood. The immediate structure of opportunities may offer a wide or narrow range of options and roles. While many of the 1996 reforms based on rules and economic incentives were aimed at the individual, the federal government now invests far more in organized training, job counseling, health insurance, and child care than ever before (Fuller et al., 2002a; Greenstein and Guyer, 2001).

Weak States but Strong Labor or Cultural Structures

Two competing accounts suggest that state action alone will do little to alter the fundamental economic and institutional contexts in which family poverty is reproduced across generations. The class-conflict tradition emphasizes that the stratified nature of jobs severely restricts opportunities for better-paying jobs among poorly educated women (Bowels and Gintis, 1976; Carnoy, 1984; Nussbaum, 1999). Beyond the economic origins of class differences, certain groups separated from mainstream society may adopt norms and behavioral scripts that lead to a "culture" of poverty. Economic and cultural conditions become intertwined, a postulate of Oscar Lewis' (1959) original model and William Julius Wilson's (1996) recent emphasis on central-city job loss and its denigrating effects on the social norms in which families are embedded. Thus mandating work or applying economic incentives alone won't necessarily alter deep-seated behavior.

Other research, however, reveals the presence of multiple role models and norms within poor communities. Anderson (1990; 1992), for example, details how Black adolescents in Philadelphia are exposed to competing adult role models: men who vary in their propensity to stay employed, maintain family commitments, and abide by coherent moral codes. Holloway et al. (1997; MacLeod, 1987) similarly describe how poor single mothers in Boston pursued work, child care programs, and better housing with varying levels of intensity. And Ogbu (1978) has shown how the perceived opportunity structure varies enormously among voluntary immigrant groups, including Latinos, versus so-called involuntary minorities such as African Americans.

This work shows how multiple cultural frameworks operate in low-income communities, and that some individuals may indeed respond to new economic incentives and normative signals. In addition, many low-income families do manage to leave the poorest neighborhoods (Jargowsky, 1997). Mobility out of poverty remains a cruel question of probability, and some individuals cycle in and out. Rising employment rates among women formerly on welfare, sustained even during the most recent economic recession, suggest that the earlier portrayal of a monolithic "underclass" was over-stated.

Formal Rules, Institutions, and Informal Social Support

The new social engineers in Washington argue that rules, incentives, or sanctions—together with moral signals now emanating from welfare offices—can alter poor women's behavior and work. How the new generation of welfare interventions is interpreted by these women is one intriguing question. In some studies, only about one-third report that they participated in key program components, such as job preparation (job club) activities, classroom training, counseling, or other support programs (Bloom et al., 2002). Still this new approach to family policy assumes that local agencies are fostering significant change in some women's lives.

Policy makers occasionally attempt to alter informal channels of information or aid informal supports. Child care is an important case, where government has contracted with community-based organizations (CBOs) to distribute child care vouchers, and much of this funding reimburses kith and kin members to watch after children. In California, for instance, well over half of the state welfare agency's $1 billion allocation for child care moves to informal child care providers (Fuller et al., 2002). Government acts in other ways to strengthen or alter informal ties, from more aggressive enforcement of child support, to family counseling, to parent education efforts.

How are women responding or using resources to help them get ahead? And do they view these resources the way policy makers portray them? In addition, these policy strategies correspond to a growing debate among scholars over the relative effectiveness of formal institutions versus informal networks in offering linkages to jobs, ways of acquiring skills, or finding work supports such as child care. Renewed interest in the notion of social capital has revived work on understanding these tacit networks and their positive elements, including trust, reciprocity, and coherent social norms (Loury, 1977; Putnam, 1995; Williams, 1981).

Others argue that these local networks are weak, only occasionally yielding steady support for women and their families. Often they fail to offer needed economic resources or resourceful institutions. From this viewpoint, the efficacy of informal networks must be seen within a class structure that reproduces differential access to jobs, education, and status opportunities (Fuller and Hannum, 2002; Portes, 1998).

We have learned about how poor women see and negotiate welfare offices, including their caseworkers and allied agencies (Berrick, 1995; Holloway et al., 1997). New evidence is beginning to shed light on how women are interpreting post-1996 policy pressures, and how these signals, rules, and resources blend into the everyday flow of their lives (DeParle, 2004). In addition, the competing theoretical accounts just reviewed helped to lend order to the mountains of interview transcripts that we compiled. Mothers told us much about how they were experiencing the pressures and supports exercised by welfare caseworkers, training organizations, and child care agencies.

Three kinds of stories emerged in this regard, to which we now turn: Accounts of recognizable pathways women were trying to travel; key people from whom they gained economic or social support; and models of action or contested ideas about how they should behave (what we came to call, "guiding signposts").

Recognizable Pathways

The slogans voiced by many policy makers capture the linearity of their thinking. The phrase "welfare to work" belies the hope that changing the behavior of low-income parents can be unidirectional. Implied in such a theory of action is the notion that reforms operate via a pathway that has a clear origin and indisputable destination. We explored with participating women whether the expectations for working—urged by caseworkers, child care counselors, housing officials, and others—led to a clear course of action. This behavior might have included attending job preparation sessions, skill training, searching for reliable child care, or stronger engagement in the labor force.

Recent qualitative studies point to an equally salient pathway focusing on how to best raise one's child and simply keep food on the table. This is what Edin and Lein (1997: p. 7) termed, "the dual demands on single mothers." Based on their interviews with 379 women, prior to the 1996 reforms, they found that, "Because virtually all the women . . . were at least as concerned with parenting as with providing, many chose not to work for a time."

Drawing from a second sample of families, after the 1996 welfare reforms intensified work pressures, Scott et al. (2001: pp. 132, 149) describe how work–family trade-offs pose a dilemma for women.

> At the heart of this tension between how to be good workers and how to be good mothers was the question of how they could best assist their children in attaining upward mobility. At the core of their decisions about work was the desire to put their children first and do the right thing for them.

This implies that women may have clear notions of theoretical pathways for their families, but the dominant one usually pertains to how to keep their youngsters safe and help them get ahead. Maximizing income—through work, welfare, or other means—certainly may be viewed as being instrumental in advancing their children's well-being.

Key People and Resources

Poor women obviously have a range of social ties, from linkages to formal agencies to informal networks of kin and friends. Much of our own interview time was spent trying to identify key members of each mother's support network and the resources they provided. We also were particularly attentive to adults or agencies that helped mothers obtain child care or connect to preschool programs.

In 1997, when San Francisco began to implement welfare-to-work reforms, the county human services agency contracted with an established CBO to operate child care programs. Each mother had an assigned child care caseworker in addition to her caseworker at the welfare office. Some women reported ongoing contact with each counselor as they proceeded through program activities and searched for a job. We explored the resources and support these agency staff provided, as well as how women drew on more indigenous ties. Earlier work shows that informal networks, such as relying on kith and kin for informal child care, can substitute for subsidies flowing through formal agencies (Weisner et al., 2002).

Guiding Signposts: Cultural Models and Contested Ideas

As we came to know these women, we heard more about their beliefs regarding the nature of jobs, welfare, and childrearing. Earlier work has detailed how low-income women certainly vary in their interpretations about staying on or off cash aid (Holloway et al., 1997). They often express beliefs about acceptable forms of child care, such as the desirability of placing their young children in formal centers versus relying on kin members or friends. And women develop their own views regarding the helpfulness of other adults in their immediate context, including caseworkers, men, and kin members.

Many of these tacit beliefs—what theorists term *scripts* or *cultural models* (D'Andrade and Strauss, 1992)—offer daily signposts for women's decisions or shifts in their beliefs and behavior. Varying cultural models may include a sequence of behaviors, adding up to a sequential set of actions. That is, several women in our full sample talked about the steps they followed to find a child care arrangement with which they were comfortable, or how they combined training, caseworker supports, and child care to accomplish their goals of getting a stable job. These behaviors may stem from the mother's implicit understanding of how to move along a pathway with associated supports and incentives (Fuller et al., 1996; Scott et al., 2001).

Claudia and LaTasha—Pathways toward
Work and Better Childrearing

Core Questions and Analytic Approach

Each of the single mothers participating in this study had at least one child, one–three years of age, at entry. Each was participating in the broader

Growing Up in Poverty Project, a three-state study of how women and their children have fared under the 1996 welfare reforms (Fuller et al., 2002b). Our qualitative sub-study described here was conducted exclusively in San Francisco.

We conducted four interviews with each woman at her home, sometimes in a cafe close to work, and, in one case, the county jail. These conversations were wide-ranging in the topics covered. After learning about their backgrounds and life histories, we explored their interactions with welfare office staff, their network of friends and kin members, and beliefs about raising young children and child care challenges, as well as how they viewed their neighborhood, housing situation, schools, and daily life within these settings. Each interview was recorded and transcribed, yielding about 1,800 pages of text. The interviews were coded for data analysis, relying on basic codes covering these aspects of their daily lives. We use pseudonyms throughout this chapter.

These women, in general, understood that government was pushing them to follow certain pathways: Leave home, find a job, perhaps do short-term training, and eventually leave the cash aid system. As we studied the transcripts, we developed a series of questions on which to focus in subsequent interviews. How do the women describe their own aims or desirable pathways? Do these mothers see certain actions leading to known outcomes, such as finding safe and reliable child care, or enrolling in training with the intent of finding a better job?

Introducing Claudia and LaTasha

The two-story blocks of tiny apartments that comprise the projects on the southern edge of San Francisco run parallel to one another on slightly inclined hills, resembling a stretch of rundown army barracks. When we arrived one evening, children and teenagers were out playing tag or tossing a ball. Others were jumping on two old mattresses that served as weathered trampolines, scattered amongst the litter and cigarette butts covering the development's browning lawns. People were friendly when we stopped by, and seemed eager to help these strangers who looked so obviously out of place.

We waited outside Claudia's unit, squeezed between two others, while her 10-year-old daughter, Khadijah, unlocked the deadbolt and swung open the steel bars first, then the front door. We noticed the adjoining apartment had been gutted by fire, leaving a charred black shell where homeless men or carousing neighbors reportedly hung out.

The colorful, immaculate interior of Claudia's apartment offered a stark contrast to the visual chaos outside. Two of her five children were stretched out on the green shag carpeting watching a loud sitcom. We sat in a spartan kitchen at a cheap wooden table. Not a speck of dust could be spotted; everything from magazine rack to pots and pans was in its proper place.

Claudia's own life had not been so tidy. She grew up in the same projects, trying to be a dutiful daughter to an alcoholic mother. Claudia, 33 years old, had left school when she was 14, in part because she had to take care of her younger siblings. She gave birth to her first child at 16, and for the past 17 years had been on welfare. Her stepfather is still in the picture: "I always remember him working and helping my mom. He stuck it out with her as long as he could because of the drinking. He was with her for, I think, ten years." Claudia's father organizes weekend outings for his grandkids and lends Claudia money when she comes up short.

Claudia's school-age kids get on the bus each weekday morning to leave the projects and head for middle-class schools. She talks often of how, over the years, she searched for a better child care arrangement for one of her children. She now eagerly participates in the city's school choice program. Although Claudia admitted suffering from bouts of depression, she is able to act decisively when her children's interests are at stake. In one interview, we asked how she makes sure that the county pays for her daughter's preschool. Claudia responded with characteristic brevity: "[I] go to work." Her fortitude in finding a job rises when it's directly in her children's interest.

LaTasha, age twenty-six in 1998, lives not far from Claudia, but in a smaller, seemingly more tranquil, set of public housing units. When we first met, LaTasha was crammed into a small two-bedroom apartment with her three children: Cale, seven, Monique, five, and Mark, almost two. Their apartment was filled with stuff, yet felt warm and homey, adorned with family pictures and sparse but comfortable furniture. The television was usually on when we stopped by to chat. The couch downstairs doubled as LaTasha's bed, since she often surrendered her own bedroom to Monique when her brothers got out of hand.

LaTasha had held several jobs before resorting to welfare in the summer of 1998. She had been a receptionist at a large bank, booked through a temp agency. Then she did data entry on the night shift in the same bank. But her infant, Mark, was getting upset during the day, not seeing his mother, and LaTasha felt bad being away from all three children. She thought that welfare would offer her a break and maybe a pathway to a better job. Although a bit reserved, LaTasha often seemed upbeat and when something was on her mind she had no difficulty expressing it. She was sure that better jobs were within her grasp once she acquired more training and stronger skills.

As a teenage mother, LaTasha had received cash aid. Her understanding of the reformed CalWORKs program included the salient fact that "I can get paid child care. They'll pay for my child care if I work and go to school."

A Fresh Trail: Get to Work First

Our conversations with Claudia revealed that she clearly understood and often acted to move along the intended pathway from welfare to work. It was not a trail that she would likely have blazed on her own, nor was it a linear path. For instance, Claudia felt she had been "bumped around into different work activities" by a succession of benign, at times warmly supportive, caseworkers. In the end, her sister-in-law found the home health worker job that, at the time of this study, she had held for over a year and reported enjoying most days. At the time of our final interview in 2002 she was earning $1,140 a month assisting elderly or disabled adults, two clients each day in their homes.

Seventeen Years on Cash Aid

When we first met Claudia, she had been on and off cash aid for almost two decades under the old AFDC program. (Her own mother, who still lives three minutes down the hill in the next housing block, was also on AFDC when Claudia was growing up, although she occasionally "worked food service jobs in the schools.") But the notion of moving from welfare to work was not a new idea to Claudia. For three years after giving birth to her first child, Karlesha, she had been on cash aid.

Claudia left the welfare rolls after the children's father assumed custody of both Karlesha and Durrell, an issue that Claudia has never felt sufficiently comfortable explaining. She went back on aid in 1989 when her daughter Khadijah was born, then tried to find work handing out flyers at a local store, followed by taking care of an elderly couple. She was called-up to find work under the GAIN experiment (Greater Avenues to Independence), California's first welfare-to-work program, but a job never panned out.

In 1998, after Claudia qualified for the new CalWORKs program, she attended an orientation session where participants were told they needed to find a job and a variety of work supports were described. Claudia reported that an optimistic pathway was presented by enthusiastic caseworkers:

> The orientation was helpful, I liked it. I went to two of them. It just filled us in on what was going on and where we were going to be a couple years from now.

Claudia's "employment specialist" set up a meeting to develop an "employment contract." She could go into a job club for help in finding work or into more specialized training at a local college. But Claudia reported,

> I wasn't quite sure what I wanted to do yet, because I hadn't had enough testing. I didn't want to go out there and just be working at a department store or something like that.

Although there was a waiting list to take the vocational interests test, Claudia had already formulated a clear view of the work she wanted:

> Hospital, working in a hospital. Working with people or kids. Pre-K children, like my daughter's age. I got lots of experience. I've been with kids all my life. There's six of us in our family, and then I have five kids. So, I think I could do that. And hospital work. I like working with people. Helping them.

Within a couple of months (late 1998) Claudia had agreed to enroll in child development courses at the local college, studying to become a preschool teacher's aide. The program involved both classroom study and nonpaid work experience in preschools. Claudia stuck with it for five months, but then concluded that "it was too much for me to handle, having kids and having to do all that work, plus turn around after school and do volunteer work."

After Claudia left the child development program, her caseworker remained encouraging and supportive.

> She suggested that if it's possible to work with something I want to do, that I should go that route, but to really think about it and stick with it. Don't give up on it, which is what I was basically doing.

Claudia was becoming clearer about the kind of job she did *not* want to do:

> Stuff like tellers—I'm not a sitting down person. I can't walk into an office and sit down and work like that. It's too quiet, and it gets to me. I need to be moving around. I don't want a minimum wage job, but something better than that would be nice.

By the spring of 1999, Claudia had left the child development program and was assigned to the Help Works program, a private firm that guaranteed its graduates would get jobs. Her same caseworker was determined that Claudia would succeed:

> I was down there (at the welfare office) all the time because I didn't know what I wanted to do or where I was at. I would have to meet with her, and she was trying to keep me busy.

Moving from one "Work Activity" to Another

The theme of "staying busy" kept arising in our conversations with Claudia. Her earnest caseworker assigned her to the Help Works program, then a computer course, provided her bus passes and made sure the local child care agency was finding a slot for Claudia's youngest. As long as Claudia remained in a legitimate work activity she could receive cash aid and work supports.

Claudia did not really see this sequence of assignments as leading anywhere. She was being "kept busy" by a caseworker who clearly cared about her long-term success. As Claudia explained,

> She was telling me that she wanted me to stay motivated and not give up. That's when she decided to put me in the computer class, just to keep me busy and to keep me going.

Claudia had a theory about her benevolent caseworker's own motivations. Through early 1999, Claudia reported that her caseworker

> might ask for a progress report . . . (but) she's letting me do it at my speed. She's not on my back constantly. As long as I'm still there (in the computer and word processing class), I really don't have to meet with her.

But by late 1999, with no job in sight, her caseworker's supervisor was reportedly

> getting on her [the caseworker] because she [Claudia] was just sitting at home, and why doesn't she have an activity. And that's when she started throwing me in all these different programs just to shut them up.

In November 1999, Claudia secured a full-time job, working as a home-care provider, assisting elderly or disabled adults in their homes. Despite the efforts of her caseworker, it was Claudia's friend, "who is kind of like family," who suggested, then recommended Claudia for the job. The friend supervised other home-care workers at the firm that hired Claudia. As Claudia remarked, Help Works did not help her find the job. "I found this job by myself. My friend said, 'Just try it, see if you like it.' "

LaTasha's View of Work—and Child Care

When we first sat with LaTasha in the fall of 1998, she was not worried about work. But she was upset over her youngest son's child care situation. Her ability to obtain subsidized care in the new CalWORKs program—as long as she worked—was a topic that surfaced time and again in conversations over the subsequent three years. Referring to her caseworker, LaTasha said,

> He's okay about everything. I call him and I tell him, "Well, I gotta work these many amount of days," and he's like, okay, just go ahead. Your child care is approved. Just send me your check stubs.

But LaTasha's caseworker, Alex, could only offer the standard menu of choices available to new welfare clients: Jobs like hotel maids, airport customer service, fast food, or a slot at the same bank where she had worked before. She wasn't satisfied with the resume building and interviewing skills taught at the job club, since she already had considerable work experience. She wanted a better job and felt that her children needed stable financial support.

> I learned how to type . . . but I would rather go to school and learn something more so I can move up and do something better. But right now, I just can't do it because I have to work in order to take care of my kids, 'cause welfare ain't doing it with three kids. . . . I ain't buying clothes, shoes, household, nothing. I feel like they learn better in

school when they're able to take pictures, or order books . . . you know, school things.

Despite having a resourceful and supportive caseworker, LaTasha continued to draw on the temp agency that had found work for her in the past:

Without the temp agency I'll probably still be looking for a job. Since I have been with them for a while, when anything good comes up, and they know that I'll be able to, they'll just call.

In the subsequent three years (1999–2002), LaTasha relied on family and friends to make a series of lateral moves in the job market. The pattern she had established prior to entering CalWORKs essentially continued—taking a new job and staying for up to eight months before getting bored or dissatisfied. She slowly improved her wages and benefits, even some flexibility in work hours. When we last spoke with LaTasha, she was making $12.36 an hour with benefits. And she was looking for something better.

In short, LaTasha continually talked about finding a better job, getting ahead. This pathway indeed had an intended direction—upward—and a set of strategies, mainly talking up job possibilities with her temp agency, caseworkers, and with kith and kin. But despite these resourceful supports and moving from job to job, after three years, LaTasha was still earning a barely livable wage of just over $12 an hour and trying to survive in an expensive city.

Preoccupied with Another Pathway

From LaTasha's earlier experience with California's GAIN program, she knew that cash aid meant free child care. When her oldest son was a toddler, she had returned to work, aided by another supportive caseworker who had driven her to various child care centers. Through the Children's Council, she gained access to a Montessori center that she loved. During our interviews, now that her youngest son, Jeronald, was preschool-age, she relied on the same agency to find a new center:

I want a school-type setting for my baby, because my other two, they went to daycares. And it was like they were going to school daycares . . . he'll be in a class with other two year-olds, not threes, fours . . . I want him to be where it's maybe five kids to one teacher . . . that's what I like about school daycares, because they're more like classrooms, like schools . . . instead of sitting around watching TV all day and never going outside or taking trips.

With three children, LaTasha often worried about child care and problems with after-school care arrangements. Over the three-year period that we visited LaTasha, she relied on family child care homes at times, including during the summers for her school-age children. If she worked night shifts or weekends, she had to rely on home-based care:

> Finding a daycare that will take him (Jeronald) the times I need . . . that's
> the only problem with day care . . . I need a daycare provider for the
> weekday, and then one for the weekends.

LaTasha's first criterion for selecting among child care options was location
and convenience, given her work schedule, which changed from month to
month. She thought highly of her caseworker at the Children's Council and
called her quite often. But in the end, LaTasha relied on places within her
neighborhood:

> I just always go by the people I know . . . That way I don't have to do
> all the background checks and all that stuff. If I know somebody's kids
> that go there, then obviously it must be a good place. Because lots of
> my cousins, they got kids and they're not just going to send their kids
> to anywhere.

To cover the weekends and after-school for her older kids, LaTasha paid her
own mother or a nearby aunt for child care help. "I usually do pay," LaTasha
said. "They probably ain't getting what they would get if they was a daycare
provider, but they're getting something [laughing]."

In sum, jobs and childrearing—including reliable child care—were
typically interwoven as LaTasha talked about her daily pathways, usually
aimed at somehow getting ahead. Her kids came first. But with new welfare
rules, the game had changed. She would not jeopardize her kids' well-being
by taking the risk of going back to school or training, particularly when her
fives years of welfare eligibility was ticking away. She was well aware of the
push to get off cash aid.

LaTasha's child care subsidy was important to her, and her preferred
solution was to enroll her youngest child in a "school-type" setting. Yet the
demands of her job and the practicalities of finding convenient day care
constrained her options. LaTasha depended on those she knew well to find
child care, similar to how she worked the job market.

Deeper Pathways—Advancing Children's Well-Being

For Claudia the eager pursuit of better options for her children took the
form of a separate pathway—not interwoven with the welfare-to-work trail
that LaTasha had followed. During each of our four interviews, Claudia
emphasized the importance of schooling and her various efforts to secure a
better child care setting or schooling for her children. For example, San
Francisco uses an open-enrollment system for choosing elementary schools,
a system that Claudia intensely engaged when each of her children entered
kindergarten.

Her commitment to reliable child care and sound schooling made us curious about why she herself had never entered high school.

Since I was the oldest, I was taking care of everybody (her five siblings) because my mom had a drinking problem. So it was all on me. That's why I tell Khadijah and Jamel, you're going to stay in school. There's no doubt about that. . . . try to (keep) your kid in school for as long as possible. Everybody from around here is like going to Lafayette School. But I'm trying to pull her (Khadijah) away from the neighborhood schools. I'm trying to make it easier (for her).

In late 2000, Claudia again talked about getting her kids out of the neighborhood:

I just don't think it would be good for her (Khadijah) to go to school around here . . . I just want her somewhere where she can meet new people.

Similarly, Claudia was untiring in her quest to find quality child care for her younger children, including a preschool for Nicole, as well as before- and after-school programs for Jamel and Khadijah. Claudia felt particularly lucky to have had her three youngest attend the Cityscape Preschool Center.

After Claudia landed her home-health-worker job, she awoke by 6:00 A.M., prepared a modest breakfast, then helped Jamel, Khadijah, and Nicole get dressed and ready.[3] By 7:45 all four "run up the hill and hopefully a bus will come, and we flag it down." Claudia dropped all three kids off at the Cityscape Center where a school bus drove Khadijah and Jamel to their elementary school, a half-hour from the projects in a blue-collar neighborhood. At day's end the bus brought them back to the center for a two-hour after-school program, and Claudia pushed to pick up all three kids by 5:30.

After being swept into the CalWORKs orientation meetings downtown, testing sessions, and then child development classes, Claudia was greatly relieved when we first met. She had just secured a full-day slot at the Cityscape Center for Nicole and places in the before- and after-school programs for the older kids. But organizing this mix had been difficult, she said.

It took me a while. That's the hardest part of the whole program. The hardest. I have a sister who still hasn't found child care. I didn't want my kids to go to somebody's home. I wanted them to be in a center. I started out with my mother. She would watch my little girl (Nicole). It was a lot of paperwork involved. They wanted you to fill out time sheets. And they take time paying your provider. So then your provider gets frustrated and wants to quit on you.

Claudia then acted independently of CalWORKs child care and went directly to the school district, visiting the "head office of the child development program." After a little "screaming" the school officials promised both the preschool-age slot for Nicole and the two school-age slots for her other children. "But it took me almost a year to find that," said Claudia.

Claudia's unrelenting pursuit of stable, center-based child care overlapped with her desire to get her school-age kids out of the neighborhood. Claudia selected an elementary school that was 30 minutes away by bus. However she admitted being fearful of the risks related to having Khadijah and Jamel waiting alone at the bus stop, or walking by themselves for the 5 minutes it takes from the bus stop to the front door:

> Around here you need somebody at the bus stop, because you never know when something's going to break out. Who would be at the bus stop to pick them up? My mom wasn't really steady, and she had things to do. She has a bad back, so I couldn't rely on her everyday. Then I had to figure out, when the other two (kids) got out of school, where are they gonna be?

In addition to the Cityscape Center's proximity and multiple services, Claudia was pleased that Nicole was involved at the center in a variety of play and learning activities.

> I like it (the center) because she's learning stuff there. She's got her reading time and her dress up time. Nap time. A little bit of everything. And she likes it a lot.

Later in the same 1998 interview, Claudia added,

> She's learning different songs. She's always picked up a lot anyway. Here (at home) before she even started up there, she'd already started singing her ABCs. So now she's counting . . . and learning different songs. And she knows about what she's eating because she eats a lot!

Claudia also got involved in community activities organized by the center, including a parenting class, monthly meetings with the staff and other women, and small-scale raffles. Claudia especially enjoyed the parenting class:

> (We learned) how to talk to them (one's children) if someone is mad, throwing a fit . . . instead of giving whippings . . . the talking, the time-outs I guess is what they call it.

Key Actors and Resourceful Ties

We next report on how LaTasha and Claudia defined sources of support in their lives—individuals and agencies that offered discrete economic or social resources along the way. We specifically asked about their friends and kin members, as well caseworkers and those working in local organizations.

Official Supports

Various people were mentioned as these women talked of their recurring search for jobs amidst the steady task of raising children. Claudia, for instance, referred often to her welfare caseworker. More frequently, she brought up information or friendship offered by kith or kin, who sometimes provided a window into official institutions. Most noteworthy, in this regard, was a sister who helped her find jobs and negotiate the tax system to receive her earned income tax credit during the years she worked.

Some nearby people were distinctly unhelpful in Claudia's life, including her mother who was often drunk. In contrast was Jamel's father who was "always telling me you can do this (get off welfare)," and the friend next door who Claudia said "always watches out for me."

Soon after Claudia entered the CalWORKs program in the spring of 1998, she began talking about her caseworker, who she called an "employment specialist." This caseworker was instrumental in continuing Claudia's cash aid, directing her to job preparation resources and training programs, obtaining new clothes for interviews, and coaching Claudia on how to keep other benefits, including Medicaid, after she began working full time. These official contacts seemed to boost Claudia's confidence and self-concept:

> We learned what things are available to us right now as far as not just child care, but they have programs that are, like, for getting clothes. To get out there and get you dressed up . . . it makes you feel motivated and stuff.

Claudia developed a tacit compact with her caseworker. By pursuing various training and work experience—the Steps Ahead job club, child development courses, a computer and word processing course, multiple vocational assessments—Claudia stayed in good stead with the welfare department. In return, the caseworker did not push harder on Claudia since she was engaged in certifiable "work activities." In late 1998, Claudia reported, "She's not on my back constantly to where there's some that are. If I'm not doing anything at the time, she tries to see what I can do."

Resentment did arise once when her caseworker held resources over her head until Claudia displayed the right behavior. Claudia was visibly angry when telling us how her caseworker "dropped [her children] from their day care" in the interim period between two different training programs. She had quit the community college courses, unable to handle studying while living solely off cash aid. When she left that program, she had to pull her children from the center until she entered another work activity.

Claudia also was furious one month with a new caseworker. To maintain eligibility for cash aid, she had mailed in two pay stubs to verify employment, but accidentally failed to include a required third one.

Instead of calling me and telling me, "Well this is the problem, and we need to know why you didn't mail in all three," they didn't call me or send a letter. They just didn't send me my grant. So I had to go through the whole running around, had to run back home, had to miss a day of work and gather up all the check stubs . . . it was just a big ole' mess.

Claudia had acquired considerable experience in gaining child care support through official agencies, going back to 1986 and her false start with the GAIN program. Initially she had applied and obtained a child care voucher through the Children's Council that reimbursed her mother to care for Nicole, who was just two at the time, and for after-school care for Khadijah and Jamel. But after several months, Claudia came to feel that all the paperwork and monitoring outweighed the material benefit accruing to her mother: "They (the child care agency) were paying her . . . and it was a big old hassle. We had to have these time sheets that had to be filled out everyday." But after she started working full time and her three children were enrolled at the Cityscape Center, Claudia said she only had to verify to the center staff that she was still employed once a year.

In 1999, Claudia heard from the Children's Council to see "if I needed help with child care." She knew that she was still eligible for child care assistance even though she was working full time: "I'm still under the [income eligibility] level . . . I'm not making enough, so I don't have to pay [for the center program]." The agency's follow-up was obviously reassuring.

LaTasha's Uneven Support from Official Agencies

LaTasha expressed mixed feelings about her caseworkers over our three years of conversations. Soon after entering CalWORKs in 1998, she reported quite positive feelings about her initial caseworker.

It seems like it's much easier now to deal with them. I mean, you're not really dealing with them that much I guess if you're working. If you're not working, then you're not dealing with them at all. But if you're working . . . it seems like they're trying to help you more than before. It's like, they're asking you what you need and, "How can we help you get this?"

But I know Mr. Barnett, he's helped me out a lot. He's my employment specialist. If they was more like him, it'd make a lot of people want to do stuff. He was like, "Well, I can help you do this and I can help you do that." Not, "You're gonna have to do this and you're gonna have to do that or you're out of here." I could just call him and be like, "Well, I need you to extend my day care for another month." And he was like, "Okay, I'm gonna call them today." I call the lady and it's done.

The respect and resourcefulness that caseworker Barnett displayed carried over even when the news was bad.

He told me before he do anything that my food stamps are gonna go down to this and my AFDC is gonna go down to this. But he's nice. He's really nice. And as long as he's my worker, then I feel like we're going to have a good relationship.

LaTasha tended to use CalWORKs as a source of income in between jobs. It also ensured that she did not lose her child care, an essential pillar of her household economy. For example, she left CalWORKs in early 2000 after she neglected to send in the form verifying employment. She then was able to stay off cash aid for a full year until she quit that job. When we last interviewed LaTasha in the summer of 2001, after a short spell on the rolls, she had again left CalWORKs and had no contact with her caseworker.

During her first episode back on aid, LaTasha experienced more negative feelings toward her caseworker:

When I went back on for those two months . . . she (the new case-worker) gave me a hard time. I was like, man, I gotta hurry up and find me a job. That's when I got this job as accounts payable for [a] health care center. And I'm like, I wouldn't be down here applying for this if I didn't need it. Obviously my rent need to be paid, and I can't get a job in time enough to have it paid on time, so that's why I'm here applying. I've had a good one [caseworker]. . . that were like my per-manent workers. [But] it was just like she was . . . oh, she made me never want to be on welfare.

LaTasha also reported parallel contacts with caseworkers at the Children's Council. She initially had problems ensuring that her child care provider was receiving timely reimbursement from the Council. She did not articulate the precise problem. But after this initial snag in 1998, LaTasha was typically upbeat about her relationship:

The Children's Council is one hundred percent different from welfare. Children's Council—I have no complaints with them ever. Now, Carmelita, that's my caseworker, my child care service specialist, she is cool. I ain't never had a problem on her. She called me just to say "LaTasha, are you ok? You need anything?" Things like that. "How's work going?" You have your one-on-one person . . . They get you your child care, they make sure your child care payments are made . . . As long as you sign them timesheets and send your own stuff in on time . . . the providers do their half and the parents do their half.

By our final interview in 2001, LaTasha was speaking to her Children's Council caseworker infrequently.

I really haven't been talking to them. Like once every six months. For me, you know, just to bring my check stubs in so they can keep my child care going.

Throughout these episodes with various caseworkers inside formal agencies, LaTasha was acquiring a range of resources. Beyond monthly cash aid and child care subsidies, she received food stamps, clothing for job interviews, and bus passes. Yet LaTasha never enrolled in a job club or classroom training, typically the beginning steps for the welfare-to-work routine. She plugged into CalWORKs when between jobs or in need of child care. And these formal agencies typically supplemented information and supports she arranged herself, mainly through the temp agency that readily provided low-wage job assignments.

Informal Support Networks—Aiding Childrearing and Work
LaTasha relied heavily on family and friends to hear about jobs and to locate child care providers. These informal networks led to various options, then she would contact CalWORKs or the Children's Council for the economic support described earlier. LaTasha's family was consistently there to provide support, with numerous examples mentioned across our interviews. Each time we visited her apartment, her mother, a cousin, or an old childhood friend was hanging out in the small living room—chatting with us, watching a movie, or getting her hair done. LaTasha's cousins and friends frequently cooked together or played with the kids at one of their houses.

On her mother's side of the family alone, LaTasha had 17 female cousins at recent count, many of whom lived nearby. Whenever LaTasha needed to go to the grocery store or run another errand she reported that it was easy, even expected, that she could drop off her kids with a relative. On weekends, when her kids stayed with their paternal grandparents, LaTasha spent even more time with old friends and kin, going to amusement parks, fairs, concerts, and nightclubs.

LaTasha's father, Jeff, provided consistent financial help over the years. Her mother, Gloria, was constantly present in LaTasha's everyday life, offering child care advice and steady emotional support. Over the course of three years we heard of how her father, mother, brother, auntie Ellen, and the kids' paternal grandparents all pitched in to help with child care. In late 1998, LaTasha told us:

> I have to be at work at six in the morning, and my kids should be at day care by five. So it give[s] me an hour to get to work, but she [the family child care provider] don't want to take the kids 'til seven. I have either my dad or my brother drop them off for me in the mornings. And then, after work, if I'm working overtime, then they'll pick them up.

LaTasha's father occasionally took all three children on trips, to Angel Island or Marine World. In 1999, when LaTasha became depressed about her cramped housing situation and resulting difficulties for her children, her mother took a two-week vacation from work to comfort and stay with LaTasha.

LaTasha made good use of her expansive social network of relatives and friends to find needed resources for herself and her children. Her youngest child, Mark, almost five in 2001, had stayed with seven different subsidized child care providers by the time of our final interview. Each time LaTasha changed jobs it shook up her child care arrangement. Most often LaTasha would check with her cousins or friends to find a new child care provider. Of the eight kids attending the Hilltop family child care home in 2001, three were biological cousins of her son Mark. "Everybody over there (are) his new cousins . . . that's his new family," said LaTasha. She reportedly had to "drag (him) out the door everyday" when she picked him up.

In contrast to LaTasha's large, supportive network of relatives and friends, Claudia expressed feelings of isolation, especially given the dangers and grim appearance of the housing projects where she lived over the years. Referring to all three children, Claudia told us, "I don't let them play outside." Talking about close-by friends, she said,

I have my next-door neighbor. But that's it. Everybody else, it's like, "hi" and "bye." That's how you have to keep it when you live somewhere like this. They tend to try to just come in to see what you have and find out what's going on, more or less.

This caution appeared warranted, given the amount of crime in the area. Claudia told us one evening:

I just recently found out about a couple break-ins. It's happening to people who even have gates on their house. They come through the walls. I have double cylinder dead-bolts. If they get in, they can't get out. Since this place [the burned-out unit on the other side of Claudia's apartment] has been empty, I'm at work constantly worrying about it. What if someone is to get in there and set it on fire?

In late 1999, Claudia told us that the shootings and violent crime had subsided significantly. "It's just gotten a lot more quiet. You don't see too much violence up here anymore." But she still wouldn't allow her children to play outside. "When I come home [from work] I am inside, and I just keep to myself."

Claudia did benefit from three or four people who provided steady support day to day. She talked about her nearby neighbor, Faye. Middle-aged, thin, and projecting a sense of confidence, Faye watched out for Claudia. When we came by to visit Claudia, Faye would somehow sense our arrival and pop out her front door. Claudia also was close to one sister, from whom she received advice and emotional support: "I mean I call her 15 times a day." In addition, one married cousin helped out whenever necessary. According to Claudia, "I can sometimes con my cousin to taking [the children] if it sounds like I'm just pulling out my hair."

Claudia's school-age kids sometimes went to her mother's apartment in the afternoons. But she wasn't thrilled with this environment, knowing that her mother still drank. "My mom lives just across the street which I don't like, because there is not activity, you know, she's [daughter] only going to be able to do her homework and watch TV. "

When we asked Claudia about how she found new jobs, she consistently reported leads from her mother, sister, or a friend. For example, her mom had worked at Costco, and a friend told her how to apply. Claudia landed her home-care job, which she still held as of our last interview in 2002, through an acquaintance that worked at the company.

Unflagging support for Claudia came from her stepfather. She told us in late 2000 about how her children would ask for Christmas presents or need new school clothes—things she could not provide.

> If I didn't have the money at the time . . . we'll call my dad, and he'll get it. He'll give me the receipts, and I'll pay him back the best way I can. He still does that, even though I'm working. I get four checks now a month, so it's easier for me to say I'll pay the bills and rent . . . and just pay him off with the child support money.

Claudia's stepfather, who "sets up and breaks down shows at the Moscone Convention Center," came up in various conversations.

> He's basically raised us. He does it all. When the washer machine broke down, I said I needed a new washer and I don't have the money. So, he ran out and bought the washer and handed me the receipt.

Claudia's stepfather also enjoys activities with the children: "We always try to go with him to the mall or somewhere . . . birthday parties, to the park, on my days off."

Guiding Signposts—Contested Ideas and Tacit Understandings

A final element of these perceived pathways emerged over the course of our conversations with Claudia and LaTasha. These were ideas or signals from their environments to which they attempted to respond. The policy logic behind work-first reforms has been that women will enter the labor force due to stricter rules and stronger incentives. These represent a mix of explicit and variably intrusive signals or rewards that are contingent upon the mother's actions. They certainly provide signposts—in the eyes of women, caseworkers, kith and kin—that indicate how each woman is doing on an intended pathway. First we examine these signals or signposts that women encounter along this understood pathway. Then we focus on signals and ideas they encounter in the child care arena.

Being on Welfare—Personal Responsibility

The morality of being on welfare was certainly debated in Claudia's social network. Her mother depended on AFDC when Claudia was growing up. In the projects, many families rely on cash aid. But Claudia expressed mixed feelings about welfare, and believed that the work-first push was positive overall. In an early interview, Claudia told us,

> Welfare reform is good, because it makes people stop sitting back and collecting it because it's free. If it wasn't for that [the work push], nobody was going to get up and start doing it.

About a year later, after she was working steadily, we asked whether she would have pursued this job in the absence of welfare-to-work pressure. She responded:

> If it hadn't happened, I really don't think I would have a job right now. Then again, I get a lot of support from his dad [her middle son's dad], and he is always the one . . . telling me that you can do this. You don't need to be sitting there and collecting it. You can be doing something.

We asked Claudia how her friends and family viewed welfare. She responded, "Some of them see it as a good thing. I have some sisters that don't like it at all." In another interview, Claudia told us that working at her low-wage home assistant job didn't really boost her net income, at least not enough to buy her children more clothes and toys.

Claudia seemed to blend these official rules and incentives with signals or understandings that she received from more trusted people in her social circle. At one point, we asked about different sources of income, and she mentioned the earned income-tax credit (EITC). Originally, she had worried that she could not file for this refundable credit, since she was on welfare. But then when she landed the Costco job, "Everybody was saying, 'Yeah, yeah . . . go ahead and do it.' So, I did. Now my sister-in-law does that for me every year." The mere presence of an incentive or signal is important, but, at times, not sufficient until it is legitimated by a friend or kin member.

Claudia implied that moving off cash aid and into steady employment was the more correct path to take, from a moral standpoint. Yet often her short-term concern was to stay in good standing with her welfare caseworker. She hated pushing her elderly or disabled clients to sign her time sheets each day, just to prove to her caseworker that she had put in the required hours. Claudia felt at times that she was being shuttled from one requirement to another—to a job club, to a new training program, to various interviews, or testing sessions. Even after she had found the home assistant job through an acquaintance, someone in the welfare network pushed her to stay in touch with the private job preparation agency. "I'm still in Help Works because even though I am working, they have to keep up with me."

Claudia talked on and off about an alternative employment pathway to become a certified nurse's assistant. But "you have to take classes. That's first off. I think it's a six-month program. I'm trying to figure it out now, to see how it can work." Over the three years that Claudia spoke of this dream, she couldn't figure out how to put together the income to sustain her family over six months, and she did not believe that her caseworker would award her that much time away from real employment.

With LaTasha it's doubtful that the work-first push altered her views of work or "personal responsibility" when it came to holding down a job. "I don't really have trouble finding a job, she told us in 1998, "I just have trouble finding a job that I like." LaTasha had worked since her late teens. Neither of her parents had ever been on welfare; most of her cousins and friends typically worked. After LaTasha became pregnant with Monique at age 15, then applied for cash aid, her mother strongly disapproved, reminding LaTasha, "You weren't on welfare (growing up). You weren't raised in the projects." Both her parents reportedly expressed relief in those periods when she went off cash aid.

What she took away from her first orientation session at the downtown welfare office was "that I can get paid child care. They'll pay for my child care if I work and go to school." This was a huge benefit in LaTasha's mind. It saved her money; it saved the hassle of having to juggle among her mother, the kids' father, or her cousins to be sure she could get to work. The incentive of subsidized child care did not necessarily alter LaTasha's moral views of work behavior, although it appeared to minimize periods of joblessness.

Like Claudia, LaTasha talked occasionally about returning to school to partake in a longer-term training program. But this alternative route felt too challenging, too unrealistic, while her children were young. She certainly never perceived that the welfare office would support that kind of educational investment.

Mothering First, Work Second

When it came to pasting together better opportunities for their children, these women displayed no lack of personal responsibility. We discussed how Claudia aggressively pushed to get three of her children into the school district's local preschool program. As her children were entering kindergarten, she purposefully played San Francisco's school choice game to find schools far from the projects.

Both Claudia and LaTasha talked much about how their children came first and work came second. Employment was one way, among several methods, of raising one's income. This translated into better housing, a few more excursions with the kids on weekends, perhaps a new entertainment center, or nicer birthday presents.

LaTasha often relied on family-based child care homes, beyond her mother's child care services. But from our first interview forward, LaTasha made clear she wanted a "school-type setting".

LaTasha used terminology that was likely acquired from her child care caseworker at the Children's Council, perhaps in parent training sessions. In our second and third years of conversation, she began using the term "provider," not the more localized usage, "daycare." She was attuned to indicators of quality, which signaled the setting was more school-like. In the summer of 2001, LaTasha was utilizing a family-based child care home for Jeronald, and her detailed description resembled a textbook on school readiness:

> It's big, it's clean, and she has a lot of children's things in her house. It's set up for kids and that's what I like. And she taught him how to write his name. They have their little food time in the mornings. She has all the little computers for them to play on . . . [she] teaches them how to write their numbers and write their names, you know, how to identify certain things. When you go to daycare, that's going to school to him. He don't call it daycare or Miss Phyllis' house, he call it school.

LaTasha, wanting to spend more time with her children during certain periods, would reflect on a clearer pathway to reach this goal:

> It's just that I can't go to college right now because my baby is too young. I can't do it right now. I'm a wait 'til he's at least four, so then I'll feel more secure about leaving, going there [community college] and trying to go to work, and not seeing him all day. 'Cause right now, I hardly ever see him. I would rather go to school and learn something more, so I can move up and do something better. But right now I just can't do it because I have to work in order to take care of my kids. Welfare ain't doing with three kids. So I have to work right now to get them things and my kids' birthdays and Christmas. I'm gonna make sure that my kids is happy.

Claudia also acquired an understanding of signals and ideas in the child care world that seemed important. She talked to us about how young children "learn more in a center," rather than what she termed, "child cares," meaning family child care homes. Even when she first entered CalWORKs back in 1998, she knew she wanted a school-like setting for her children.

> They gave me a list of child cares . . . [but] I was not interested really because . . . I wanted her [daughter] in a center. I figured, you know, she can learn more in a center than going to somebody's house everyday. Besides that, I don't trust anybody's house. I liked the way the classroom was set-up . . . little sections, like a play area for the kitchen, or the little library has shelf with books and a fish tank, and a couch. They have a section called the dollhouse [with] clothes that people donated for them to play in. Then, the teacher, she was really friendly, really nice.

She got really close to Arnelle. She see her passing in the hallway, they hug, stuff like that.

Gaining Respect

Finally, the notion of being respected in everyday contacts with caseworkers and agency staff arose often in our conversations. Claudia tended to be less confident, more reticent to push back. One evening, we got talking about public housing. Claudia's dream was to escape the south-side projects in which she had spent her entire life. She had applied for her Section 8 housing voucher by the summer of 2000. But "because they know I'm in low-income housing, I'm like last priority."

What really got to Claudia was the lack of respect displayed by housing officials: "They act like they don't have to help. They're rude, very unprofessional. They kept turning me down." In contrast we have heard how welfare and child care caseworkers were generally seen as supportive and resourceful by both women. Claudia and LaTasha constantly expressed their feelings toward specific caseworkers, and felt much better about those who were attentive and respectful.

Circuitous Pathways, Constant Uncertainties

This kind of in-depth, qualitative evidence is based on the stories of just two welfare-to-work mothers. We must be careful about making strong inferences regarding wider populations of low-income mothers. As we have documented, these reports of two mothers' experiences have shown similarities and differences as they moved through San Francisco's reformed welfare program. Still, Claudia's and LaTasha's stories offer suggestive evidence that points to a pair of tentative hypotheses, which should be investigated with larger samples of families.

First California's version of welfare reform—particularly San Francisco's program—prompted novel action by Claudia and LaTasha. Both women felt the new rules and pressures, along with additional work supports, resources, and options, which they never experienced during their earlier involvement with the AFDC program. Both clearly felt that work expectations had risen; their welfare and child care caseworkers reinforced these demands while offering steady assistance and oversight.

The first hypothesis follows from this reasoning: *Novel welfare-to-work pressures and supports were insufficient to lead either woman down a linear path that resulted in steady, motivating employment.*

LaTasha continued to accept and then withdraw from cash aid, depending on her current luck in the job market. Claudia landed the home health care job after a series of training and counseling sessions, only to grow bored and dissatisfied with her new occupation after a year. Neither woman felt that she could afford a training program for more than a few weeks, nor move up the employment ladder beyond earning $10–12 per hour. This realization, surfacing toward the end of our three years together, seemed disheartening though not surprising as they described how they may have reached the end of the line regarding work.

So, although these women understood the tidy pathways intended by policy makers, their actions often resulted in a circuitous path that took unexpected twists and turns. The winding pathways that Claudia and LaTasha reported are certainly less linear, bent by many more unpredictable pressures than earnest policy makers may expect.

Second the mere amount of talk about their children, the challenges of raising kids alone, and the strategic maneuvering through the child care system all suggest that far deeper tracks were being carved in their parenting route. As LaTasha told us a few times, "My kids come first." Even Claudia, at times timid in challenging agencies, repeatedly pushed for better child care arrangements and worked the city's school-choice scheme to get her older kids out of the projects and into better schools. This determined focus on advancing children's well-being is consistent with an earlier study by Scott et al. (2001), which revealed how many mothers are primarily motivated to advance their children's interests. From this base, they piece together sources of income that advance this goal.

A second hypothesis flows from this line of reasoning: *Welfare-to-work policies, combined with mothers' drive to advance their children's well-being, motivated them to hold down paid employment.*

Our study suggests the importance of additional research—both ethnographic and quantitative work—that delves into how women understand their responses to novel policy messages. Both Claudia and LaTasha felt quite good about a subset of their caseworkers. Both women understood the role of their employment specialist, that is, the main caseworker who helped in finding a job. But overall Claudia and LaTasha felt better about their child care caseworker than their employment specialist, although this may be linked to the importance they placed on finding a reliable caregiver or preschool. Both women became quite discerning in how they assessed the qualities and learning agendas of home- or center-based child care programs.

The hazy boundary between agency support and that received via informal networks is important to emphasize. Policy makers tend to focus on improving formal welfare agencies; instead scholars have been preoccupied with informal kinds of social capital. Our findings suggest that these two worlds sometimes overlap. Kinship linkages to child care providers or preschool teachers is one case in point. Claudia and LaTasha also acquired information about jobs and training possibilities from caseworkers and friends or kin, leading to a mix of employment possibilities.

Claudia also reported on her welfare caseworker's earnest desire to keep her busy in some activity, even when the training sequence was illogical or when she was pressured by a private training program to keep attending, even after finding a job. The emphasis placed on an allowable work activity by the federal TANF program creates incentives to look busy, to make sure one's client is signed-up for something. But the haphazard, even nonsensical string of activities encouraged by the welfare office appeared to undercut the program's overall credibility in Claudia's eyes.

We found little evidence that the welfare-to-work push deepened these women's moral commitment to paid jobs, although it may have raised their self-esteem and efficacy in negotiating a wider range of firms and agencies. When work advanced the household economy, especially in ways that benefited their children, Claudia and LaTasha reported positive feelings about going to work each day. Finally securing a full-time job appeared to boost Claudia's belief in herself—that she could work steadily and raise her family with some degree of success.

Still, both women repeatedly told us how they felt stymied in getting further ahead. LaTasha remained tied to her temp agency. Claudia saw no clear route for getting into nursing school, her long-term dream. But her dream of escaping the projects did come true. We called Claudia in 2003, since a reporter covering our study was eager to interview a participant. Claudia proudly told us that she had moved out of the City and now lived within walking distance of the beach.

Finally the work supports made available through CalWORKs after the 1996 federal reforms mattered a lot in their lives. Strong and steady child care support was certainly noticed and highly valued by both women. LaTasha went back on the welfare rolls when her earnings dropped and she worried regularly about losing her child care subsidy. The smaller supports—bus passes, a nice set of job clothes, help with keeping medical insurance—seemed to boost both women's respect for and trust in their caseworkers.

In recent years, the persisting debate over welfare in America has shifted in favor of legislating even tougher work rules that promise "to allow more families to realize the dignity of work" as George W. Bush likes to put it. As talk of additional reforms persists, it's worth considering whether the welfare system might become more motivating if it tapped into what really appears to energize women like Claudia and LaTasha: Finding ways to improve the conditions in which they are raising their children. The dignity and emotional rewards of raising one's children may present a more fulfilling pathway, if the only other alternative is simply a low-wage, unfulfilling job. Ironically conservative policy makers appear to be more eager to mete out stiffer versions of tough love—through more intense work requirements—than strengthen women's ability to become resourceful mothers.

Notes

An earlier version of this chapter was presented at *The Daily Lives of Poor Families: Policy Implications of Qualitative Inquiry*, a conference held at the University of California, Berkeley, November 2001. The Haas Jr. Fund, San Francisco, and the Berkeley Center for Child and Youth Policy supported the forum. Special thanks to Hedy Chang, Amanda, Feinstein, and Cheryl Polk. Sandra Park assisted with the data analysis. This chapter stems from the Growing Up in Poverty Project, based at Berkeley, Stanford, and Columbia University, supported by the Casey, Packard, Spencer, and MacArthur foundations, the Haas families, the U.S. Department of Education, and the Department of Health and Human Services.

1. In 1996, about 90 percent of all families receiving cash aid were headed by a single mother; the focus of this chapter, therefore, is on single mothers. This has changed significantly in recent years with the rise of "child-only cases," where the guardian may be a grandparent or another adult who receives cash aid for the child's care.
2. California Work Opportunity and Responsibility to Kids program, California's version of the federal PRWORA legislation.
3. Over the two years that we interviewed Claudia, her oldest children, Durrell and Karlesha, ages 15 and 17 in 1998, were still in the legal custody of their father. Claudia paid $200 monthly in child support to the father.
4. The intentions of federal policy makers in this regard are discussed in Fuller et al. (2000b). The theoretical underpinnings for examining the tacit understandings or taken-for-granted "cultural models" of action are examined in Holloway et al. (1997).

References

Anderson, E. (1992). The story of John Turner. *The Public Interest, 32*(108), 3–34.

Berrick, J. D. (1995). *Faces of poverty: Portraits of women and children on welfare.* New York: Oxford University Press.

Blank, R. and Haskins, R. (ed.) (2001). *The new world of welfare.* Washington, DC: Brookings Institution.

Bloom, D., Adams-Ciardullo, D., Hendra, B., Michalopoulos, C., Morris, P., Scrivener, S., and Walter, J. (2002). *Jobs first: Final report on Connecticut's welfare reform initiative.* New York: Manpower Demonstration Research Corporation.

Carnoy, M. (1984). *Political theory and the state.* Princeton: Princeton University Press.

Collins, A., Layzer, J., Kreader, J., Werner, A., and Glantz, F. (2000). *National study of child care for low-income families: State and community sub-study interim report.* Cambridge, MA: ABT Associates.

D'Andrade, R. and Strauss, C. (eds.) (1992). *Human motives and cultural models.* New York: Cambridge University Press.

Deparle, J. (2004). *American dream: Three women, ten kids, and a nation's drive to end welfare.* New York: Viking Books.

Durkheim, E. (1938). *The rules of sociological method* (trans., S. Solovay and J. Mueller.). New York: Free Press.

Edin, K. and Lein, L. (1997). *Making ends meet: How women survive welfare and low-wage work.* New York: The Russell Sage Foundation.

Fuller, B. and Hannum, E. (2002). Scaffolds for achievement? Institutional foundations of social capital. In B. Fuller and E. Hannum (eds.), *Research in sociology of education* (pp. 1–12, vol. 13). Oxford: Elsevier.

Fuller, B., Kagan, S. L., Caspary, G., and Gauthier, C. (2002a). Welfare reform and child care for low-income families. *Future of Children, 12,* 97–120.

Fuller, B., Kagan, S. L., and Loeb, S. (2002b). *New lives for poor families: Mothers and children move through welfare reform.* Berkeley and New York: University of California, Berkeley (PACE Research Center).

Giddens, A. (ed.) (1986). *Durkheim on politics and the state.* Stanford, CA: Stanford University Press.

Greenstein, R. and Guyer, J. (2001). Supporting work through Medicaid and food stamps. In R. Blank and R. Haskins (eds.), *The new world of welfare* (pp. 335–363). Washington DC: Brookings.

Haskins, R. (2001). The effects of welfare reform on family income and poverty. In R. Blank and R. Haskins (eds.), *The new world of welfare* (pp. 103–130). Washington DC: Brookings.

Holloway, S., Fuller, B., Rambaud, M., and Eggers-Pierola, C. (1997). *Through my own eyes: Single mothers and the cultures of poverty.* Cambridge, MA: Harvard University Press.

Howard, C. (1997). *The hidden welfare state: Tax expenditures and social policy in the United States.* Princeton NJ: Princeton University Press.

Jargowsky, P. (1997). *Poverty and place: Ghettos, barrios, and the American city.* New York: The Russell Sage Foundation.

Katz, M. (1986). *In the shadow of the poorhouse: A social history of welfare in America.* New York: Basic Books.

Lewis, O. (1959). *Five-families—Mexican case studies in the culture of poverty: San Juan and New York.* New York: Basic Books.

Loury, G. (1977). A dynamic theory of racial income differences. In P. Wallace and A. LeMund (eds.), *Women, minorities, and employment discrimination.* Lexington, MA: Lexington Books.

MacLeod, J. (1987). *Ain't no makin' it: Leveled aspirations in a low income neighborhood.* Boulder, CO: Westview Press.

Mead, L. (1992). *The new politics of poverty.* New York: Basic Books.

Michalopoulos, C. and Berlin, G. (2001). Financial work incentives for low-wage workers. In R. Blank and R. Haskins (eds.), *The new world of welfare* (pp. 270–286). Washington DC: Brookings.

Murray, C. (1984). *Losing ground: American social policy, 1950–1980.* New York: Basic Books.

Nussbaum, M. (1999). *Sex and social justice.* New York: Oxford University Press.

Ogbu, J. (1978). *Minority education and caste: The American system in cross-cultural perspective.* New York: Academic Press.

Portes, A. (1998). Social capital: Its origins and applications in modern sociology. *Annual Review of Sociology, 24,* 1–24.

Putnam, R. (1995). Bowling alone: America's declining social capital. *Journal of Democracy, 6,* 65–78.

Scott, E., Edin, K., London, A., and Mazeliz, J. (2001). My children come first: Welfare-reliant women's post-TANF views of work-family trade-offs and marriage. In G. Duncan and P. Chase-Lansdale (eds.), *For better or for worse: Welfare reform and the well-being of children and families* (pp. 132–153). New York: The Russell Sage Foundation.

Weaver, R. K. (2000). *Ending welfare as we know it.* Washington, DC: Brookings Institution.

Weisner, T., Gibson, C., Lowe, E., and Romich, J. (2002). Understanding working poor families in the New Hope Program. *Poverty Research News, 6,* 3–5.

Wilson, W. J. (1996). *When work disappears.* New York: Alfred A. Knopf.

CHAPTER THREE

Where Poverty and Parenting Intersect: The Impact of Welfare Reform on Caregiving

LAURA FRAME

Public policies impact individual lives, but the task of identifying those effects can be a challenge. In the case of welfare reform, locating the effects of changed welfare policies on parenting quality is complicated by the fact that most welfare policies do not directly target parenting behavior, and most welfare programs are not parenting interventions, per se. Rather the federal welfare reforms of the 1990s were largely intended to influence workforce participation and family income, as well as to encourage marriage, and to thereby affect parenting through indirect routes. Still changes in welfare laws have important implications for children and parents, and parenting remains a primary avenue through which poverty conditions—and the welfare policies that influence them—affect children.

In their review of the literature on welfare reform and parenting, Chase-Lansdale and Pittman (2002) outline a complex model of the determinants of parenting. In this model, parent characteristics, child characteristics, family economic resources, and family structure/size have an effect upon the more proximal influences on parenting, specifically the quality of marital or partner relationships, the quality of kin and social networks, and parental mental health. The latter influence—parental mental health—figures prominently in much of the literature on parenting and socioeconomic conditions.

The links between economic hardship and parental psychological distress have been well established, and the relationship between parental mental health and parenting quality has been similarly well supported (Elder, 1974; McLoyd, 1990; McLoyd and Wilson, 1990, 1991). Further parental psychological processes have been demonstrated to be important mediators between poverty and parenting, and parenting behavior plays a key role in mediating the effects of poverty on children (Conger et al., 1984;

Duncan et al., 1994; Garrett et al., 1994; McLeod and Shanahan, 1993; McLoyd, 1990, 1998; McLoyd and Wilson, 1990, 1991).

In parenting-related studies, parental mental health has often been examined in terms of stress, reports of psychological distress, or diagnosed mental health problems (e.g., depression). This Chapter offers a research-based framework for understanding the impact of welfare policies on parenting, which elaborates in some detail the psychology of caregiving (parenting) and its role as a mediator of parenting behavior in poverty conditions. It draws upon a "theory of caregiving" proposed by Solomon and George (1996; see also George and Solomon, 1996).

In this theory, caregiving behavior is psychologically guided by parents' internalized sense of themselves as caregivers, their child, and their relationship with their child; and also by their capacity to process information and emotions relevant to the parent–child relationship. Parenting behavior is thus related to parental capacities to think and feel about their child, their child's needs, and parenting issues. A parent's subjective experience of life events or conditions is understood to impact caregiving, and, at the extreme, "assaults to the caregiving system" (Solomon and George, 2000) may overwhelm, disorganize, and significantly disable parenting capacities. Thus welfare reforms' effects on parenting quality—specifically, the provision of basic forms of care and protection to children—are considered in terms of their role in shaping the context in which parenting occurs, and how it is experienced.

Description of the Study

This longitudinal, qualitative study examined the links between urban poverty-related conditions and the quality of parent–child relationships, specifically the care and protection of infants and toddlers. The study was conducted between 1999 and 2001, allowing a couple of years for the implementation of welfare reforms. The study's focus was on families likely to be socially and economically precarious under the conditions of welfare reform, including long-term welfare recipients and other families involved in the public child welfare system.

A theoretical sampling strategy was used such that families were purposely selected to be economically poor, and likely to represent various points on a continuum of parenting quality. To meet this purpose, sampling and recruitment occurred through two sources. The first was a previous survey sample of welfare recipients who had participated in the University of California at Berkeley's UC DATA/Survey Research Center study of welfare reform experiments in the 1990s. Participants received welfare cash grants in 1993 and again in 1998, with either continuous or discontinuous involvement between those years.

The second sampling source was the Alameda County Social Services Agency, Department of Children and Family Services—the public child welfare services agency. All parent participants were required to live in Alameda County, California, to have relied on TANF as a primary source of income, and to have at least one child under age 3 at the time of recruitment into the study. Families recruited through the public child welfare agency were receiving child protective intervention due to child neglect. A total of ten families were recruited for participation; four through the UC DATA sample, and six through the child welfare agency. Participating adult subjects were paid $25 per interview. All ethical considerations, including those related to remuneration, were regularly discussed with the research team and addressed directly with participants, where necessary.

The study utilized ethnographic methods, with data collection scheduled to occur approximately monthly in field visits with families for about a year, and efforts at follow-up at the end of the second year. Because participants entered the study on a "rolling" basis and there was variability in engagement, the number of contacts and length of the data collection period varied somewhat. Although one participant dropped out after two interviews, most of the nine other families remained involved in data collection for 10–14 months, and most completed between nine and thirteen interviews during the initial data collection period. (There were 2 subjects involved for 4 and 8 months, and three subjects who completed six–eight total interviews.)

Data collection took place in families' homes and other locations (the local park, fast-food restaurants), with the researcher taking an observer–participant stance. Relationships between the researcher and families varied naturally in terms of quality and intensity, but all families were interviewed about the same general set of topics. Interviews and observations, using topic guides and, in some cases, semi-structured interview formats, focused on the quality of parent–child relationships, parents' experiences of parenting their children, families' economic circumstances and socioeconomic histories, and experiences with public welfare and child welfare systems. Special attention was paid to the care and protection of the youngest children. All interviews and researcher observations were audiotaped and transcribed, verbatim.

A qualitative software program, Atlas.*ti*, was used to manage the extensive notes in the analysis process. Data analysis combined inductive and deductive approaches; the study was theory-guided, but not theory-driven. It made use of sensitizing concepts (see Beeman, 1995; Patton, 1990) from existing theory and research, but allowed room for emergence of fresh ideas. Notes were coded in detail across a variety of topics, including aspects of parent–child interactions and living environments with respect to the care and protection of children (e.g., hunger, illness, injury, environmental safety); parents' subjective experiences of living in conditions of poverty (e.g., fears, hopes, stresses); economic and welfare-related circumstances (e.g., grant amounts, sanctions, and time limits); and the impact of welfare and child welfare systems on economic stability and parenting quality. Themes were identified using an iterative process of "constant comparison"

(Strauss and Corbin, 1990), and codes were gradually grouped into categories. Reliability and validity were insured by following a number of strategies recommended by Miles and Huberman (1994) and Padgett (1998).

The Participants

All families lived in urban areas of Alameda County, California. Alameda County is an ethnically and economically diverse county, with high poverty and unemployment rates in its urban centers, which include the City of Oakland. Some aspects of California's welfare-to-work program, CalWORKs, were implemented relatively slowly in Alameda County during the early study period. Conversations with key informants in the welfare department confirmed this, and suggested administrative explanations. The pace of implementation was evident in the experience of a study participant, who reported, for example, contacting the CalWORKs office in 1999 to sign up for a welfare-to-work plan, and not receiving a return telephone call or letter within the study period. Some features of the welfare-to-work program in Alameda County, such as sanctions, also were not fully implemented during the study period. At least one study subject who was not working the required number of hours did not receive a sanction during the study.

The study subjects included nine mothers and one father; although some had partners during the study, all were the primary or sole caregiver of their children. Seven parents were African American, two were Latina, and one was Caucasian; in nearly every case, their children were the same race as their parents. Parents ranged in age from 28 to 40, with the majority in their mid-thirties at study entry. In addition to having at least one infant or toddler, all parents except one had at least one other child; one parent had two, and the others had between three and five living children. Of the six families involved with the child welfare system for reasons of neglect, all had reunified with their youngest child (from foster care) at entry into the study. All of the child-welfare-involved parents had experienced years of drug addiction and were in recovery; many had served time in jail or prison. Four of these parents had lengthy experience with the child welfare and foster care systems, including termination of their parental rights on older children.

Most of the study subjects were long-term welfare recipients. With the exception of the father in the study, who had received TANF for a total of 2 months, the sample's welfare history dated back 10 to 20 years. The actual number of years that subjects had received welfare were somewhat fewer, as all but one parent had cycled off and on welfare during their history. During the study, seven of ten families were affected by the family cap provision, and therefore did not receive cash aid for their youngest child. Three parents had completed high school and some community college. Of the remainder, two had obtained their GEDs, and five did not complete high school.

The employment history in the sample ranged from none other than street skills (prostitution, drug dealing) to many years of intermittent low-wage work experience. Only one parent of ten actively used welfare-to-work training to obtain a job; most who secured employment did so through friends and personal contacts. One parent attended half an orientation session and never returned to CalWORKs, another completed an initial set of "job club" meetings and like one other parent, enrolled in community college to meet her welfare-to-work requirements. All six of the families who were child-welfare-involved, and two others, utilized CalWORKs-subsidized child care. No families reached welfare time limits, to their knowledge, during the study period. One was sanctioned during the first year of data collection for work nonparticipation.

Findings: Impacts of Welfare Reform on Caregiving

For parents in this study, features of welfare reform were simply part of the experience of raising children in poverty, and the impact of specific reforms were embedded into daily concerns for their children. When parents were asked about particular aspects of welfare reform, they often offered an opinion that was thoughtful, but somewhat abstract. The more revealing observations about welfare reform occurred while examining the mundane details of parenting and providing. Grant amounts were reported to vary unpredictably. Letters from the welfare agency arrived or did not arrive, were lost and relocated, were interpreted, misinterpreted, ignored, or worried about.

Discussions about welfare to work were contextualized by the cost of transportation, child care availability, and the desire to give their children a basket of candy on Easter Sunday. Welfare did not lift these families out of poverty, and living conditions did not dramatically change for those who moved from welfare to work. Thus parents' experiences of welfare reforms appeared to be less about the explicit "messages" of reform than they were about the daily experience of parenting their children, given their economic conditions.

Welfare reform's impact on parenting capacity and quality can be understood in terms of: (1) The material realities of parenting in poverty conditions, and parents' means of coping with those strains; (2) the psychological experience of parenting in poverty conditions, and parents' capacities to adaptively cope with those experiences; and (3) the severity of poverty conditions. The experience of raising children in conditions of poverty is not simply one of "generic" stress or distress. Rather much of parental stress is located at the *intersection* between poverty conditions and aspects of parenting. This is true in terms of the material realities of parenting in poverty conditions, and the psychological experience of doing so. Thus welfare reforms have the potential to either exacerbate the negative conditions of poverty in which children are raised, or to offset them, and, perhaps, facilitate adaptive parenting behaviors. Each of these influences on parenting quality is described here and illustrated with examples from the data.

The Material Realities of Parenting on Welfare, and in Urban Poverty

Urban poverty-related conditions are present in the concrete, moment-to-moment realities of caregiving, influencing the nature and intensity of the demands placed on parents, and the threats to their children's well-being. The families in this study experienced material realities that can be grouped into five general categories, discussed below.

Material reality #1: Low Income and Restricted Resources Limit Parents' Capacities to Meet Children's Basic Needs. The costs of food, clothing, diapers, shelter, and utilities exceed TANF grant amounts and supplemental, in-kind supports [Food Stamps, Women, Infants, & Children (WIC) vouchers], as well as the combined income of welfare and much low-wage work. The cost of diapers, for example, was an often-encountered example of the intersection between poverty and children's needs. More than one parent talked of needing to toilet train her child early, because she could not afford to purchase diapers. To have limited resources is often to be forced to accept substandard housing, such as the house of one study subject (Francesca[1]), which was leaking, mildewed, had bars improperly and dangerously installed on the windows, and rats that were entering the living area. Each of those hazards directly threatened Francesca's children.

Material Reality #2: The Dangerous Conditions of Many Poor, Urban Neighborhoods Pose Threats to Children's Safety and Well-Being. In many urban areas, affordable housing is located primarily in areas of concentrated poverty. Thus a number of the parents in this study lived in neighborhoods where there was clear evidence of drugs, gangs, and criminal activity, in addition to the generally disintegrating physical state of the environment. Regina, who lived in an environment most closely resembling a suburb, said that she would not take her toddler to the nearby park because,

> It doesn't look like a park for kids. It's more like a park for adults. [They] play cards, they drink . . . they throw the [used hypodermic] needles too and they leave them all over the place.

Leticia also worried about living alone with her child:

> So much happening. I don' wan' nobody to come in my house killin' me, you know . . . if I got one a them iron gates like that an' bars on my window, I probably wouldn't be so scared.

Material Reality #3: Institutional and Structural Obstacles Restrict Access to Opportunity or Make the Road to Economic Success More Challenging. These obstacles increase the competing demands parents face, as they work to shape the social and economic environment for their children. Without economic freedom, a parent has little power in the face of those who do, such as landlords, for example, who might choose to evict them at any time or balk at making necessary repairs. Both Francesca and Leticia dealt with problematic, unresponsive landlords, and several other participants (Kenisha, Jennifer, Anna) struggled with locating affordable housing and/or landlords who would accept a Section 8 voucher in a tight, expensive rental market.

All these parents relied on social welfare institutions for part of their economic survival. Characteristic of these institutions was a tendency toward bureaucratic inertia, and snafus such as delayed welfare checks and mistakes in Food Stamp amounts. Such problems are difficult to ameliorate when a parent's identified contact is a social worker named in the paperwork as "B. Center" (for "Benefits Center"). All of these institutional obstacles take significant time, energy, and persistence to manage successfully.

Material Reality #4: There are Often Persisting Effects of Deprivation Over a Parent's Lifetime, Effects That Further Limit the Opportunities Open to Them and Their Children. To be a long-term welfare participant, as many of these parents were, is often to have limited skills for use in the paid labor market. For a number of parents in the study, poverty played an important role in their historical background, intertwining in relationships with family members, the educational system, and future opportunities. The effects of poverty over several generations were especially clear in cases where the parent's family of origin was not only poor, but also addicted to substances and/or abusive.

Leticia, who spent most of her childhood in foster care, had no relatives on whom she could rely (all were very poor and many had been using drugs for years). In this family context, she dropped out of school in the ninth grade, and has relied on public assistance or illegal activity for income during most of her adult life. As she put it:

> My mom, she was an' addict, you know. She couldn' teach me nothin' . . . didn' tell me to go to school an' get a education an' all that stuff, so—that has a lot to do with the way I came up an' all that I been through. An' [when] . . . you grown, though, it's basically on you. It's what you wanna do with your life. I didn' wanna do nothin' with my life but use crack an' that was it . . . I didn' finish high school.

Leticia saw herself as only having the skills to be a housecleaner; her limited education and multiple criminal convictions made alternatives seem impossible. Additionally, her family's poverty history was embedded in her social support network, so she did not have social contacts who might assist her in exiting poverty.

Material Reality #5: The Cumulative Effects of Poverty Conditions Can Influence Children's Behavior, Development, and Health Issues. There were cases of very young children's asthma that was likely exacerbated by poor housing conditions, dental problems that worsened because of substandard or limited health care access, and poor nutritional habits. Any child-health problem that seemed to have poverty's stamp on it may have been intensified because of the parent's inadequate response in obtaining health care, in addition to any problems of access to care. Yet the child-health and behavior problems faced by parents were shaped and influenced by poverty-related factors. Francesca's oldest child, for example, had serious behavioral problems stemming from years of instability and insecurity in her family relationships and other aspects of her environment.

The Material Realities and Parental Coping

Parents have different ways of managing the material strains of living on welfare, and this can influence the quality of their parenting. For the parents in this study, adaptiveness depended to a large extent on their ability to successfully enter the labor market. Some parents had skills and the necessary work supports such as family and child care. This was the case for Glen, a construction worker, and Kenisha, who held several clerical positions. Both of these parents had obtained their GED and had significant work experience in spite of years of drug use. Because of their employment and the stresses it entailed, both parents were generally physically and emotionally drained and had little time for their children. However they felt good about themselves because they were able to pay the bills, enter society as a "legitimate" member, and imagine a future for their children.

For parents who did not possess the skills and supports necessary to enter the workforce or sustain employment, it was necessary to turn to some other source of economic support in order to survive on welfare. Options available to these parents included additional sources of government assistance, private agency or charity help, their church or a recovery program, and their family, friends, and partners—if these forms of support were available. Some sold their Food Stamps for cash.

For several parents in this study, the primary means of increasing their income were dangerous ones (prostitution, panhandling, petty theft, drug dealing). Several mothers talked of how, in the past, they had exchanged sex for money, food, or diapers—either by "walking the streets," as one parent put it, or in less formalized terms with "sugar daddies," or giving sex to a boyfriend. One mother had gone to jail for stealing toys for her daughter's birthday and other items for herself. Each of these alternatives was fraught with potentially negative consequences. For parents in recovery from drug addiction—as were all six of the families involved with child welfare services and at least one of the other parents—these other means of balancing the economic ledger had special potential to jeopardize the day-to-day stability of parenting their children.

This was the case for Leticia,[2] mother of four who had an eighth-grade education and had grown up in foster care. Before the study began, she had never held a job because she had spent her entire adult life using crack cocaine, and had been in and out of prison. Although during the study she obtained the first job of her life, cleaning houses, and held several subsequent custodial jobs thereafter, her situation was tremendously precarious. She explained early on that her entire family was dead, incarcerated, or using drugs, and so she could not turn to them for help when she needed it. Her three oldest children had been removed from her years before. Her relationship with her youngest child—a toddler, with whom she reunified when she entered drug treatment—was very positive and he was developing well in her care.

But she did not possess the skills to work the minimum number of hours required under the federal TANF legislation, explaining that "a lotta times I be so beat! . . . I might skip a half a day or I might call in. I always miss some . . . during every week." Thus within the two-year period, it is likely she was sanctioned for work nonparticipation. She also got pregnant and had a fifth child, a daughter, for whom she was subject to the family cap. This meant that she and her two children were most likely living on an official welfare income of $319 per month.[3] Soon after her youngest child's birth, Leticia resumed contact with a relative who was actively using drugs. She started using drugs again and disappeared. As a result, both children were placed in foster care.

Although there may have been many contributors to Leticia's downfall as a parent, it is likely that her economic circumstances rendered her especially vulnerable to making desperately poor choices. Leticia was not a parent with skills or interpersonal supports to sustain involvement in the (legal) labor market. Therefore it was extremely difficult for her to succeed in the current welfare-to-work environment without significantly greater institutional support.

The Psychological Experience of Raising Children on Welfare, in Poverty

The material realities of living in poverty described earlier contain important psychological implications for parents. Poverty conditions shape the concerns parents have about their children, affect parents' sense of themselves as caregivers, and influence their beliefs about relationships between their children and themselves. The psychological realities of parents in this study, in terms of raising their children in poverty, can be grouped into five general categories. Each of these deeply affected parents.

Psychological Reality #1: The Impact of Facing Serious Difficulties in Providing the Necessities of Life for Their Children. This included not being able to feed children, or feed them well, and worrying daily about whether the rent would be paid or the family would soon be homeless. As Maria explained, with some embarrassment,

> There's always times when I run out of . . . milk and diapers. And I hate that . . . if I don't have the money for it, which I try to keep a little chunk change running around the house in case of situations like that.

Psychological Reality #2: A Sense of the Limited Educational, Cultural, and Material Opportunities That a Parent Can Provide in Conditions of Poverty. Several parents spoke wistfully of the desire to offer their children exposure to experiences such as horseback riding or swimming lessons but lacking the money to do so. Kenisha, for example, is very aware that money buys access to the culture of ideas, art, and the experience of travel. She wishes for

> the money to like, put them in little schools . . . like maybe take piano classes an' start really workin' with their mind—you know . . . so they can learn things an' they won't be scared to do things—won't have any limitations . . . Money's important but if you don' have it, you still want the bes' for your kids so it takes time an' it takes a lotta energy an'. . . determination . . . to keep goin' an' to use what little resources you have to make it work with nothin', you know. An' that's what I kinda hate 'cause I been so wore out . . .

Psychological Reality #3: Limited Time and Emotional Availability to Offer Children. Parents talked of an awareness of just being too tired—at the end of a long day and a long bus ride—to play with their children. This was especially true for the parents moving from welfare to work, and was perceived as a major drawback by parents who appeared to be succeeding—at least in the short run—in the welfare-to-work environment. Janet, who was pregnant with her third child while working and attending community college as her welfare-to-work activity, explained:

> The only thing that I haven't been able to give Ronald is enough time as far as playing with him, you know, and probably read more to him. And what gets in the way is I'm too tired, I am too tired. In the course of a day I'm just burnt out.

Others, such as Kenisha (employed full time in a clerical position), worry about the effects of their work-related demands on their parenting:

> I don' feel like I can give them . . . the time that they need right now. I feel like I'm so bummed out an' stressed out, you know. An' that's one thing you oughtta be able to give them if you don' have nothin' else is your time an' your attention . . .

Jennifer wishes for more time for activities with her children, time that is limited because of her full-time receptionist job, and activities that often cost money. Speaking of her search for an apartment, she says:

> I've just got to find one [an apartment] that I can afford. I can't just jump into *any* one, otherwise we won't have no—what do you call that? Not leisure time—[chuckles]—but, you know, fun time for the kids. Everything would be for bills and food and that's it.

Psychological Reality #4: Challenges to Protecting Children From Harm. The parents in this study were keenly aware that money buys some measure of protection for one's children. These parents worried about their children being molested or otherwise harmed by someone in the neighborhood or in child care. Many worried about their children becoming involved with drugs at a young age. This awareness—that because of their economic conditions they faced limitations in protecting their children—was disturbing to these parents, even for those who were *used* to living in dangerous environments. Jennifer expressed her concern over the necessity of raising her children in an urban setting characterized by poverty and crime:

> It's dangerous. They got, you know, people sellin' drugs right at this store, gunshots every night jus' right in front 'a the house. The person across the street got shot an', you know—an' this is—I don' want my babies—you know, Geez.

In spite of her fears, Jennifer cannot afford to live in the community of her choice, and is left with few options. "If I had to, temporarily [live in the dangerous neighborhood], I would. It's jus' I'd jus' be really protective," she says. Kenisha talks of wishing she could purchase better quality child care, explicitly for the purpose of protection. Previously her son DeMarco was injured in child care, which Kenisha attributed to substandard care. This experience contributes to her feelings of inadequacy.

> I don' have the time an' the money to take off work to give my boy . . . the bes' place that's suited for him that . . . where I feel comfortable that he's gonna be really looked after.

Instead she feels "I hafta jus' grab the firs' thing I can get if it's a vacancy, you know." To make up for what is lacking, she is driven to work as hard as possible to get out of poverty, even at significant cost to herself: "This is what the kids need [for me to work] an' even though you might hafta wear yourself out tryin' to do it, you hafta do it."

Psychological Reality #5: A Limited or Foreshortened Sense of Children's Futures. Living in conditions of poverty influenced these parents' hopes, dreams, expectations, and fears about their children's futures. Parents hope that their children will *survive*; and that if they do, they will follow a positive life trajectory such as graduating from high school (instead of becoming pregnant during adolescence and then relying on welfare, or worse, going to jail). And ultimately, as Maria termed it, she hopes that her child will "take care a' mama."

The starkest version of this concern was voiced by Anna, mother of 15-month-old Darnell. Asked about her wishes for her child 20 years from now, Anna responded with quick matter-of-factness:

> *Anna:* Um, to be a football player, put his momma in a mansion with lotsa millions! (*holding him in the air briefly, then lowering him to her lap*) That he gonna be graduated from high school, you know, make his decision what he wanna do in life, what he wanna be in life . . . Um—that he, that he's alive.

Interviewer: That he's alive?

Anna: Yeah, that he live to see 20 years from now. Most kids don't.

These kinds of concerns form the context of childrearing for urban parents on welfare.

The Psychological Impact and Parental Coping

All of the parents in the study experienced some combination of material and psychological poverty-related concerns, and all had an emotional response. Feelings ranged from worry to anxiety; from exhaustion to emotional deadness or depletion; from anger to resentment and depression. Across the group, each parent's sense of herself as a parent, and her relationships with her children, were affected in some way by these poverty-related concerns and the powerful feelings they evoked.

Parents develop different psychological "strategies" for coping with such strains, and these strategies may be adaptive or maladaptive, in terms of the resulting impact on parenting quality. A parent's sense of herself as competent could be negatively affected by the struggle to meet her children's basic needs. This was true, as well, for parents' awareness of the limited educational, cultural, and material opportunities that they could provide (including toys), and of their limited physical and emotional availability. Parents' sense of well-being and efficacy as parents could be fundamentally challenged, when faced with conditions that directly threatened their children's safety, especially when they felt they had limited or no ability to protect them.

The extent to which these feelings seemed linked to less-than-adequate parenting appeared to depend on the nature of a parent's psychological defenses. Some parents in the study felt these worries and strains, yet did not seem to lose their sense of themselves as capable parents. These parents had the internal resources to cope in adaptive ways with the powerful affect generated by threats to their children and their parenting. Their relationships with their children tended to have more positive qualities. They were able to think and talk about what their children needed, and were able to enjoy their children more consistently.

Janet, for example, talked of many of these worries, but retained a strong sense of herself as a parent, one with agency and sensitivity to her son's needs. She experienced considerable financial strain, multiple responsibilities, and consequent tiredness and irritability. Janet is an African American mother who gave birth to her third child near the end of the study. Perpetually in debt, every month Janet paid one-half of her bills, with the exception of her rent, which she paid in full. "That way I'm always behind but I've (paid) just enough to keep everything running."

Although she regretted the impact of her work and school involvement on her emotional availability to her toddler, Janet maintained some perspective about what she offered him. An integral part of Janet's identity as a parent involved her status as head of household and breadwinner, and she chose the word "dependable" to describe herself as a parent, because, she said:

> They can depend on me. They may not ever be able to depend on their daddies but they can depend on me to make sure they have . . . a house to come to, a bed to lay in, food to eat, and clothes to wear. Uh huh. And activities at school, I'm there . . .

Janet was aware of the potentially negative influences her son might confront, should he continue to grow up in poverty. However she was able to frame her wishes for him in positive terms.

> I want him to really learn to be independent. To be independent and to be educated and to know what he want to do in life, not just be . . . out there not knowing. [20 years from now] . . . he should be well grounded in a career and really stable.

Thus the conditions of poverty in which Janet raised her children affected her, but were not psychologically debilitating. Janet had a high school degree and a consistent employment record, and had no history of substance abuse or serious mental health problems. Throughout the study period, she was able to take advantage of what the welfare-to-work program had to offer her, returning to school to obtain an early childhood education credential, utilizing the child care subsidy through the university day care center where she completed her internship, and making realistic plans to leave welfare as soon as she could shift to full-time work. Janet regretted her historical dependence on the welfare system and did not feel it "owed" her anything, but viewed welfare reform, overall, as an opportunity to exit the system.

> I feel so much better when I'm working. I feel like I'm independent and a strong woman . . . . I'm going out and working for my family. I'm not getting a handout. So I really feel a sense of accomplishment and then I think I've been a good role model for my kids.

Janet had no trouble responding to her toddler's care and protection needs, as well as most of his emotional needs, and the poverty conditions they experienced did not appear to fundamentally impinge upon their relationship. But for other parents, feelings of inadequacy or helplessness threatened to undermine any positive sense of self, or of their relationship with their children. These parents tended to experience their relationships with their children as overly demanding, or as depleted and void of positive qualities. In some cases, a parent's apparent inability to cope with these psychological threats seemed linked to a kind of distortion of children's needs, so they were seen as unreasonable, unnecessary, or not "seen" at all. Although poverty conditions were certainly not the only influence upon these parents' relationships with their children, poverty-related concerns were pervasive in their day-to-day interactions, and affected their relationships through parents' thoughts and feelings about themselves, their child, and their relationship with their child. Maria is one such example.

An African American mother of four who has only worked for a few weeks or months at a time in the past 12 years, Maria has largely relied on welfare and illegal forms of support (including petty theft). In 10 interviews over 12 months, no playfulness was ever observed in Maria's household between her and her children. She was generally irritable and tense with them, and behaved as if her children were drains on her, and hopelessly demanding. During one interview she said:

> Right now I'm not in a situation to give neither one of my kids, not even myself, anything 'cause I'm not working. I was receiving a paycheck every other week, so now I'm depending back on AFDC [TANF] . . . right now I can't provide anything. I'm flat, completely broke. I can't give them nothing, but they don't have to want for anything either. They don't need anything right now. They have clean clothes.

Over time, Maria revealed that she felt fundamentally inadequate as a parent, unable to give her children a life different from the one she had led. She relied on her 11-year-old son to keep his allowance on hand, in case she needed to buy milk at the end of the month. Notice that Maria says, at the end of this passage, "They don't need anything right now." This was typical of Maria's response to her children's needs and wants: To deny that they existed. It may have been Maria's strategy for coping with the feeling that she couldn't provide for her children the way she would have wished. Although this means of coping may have been psychologically adaptive for her, Maria's children appeared to experience her as withholding and unavailable.

In another case, a parent's inability to develop an effective coping strategy seemed to suggest that poverty-related parenting stressors were simply overwhelming, making effective parenting virtually impossible. For Francesca, economic strains generated fear of failure as a parent, and she felt profoundly inadequate, helpless, and ineffective at meeting her children's needs. Francesca is a Latina mother of three, whose eldest child had been removed from her years earlier and placed with a relative. During the study, Francesca described herself as a "responsible" parent, but emphasized the financial strain involved: "It's hard," she would say, "I'm so behind on my bills." She had spent the past several years homeless with her children, panhandling and prostituting to support the family before entering a recovery program and resolving to live on public assistance, instead. She often spoke of how "nervous" she was as a parent, and spontaneously talked of her economic strains and related fears:

> Havin' to do everything on my own . . . the bills . . . worryin' if I'm gonna make it at the end of the month . . . I end up kinda takin' it out

on the kids, you know, because I get so . . . stressed out that . . . I don't hit 'em but I'll snap at 'em, like, "Jus' leave me alone, guys, God, can' I have a break?"

The high levels of anxiety and aggravation she described were consistent with observations about her relationships with each of her children. Although Francesca could be warm toward her children, she was inconsistent and prone to utterly disorganizing anxiety, which seemed to make the children anxious, clingy, and demanding. Many factors, including a history of mental health problems, explained Francesca's ongoing problem with anxiety, but it was clear that poverty-related stressors frequently exacerbated her difficulties, especially when those stressors had particularly serious implications for her children. This created a vicious cycle of negative interactions between Francesca and her anxious children, for whom homelessness had been an experience of repeated exposure to deprivation and danger.

The Role of Welfare Reforms on Parenting Quality

What role do welfare reforms play in shaping conditions of poverty, and in influencing parenting quality? The impact of welfare reforms on parenting quality largely depends upon a parent's coping skills, and the supports she/he has available for managing both material and psychological strains of parenting in poverty. And as suggested earlier, in some cases, the effect of welfare reforms may be to impose such severe economic strains that some parents' caregiving capacities are lost entirely. Thus within a range of poverty conditions, specific reforms can have the effect of exacerbating negative conditions for raising children, or of offsetting them and potentially promoting positive parenting. This framework is used next to describe and illustrate the effects on parenting of the family cap, subsidized child care, and welfare-to-work requirements.

The Family Cap

In this study, the outstanding negative feature of welfare reform was the family cap, which affected seven of the study families. By reducing welfare benefits relative to family size, the family cap made it very difficult for parents to provide the basic necessities of life for their children (e.g., food, clothing, diapers, housing, and transportation to the doctor). The family cap presented parents with additional challenges in providing material, cultural, and educational opportunities for their children. By limiting parents' purchasing power, low grant levels also contributed to difficulties protecting children from harm (e.g., by forcing families to live in dangerous neighborhoods).

All of these conditions affected the physical and psychological well-being of families, with a range of effects. For those who relied on TANF while transitioning to work, the family cap created material and psychological strains during that transition process. For parents such as Francesca or Leticia, however, whose limitations in the face of poverty conditions were especially clear, the family cap made the choice between bread and diapers—and the resulting impact on parenting quality—even more of a reality. Thus the family cap's effects are an example of how *severe* poverty conditions can render effective care and protection of children a virtual impossibility.

On the whole, parents in this study experienced poverty-related conditions as chronic stressors. In spite of this, the caregiving capacities of most were not fundamentally impaired (they did not neglect or abuse their children such that the intervention of child protective services might be required). Parents' capacities to care for and protect their children appeared related to their subjective experience of parenting in poverty, the emotional states that were generated, and their capacity to marshal adaptive internal defenses and coping mechanisms.

But depth of poverty also mattered. In this sample of economically poor families, the poorest experienced the most psychological strain and their parenting suffered the most. For the poorest parent, Francesca, poverty itself appeared to interfere with her parenting capacities to such an extent that it could be called an "assault to the caregiving system," in the terms of Solomon and George (1996). At times, Francesca appeared virtually defenseless against the effects of poverty, both psychologically and materially. As a parent, she teetered on a precarious edge in caring for her children.

Thus it appears that severe poverty conditions can overwhelm some parents' psychological and material coping skills, and render them incapable of effectively caring for and protecting their children in spite of the love they may feel for them. Welfare reforms such as the family cap, which facilitate severe poverty conditions, will also impinge upon and potentially disable the caregiving capacities of some parents—with serious consequences for children.

Subsidized Child Care

In marked contrast to the family cap, the increased availability of subsidized child care was a welfare reform that made it more possible for parents to manage the logistics of employment, and also to manage their budgets. In more than one case, parents were concerned that they were not able to "shop around" for higher quality day care and that therefore their kids might be at risk. However for several families in the study, the use of day care increased children's access to educational and social experiences they might not have otherwise received. Thus, in spite of the understandable worries generated by the need for day care, this aspect of welfare policy appeared to confer significant benefits on families—and thereby support parenting indirectly. This was true for Glen and his child.

Glen, a single African American father who was reunited with his three-year-old daughter Tasha while in recovery from drug addiction, received a TANF grant and MediCal[4] for two months, before returning to his previous work as a carpenter. This was a seasonal union job, which provided him with a relatively substantial hourly wage (and health insurance for both of them), but lacked stability. CalWORKs paid for child care upon his return to work, and this was an essential form of support for Glen, whose job required him to take Tasha to day care before 6 A.M. The day care program transported Tasha to a nearby preschool between 11 A.M. and 2 P.M. daily, where Glen was happy to report that Tasha was offered "more in-depth teaching."

Glen's apartment was affordable but unsubsidized, and he worried about his ability to pay both his current and prior bills, in order to repair his credit. (Credit was especially important to Glen because he wanted to purchase a car to ease his transportation difficulties.) During the study, an attack of chicken pox kept Tasha out of child care for two weeks and Glen home from work; this hurt his tight monthly budget and he worried about losing his job. The cost of Tasha's day care was $600 per month, paid for by the CalWORKs program. If CalWORKs had not paid for care, Glen would have paid a reduced rate of $300. Even with a steep subsidy such as this, Glen wouldn't have made it financially.

In late 1999, Glen's income reached a point where he was required by CalWORKs to pay a percentage of day care costs (totaling $50/month). Although still far less than the $300 he would pay without assistance, Glen still struggled to pay this additional amount, making clear the benefit of the child care subsidy. Additionally Glen offered a realistic assessment of what was needed to maintain his well-being as a parent, and what was good for his relationship with Tasha. On one occasion, he spoke of his experience of leaving her at day care:

> I was ready to go out the door and she ran after me, "Daddy, daddy, no, I wanna be wit 'chu, want go home wit 'chu." I said, "I'm not goin home, Tasha." . . . I was tryin' to figure out a way to get past that, 'cause I . . . I want her to love her daddy, but I don't want her to be like, oh, boy, I can't separate . . . I need a break some time, everybody need a break sometime.

Subsidized child care, when of a quality that satisfies parents and meets children's needs, appears to offer crucial supports, which promote positive parenting for poor families.

Welfare-to-Work Requirements

Working increased a family's material costs for such things as clothing, supplies, and transportation, and also presented parents with additional logistical challenges such as managing transportation and time. Depending on their skill level and work experience, some parents experienced a moderate increase in employment income, while for others, the increase was negligible. Working was associated with a decrease in parents' physical and emotional availability to their children. In some cases, however, the change led to an increase in self-esteem as a parent (as a provider for the children or as a legitimate member of society)—which in turn appeared to have a positive impact on parents' relationships with their children. For a time, this was true for Regina.

Regina, a mother of five, lived with her boyfriend, a house painter who managed the household funds. She had not finished high school and had very little work experience. Early in the study, Regina's description of her daily activities consisted of: "I don' do nothin'." Unable or unwilling to plan daily activities outside of the home, Regina said, "All I do is watch TV, really . . . I just watch anything that comes on." In early interviews, Regina showed very little emotion other than irritation, communicating for the most part in a clipped monotone. Her three-year-old daughter, Lela, was not attending preschool and spent her days watching Nickelodeon. The home was often dark, with the shades drawn, and the children never played during interviews.

Relationships between Regina and her children seemed to be, at best, either empty or strained. She seemed to view her children's behaviors as efforts to annoy her, and was observed several times dismissing or ignoring their bids for attention or help. She did not appear to enjoy their company, and seemed to resent their needs. Over time, Regina revealed in a variety of ways that her children demanded more of her than she felt able to give, both economically and emotionally. She responded by placing emotional distance between her children and herself.

However an unusually bright period in Regina's life began, apparently, as a result of welfare reform. In the fifth interview, a hint of energy and of positive self-esteem emerged when she described entering her welfare-to-work training program in flower arranging. She talked of how the instructors were "nice" and then, with pride, of how quickly the class was learning:

> We're doing our first funeral tomorrow . . . we've only been in there two weeks, and they usually don't do them that fast . . . I'm learning. [They] taught me how to make bows. How to cut flowers, how to take care of them.

Involvement in welfare-to-work activities helped to lessen Regina's depression. Her children noticed a difference, and her relationships with them improved in ways that Regina was able to articulate.

> I'm getting out of the house, I'm not just sitting here locked [in] all the time . . . And now . . . I like it—because I'm not all mad all day . . . the day goes by faster now . . . I look forward to the next day . . . and before I didn't . . . [The kids used to] stay away from me. Now they go in the room with me and everything . . . [the kids tell me] that I seem like a happier person now, that I'm not always yelling at them. I used to always yell at them.

After months of stating, "I don't plan nothin'," with her job training program Regina got an appointment book and seemed to welcome another interview, adding that "When you come again my house will be all full of flowers." Unfortunately her positive tone was short-lived. When the training was completed Regina did not immediately obtain a florist job and instead began working for a grocery chain. She expressed many complaints about this work, especially the supervisor's insistence that she improve her punctuality and the neatness of her appearance. Regina's resentment over her role as mother resurfaced in an interview, with a comment that she hoped her daughter would "live her life" by completing school early "instead of having a kid and then staying home watching it."

As this example of Regina and her children suggests, the relationship between welfare-to-work activities and parenting is not simple, but rather an interplay of personal, relational, and environmental factors. Still it was clear that poverty conditions both reflected upon and reinforced the depressed conditions of their family life, and Regina's depleted psychology of parenting. In this particular case, moving from welfare to work appeared to promote more positive conditions for parenting, if only briefly. For each parent undergoing this transition, the psychological and material costs and benefits will likely form a complicated, and unique relationship to their parenting.

Welfare Policies that are Sensitive to Parenting and Children's Well-Being

This study elaborates on the role of psychological processes in mediating the relationship between poverty and parenting behavior. Welfare policies are understood as influences on poverty conditions, exacerbating or offsetting the risk-laden conditions in which parenting occurs for poor families. Poverty conditions, in turn, are seen as having material and psychological implications for parents, and outcomes in terms of parental behavior will depend upon material and psychological coping abilities, as well as depth of poverty.

Several caveats are in order. Although the study was intended to be theory-generating, given the design, the findings presented here are not generalizable. This model for understanding the impact of welfare reform is based on intensive study of a small sample of predominantly African American families living in a high cost-of-living, urban environment in Northern California, soon after the passage of the federal welfare reform bill. These families were economically precarious, most were long-term welfare recipients, and many had struggled with their parenting to such an extent that the child welfare system had intervened.

Additionally this chapter has isolated—somewhat artificially—poverty and welfare policy as influences on parenting. Certainly relationship quality for each parent–child dyad was influenced by a variety of other factors, including but not limited to children's characteristics and, in some cases, parents' histories of substance abuse. Similarly parental mental health is undoubtedly affected by many life experiences and factors other than parenting. Acknowledging these caveats, however, the findings support the notion that conditions of poverty, and the welfare reforms that shape them, can generate specific kinds of psychological distress in parents. Although with a somewhat different focus, these conclusions are consistent with those reported elsewhere about the effects of economic stressors on parents (Edin and Lein, 1997; Halpern, 1990; McLoyd, 1990), as well as the association between poverty-related psychological distress, and less positive relationships with children (McLoyd and Wilson, 1991). Similarly the results support the view of this psychological distress as a "normative and situational response to economic hardship" (McLoyd, 1990, p. 313).

These findings suggest that policy makers concerned about parenting for low-income families need to attend to the frightening realities of living poor and raising children, perhaps more than the psychological messages of welfare to work. In this study, parents were concerned with being good role models for their children, but their more immediate, compelling concerns had to do with issues of basic care and protection, emotional and physical availability, and the creation of simple opportunities for their children. Consistent with these findings, future efforts at welfare policy reform should be designed to promote material conditions that make it possible for families to survive, and a psychological context in which the care and protection of children can coexist with the demands of welfare to work. Certainly many structural changes and cultural priority shifts would be necessary, beyond changes in the welfare system, for children and parents living in poverty to live safer lives and experience greater opportunities for success. But within the framework of welfare reform, some recommendations can be made based upon the data and the framework presented here.

Welfare policies that exacerbate poverty conditions, and thereby strain parents' material and psychological resources, are likely to have a negative impact on parenting in some families. Given that the level of cash assistance provided to families is one basic aspect of the daily experience of poverty, a minimum standard should be considered at the federal level. Ending the family cap and other sanctions would be one means of ensuring a more adequate safety net, and promoting the care and protection of children. Additionally the family cap has special relevance for very young children, given that each new birth in affected families insures a lower income relative to family size, thus intensifying poverty conditions during the period when key aspects of development are most sensitive to poverty's effects (see Duncan and Brooks-Gunn, 1997).

Also parents' capacities to enter the labor market and sustain employment are crucial aspects of coping with the material realities of living in poverty under welfare reform. Thus services to promote job retention through supportive follow-up with parents should be considered, along with supportive services for parents with very limited work experience, or added impediments to entering the workforce (such as criminal convictions). Welfare policies sensitive to parenting and child well-being will effectively account for the vulnerabilities and limitations experienced by some parents receiving welfare. Provisions for mental health, substance abuse, and domestic violence treatment may offer some help in this regard.

However, in this sample, it was apparent that more proactive, individualized interventions would have been necessary to prevent the negative outcomes experienced by some families, such as Leticia's. For families involved with the child welfare system, coordinated efforts by welfare and child welfare programs may be useful, if such efforts are able to prevent poverty conditions from becoming so severe that parenting capacity is impaired, or children are placed at extraordinary risk.

These findings also speak to the importance of parents' feelings and thoughts about being parents, as underlying motivators (or impediments) to economic choices and behavior. Infusing a more explicit parenting-centered focus into the discourse about welfare would acknowledge that TANF is an important governmental support for *families*, and that therefore such a focus might prove advantageous in designing more effective welfare policy. For example, the quality of subsidized child care is likely to be a significant consideration in parents' successful transition from welfare to work. Further affordability of child care will be critical in order for parents to remain employed and able to pay the bills, while simultaneously feeling that their children are safe and well cared for.

Chase-Lansdale and Pittman (2002) point out that some states are using flexible TANF funds to design parenting-related programs. They also suggest that thus far, research on certain dimensions of parenting has found welfare reform's only indirect impact to be on "gatekeeping"—the enrollment by employed mothers of their children in formal child care and after-school programs. Although the creative use of TANF block grants are one means of promoting parenting, the existing policy framework itself must be made more parent- and child-friendly. Welfare policy makers may be able to harness the power of the parent–child relationship by acknowledging, in tangible ways, the importance, to parents, of educational, cultural, and material opportunities for their children, in addition to ensuring that children can be protected from harm.

Notes

Funding for this study was provided by the California Social Work Education Center (CalSWEC) and the Stuart Foundations.

1. In each case, pseudonyms are used and necessary details have been changed to protect confidentiality.
2. Leticia's circumstances are described in greater detail in Frame and Berrick (2003).
3. Information on Leticia's income during this period was pieced together from key informants and based upon knowledge of administrative practices; our contact with her ceased when her children were placed in foster care.
4. MediCal is California's version of the Medicaid program, a health insurance program for poor families.

References

Beeman, S. (1995). Maximizing credibility and accountability in qualitative data collection and data analysis: A social work research case example. *Journal of Sociology and Social Welfare, 22*(4), 99–114.

Chase-Lansdale, L. and Pittman, L. D. (2002, winter/spring). Welfare reform and parenting: Reasonable expectations. *The Future of Children, 12*(1), 167–185.

Conger, R., McCarty, J., Yang, R., Lahey, B., and Kropp, J. (1984). Perception of child, child-rearing values, and emotional distress as mediating links between environmental stressors and observed maternal behavior. *Child Development, 54*, 2234–2243.

Duncan, G. J. and Brooks-Gunn, J. (1997). *Consequences of growing up poor.* New York: The Russell Sage Foundation.

Duncan, G. J., Brooks-Gunn, J., and Klebanov, P. K. (1994). Economic deprivation and early childhood development. *Child Development, 65*, 296–318.

Edin, K. and Lein, L. (1997). *Making ends meet: How single mothers survive welfare and low-wage work.* New York: The Russell Sage Foundation.

Elder, G. (1974). *Children of the great depression.* Chicago: University of Chicago Press.

Frame, L. and Berrick, J. D. (2003). The effects of welfare reform on families involved with public child welfare services: Results from a qualitative study. *Children and Youth Services Review, 25*(1/2), 113–138.

Garrett, P., Ng'andu, N., and Ferron, J. (1994). Poverty experiences of young children and the quality of their home environments. *Child Development, 65*(2), 331–345.

George, C. and Solomon, C. (1996). Representational models of relationships: Links between caregiving and attachment. *Infant Mental Health Journal, 17*(3), 198–216.

Halpern, R. (1990). Poverty and early childhood parenting: Toward a framework for intervention. *American Journal of Orthopsychiatry, 60*(1), 6–18.

McLeod, J. and Shanahan, M. (1993). Poverty, parenting, and children's mental health. *American Sociological Review, 58*, 351–366.

McLoyd, V. (1998). Socioeconomic disadvantage and child development. *American Psychologist, 53*(2), 185–204.

McLoyd, V. and Wilson, L. (1990). Maternal behavior, social support, and economic conditions as predictors of distress in children. *New Directions for Child Development, 46*, 49–69.

McLoyd, V. and Wilson, L. (1991). The strain of living poor: Parenting, social support, and child mental health. In A. C. Huston (ed.), *Children in poverty: Child development and public policy* (pp. 105–135). England: Cambridge University Press.

McLoyd, V. C. (1990). The impact of economic hardship on Black families and children: Psychological distress, parenting, and socioemotional development. *Child Development, 61*, 311–346.

Miles, M. B. and Huberman, A. M. (1994). *Qualitative data analysis: An expanded sourcebook* (2nd ed.). Thousand Oaks, CA: Sage Publications.

Padgett, D. K. (1998). *Qualitative methods in social work research: Challenges and rewards.* Thousand Oaks: Sage Publications.

Patton, M. Q. (1990). *Qualitative evaluation and research methods* (2nd ed.). Newbury Park, CA: Sage Publications.

Solomon, J. and George, C. (1996). Defining the caregiving system: Toward a theory of caregiving. *Infant Mental Health Journal, 17*(3), 183–197.

Solomon, J. and George, C. (2000). Toward an integrated theory of maternal caregiving. In J. D. Osofsky and H. E. Fitzgerald, (eds.), *WAIMH handbook of infant mental health (Volume III: Parenting and child care)* (pp. 323–368). New York: John Wiley & Sons.

Strauss, A. and Corbin, J. (1990). *Basics of qualitative research: Grounded theory procedures and techniques.* Newbury Park, CA: Sage Publications.

SECTION II

Policy Effects on Poor Children

CHAPTER FOUR

Effects on Children as Parents Transition from Welfare to Employment

PAMELA A. MORRIS, ELLEN K. SCOTT, AND ANDREW S. LONDON

The only thing I really wanted to do was to be home with my [youngest] son. Until he got older to go to school . . . Well, they do know I am working now . . . They know well, it's better for me, mommy, to work than to stay home . . . Now that I've started working, now my son, he trying to find a job [laughs].
—Renee, a 27-year-old African American single mother of three children who was working as a nursing assistant.

How can welfare and employment policies help families cope better as parents as they make the transition from welfare to employment? Our research addresses this question by integrating two very different, but complementary, lines of research—random assignment social experiments on the effects of welfare and employment programs on low-income adults and children, and longitudinal, qualitative interview studies of families who experienced the 1996 welfare-reform changes. Together, these studies point to the benefits for children of policies and programs that increase family income as they increase employment.

The debate over how best to support low-income children has been influenced over the past 30 years by an evolving public and political consensus that single mother welfare recipients should work. Efforts to promote parents' economic self-sufficiency culminated in the 1996 Personal Responsibility and Work Opportunity Reconciliation Act (PRWORA), and associated policy changes designed to support the employment of low-income families (e.g., the expanded Earned Income Tax Credit and child care subsidies).

In the context of evolving welfare policy both at the state and federal level, understanding how policy can help families cope with the transition from welfare to employment is critical. Proponents of recent welfare reforms have argued that increased parental employment will benefit children by increasing parents' self-esteem and providing children with positive role models. Skeptics worry that greater work responsibilities may harm children by increasing parents' stress, reducing the amount of time parents can spend with their children, and increasing the amount of time children spend in low-quality child care arrangements. For parents unable to maintain consistent employment, many worry that the loss of a financial safety net due to welfare time limits may also adversely affect children. In this chapter, we synthesize the results of both quantitative experimental and qualitative research about how low-income children fare as their mothers spend more time in the labor market and attempt to strike a new balance between work and parenting. The findings presented emerged from the Next Generation Project, a collaboration between researchers at MDRC and several leading research institutions. The project examined the effects of welfare and employment programs on families and children.

We focus on the effects of parents' transitions from welfare to employment on their young children, and use children's well-being as a marker of successful coping for the family.[1] Based on the project findings, we conclude that policies that effectively increase parental income as they increase employment—as opposed to those that increase employment but not income—improve the well-being of young children and are, therefore, the most promising for helping families cope.

What Do We Already Know?

Effects of Maternal Employment. Despite considerable rhetoric concerning the benefits for children of parental employment, nonexperimental developmental research points to few unique effects of maternal employment on low-income children, after accounting for correlates of employment. For low-income families headed by single mothers, in particular, the associations between maternal employment and children's cognitive and social development tend to be neutral or positive (Harvey, 1999; Vandell and Ramanan, 1992; Zaslow and Emig, 1997). Other research suggests that differences between the children of employed and nonemployed mothers, respectively, appear to be due as much to differences in employed and unemployed mothers' characteristics as to their work status (Zaslow et al., 1999).

Several lines of research do suggest that some caution may be in order when assessing this evidence. First most mothers who leave the welfare system take highly routinized jobs that pay very low wages and afford little autonomy. These kinds of jobs appear to have negative effects on women's emotional well-being and, in turn, on their children's development (Moore and Driscoll, 1997; Parcel and Meneghan, 1994, 1997). Second some welfare programs increase employment by *requiring* parents to go to work. Research suggests that maternal employment may have more positive effects on children when mothers want to work, as compared to the effects when parents feel they have to work (Alvarez, 1985; Farel, 1980).

Finally research comparing children of employed and nonemployed parents ignores the dynamic quality of employment (Yoshikawa and Hsueh, 2001). Transitions into and out of employment may have a very different pattern of effects for children than employment status per se. Notably previous research on changes in income and employment has focused on the negative impact of unemployment, job loss, and financial insecurity rather than whether *increases* in income and *entry into* work can affect children's development. The available literature provides little evidence that would allow us to make confident predictions about whether such transitions to employment are, on average, positive or negative for young children.

Effects of Income. While there is some uncertainty about how increases in maternal employment may affect children, increasing income *along with* employment is more likely to bring about positive effects on children. Net of other correlated factors, such as low parental education, poverty has been found to have small but consistently negative effects on children's development (Duncan et al., 1994; Duncan and Brooks–Gunn, 1997; Mayer, 1997; McLoyd, 1998), and persistent and deep poverty has been shown to be more detrimental to children than transient poverty (Bolger et al., 1995; Duncan et al., 1994). Additionally poverty in early childhood appears to be more detrimental than poverty in middle childhood or adolescence (Duncan and Brooks–Gunn, 1997).

In addition to increasing the resources parents can provide to their children, increasing family income can benefit children by reducing parental stress and affecting parenting behaviors, as well as by increasing cognitively stimulating experiences in the home (Bradley and Caldwell, 1984; Smith et al., 1997; Sugland et al., 1995; McLoyd et al., 1994). Overall the available evidence suggests that family income is more consistently predictive of children's academic and cognitive performance than their behavior and health problems (Duncan and Brooks–Gunn, 1997; Klerman, 1991; Korenman and Miller, 1997).

Parenting as a Mediator of the Effects of Employment and Income

Family income and maternal employment may affect children through changes in parents' emotional well-being and parenting behavior. Financial strain has been found to negatively impact children through marital conflict in two-parent families (Conger et al., 1997), and through depression and negative disciplinary practices in single-mother families (McLoyd et al., 1994). Elder's seminal work on economic hardship during the Great Depression identified a link between job and financial loss and punitive, inconsistent parenting behavior (Elder, 1974, 1979; Elder et al., 1984).

Later work provides evidence that the relation between economic changes and parenting is mediated by changes in parents' emotional well-being (such as depression). McLoyd's work further expanded this model for relevance to Black families (McLoyd, 1990), and provided a test of this model among single-parent families. Her findings suggest that the financial strain and psychological distress associated with job loss affect parenting behavior and, ultimately, adolescent well-being (McLoyd et al., 1994; see McLoyd, 1998, for a review).

In sum nonexperimental research on the effects of employment and income on child well-being suggests that increases in employment may have few effects on children, while increases in income will likely benefit children's development. Additionally change in parenting is likely to be a key intervening mechanism linking changes in employment and income and children's well-being. However the nonexperimental nature of the research reviewed makes it very difficult to disentangle the positive effects of employment and income from unmeasured differences between families, such as differences in parents' educational status or family structure.

In this chapter, we examine the effects of programs that increase employment, and sometimes income, in the context of random assignment evaluations. The random assignment design ensures that any systematic differences in children's outcomes can be confidently attributed to the program and the targets of the intervention—the change in parental employment and income—and not to unmeasured characteristics. We also examine evidence from longitudinal, qualitative interview studies. The qualitative research allows us to better understand the pathways by which increases in employment and income may be affecting children's development, and whether there are offsetting influences on parent and child well-being.

A Review of the Studies

Quantitative Experimental Studies

In this chapter, we draw on the results of a set of seven experimental studies that together evaluate the effects of thirteen programs aimed at increasing employment among low-income and welfare-reliant families. All of the programs described in this chapter were aimed at increasing parental employment among low-income families, while some were aimed explicitly at both increasing employment and increasing income. Because the policies and programs are aimed at parents' economic outcomes, and because random assignment procedures were utilized, effects on children will only arise indirectly as a result of changes in parents' employment and income (and related factors). Thus we can utilize the results of these experimental studies to make inferences about the effects of different kinds of programs on children when parents move from welfare to employment.[2]

All of these studies utilized a random assignment research design to assess the effects of a particular constellation of policies. That is, families were assigned at random (through a lottery-like process) to either a program group or a control group. The program group was subject to the rules and benefits of the new program, while the control group was subject to the prevailing welfare benefits package and rules (AFDC in the case of the U.S. studies and Income Assistance in the case of the Canadian study) or other benefits widely available to low-income families. Because the two groups did not differ systematically at the beginning of the study, any differences between them or their children found during the study can be reliably attributed to differences between the groups' experiences in their respective programs. Differences between the average values in the program and control groups are computed and referred to as the "impact" of the program. Here we compare impacts within and across program models. Notably one drawback of this approach is that differences in cross-program effects may be due to factors (e.g., samples) other than the variation in program approaches and their resulting impacts on parental economic outcomes.

Extensive assessments of young children were collected in each of the studies. Outcomes were examined for children of single parents (primarily single-mother welfare recipients) who were of preschool age or early school age at the time of their parents' random assignment (approximately 3–9 years old at random assignment).[3] These children had reached middle childhood (approximately 5–12 years old) by the end of the follow-up period, from 2 to 5 years later. This age group was chosen as the basis for the cross-study analysis to maximize the comparability of the samples across the programs and because this age group was the subject of a set of detailed questions about children's well-being in all the studies.

To increase the comparability of the results found in the different studies, we examined a subset of measures, which was similar across studies and represented the range of children's outcomes that might be affected by welfare and employment policies: Achievement or cognitive functioning, externalizing ("acting out") behavior problems, positive behavior, and health. These data allow for a reasonable comparison of program impacts across studies.

All of the treatments were designed as "employment" treatments of one form or another—all were intended to reduce welfare and increase employment, without direct intervention components targeted at parents' mental health, parenting, or outcomes for children. Although many policies were tested, the approaches can be grouped into two categories: *Earnings-supplement policies* that are designed to encourage work and increase income via "make-work-pay" strategies (supplementing the income of those who work); and *mandatory employment services and time-limited programs*, which attempt to encourage work via sanctions and benefit termination strategies (for more information on these program models, see Bloom and Michalopoulos, 2001; Morris et al., 2001).

Qualitative Research

The qualitative portion of this analysis comes from data collected under the auspices of MDRC's project on Devolution and Urban Change (henceforth

"Urban Change"). Urban Change employed a nested, multicomponent, longitudinal design and uses a variety of data collection and analytic methods to assess how poor families have fared under welfare reform in four urban areas (Cleveland, Philadelphia, Los Angeles, and Miami). [For more details about the study design, see Quint et al. (1999)]. All data are drawn from residents of the poorer neighborhoods of these large cities (more than 30 percent of neighborhood residents were poor or more than 20 percent received welfare in 1990).[4]

The analysis presented in this chapter is based on data from the ethnographic component of Urban Change in Cleveland and Philadelphia. In each city, participants resided in one of two neighborhoods (one African American and one predominately White) that had a "moderate" level of poverty concentration (30–39 percent), or in an African American neighborhood where poverty was even more highly concentrated (40 percent or more of its residents were poor). The combined, two–city sample includes 75 welfare recipients. Participants were recruited using a variety of methods (e.g., referrals from grassroots community organizations or other study participants, flyers, contacts on the street, and by going door-to-door). Potential participants were screened in order to recruit a sample that reflected the heterogeneity of welfare recipients, and that was dispersed residentially within the boundaries of the neighborhoods.

At the beginning of the study, all respondents relied on cash welfare benefits, and were primarily unmarried women. About half of the sample demonstrated characteristics of short-term welfare recipients (e.g., a high-school diploma or GED, at least two years of formal-sector work experience, and/or two or fewer children). Residents of housing projects were excluded from the sample, and very few women in the sample received Section 8, other forms of subsidized housing, or SSI.

Between 1997 and 2000, three in-depth interviews were conducted with each respondent in a semi-structured, conversational manner covering common themes, with shorter interim interviews conducted throughout each year. For the analysis presented here, we use data from the baseline and first main follow-up interviews, most of which were conducted in 1998 and 1999 and took place approximately one year apart. Building on the work of Edin and Lein (1997), questions were aimed at assessing the changes in women's daily lives as they engaged in the process of moving from welfare to work. These included qualitative and quantitative assessments of changes in income and employment, as well as qualitative assessments of changes in family interactions and changes in family and child well-being. All interviews were tape recorded and transcribed verbatim, and interviewer field notes sometimes supplemented these interviews. Data were coded electronically and analyzed using standard qualitative analysis techniques to identify common themes.

Observed Employment and Income Patterns

Between the baseline and first main follow-up interviews, 61 percent of the 75 women in the qualitative study engaged in some formal sector work.

However, in this period, only 17 percent had been working and not receiving welfare for more than six months. The remainder of those who did any paid, formal-sector work in this period showed lower levels of work activity and greater welfare reliance. Most of the women who worked were in low-wage jobs without benefits. They often worked odd shifts and part-time, sometimes patching together multiple jobs in order to make ends meet. Later we discuss how these increases in employment affected parenting and child well-being.

With regard to income changes, overall 72 percent experienced some increase in their average monthly income, with a mean increase of $233 (median = $164). At baseline, women's annual income from all sources combined was $11,952, and at follow-up, it was $14,748. Women who worked more than six months without relying on welfare were most likely to increase their average monthly income. Of women in this category, 92 percent increased their income, and these women were the most likely to have an increase of $350 or more (69 percent did). Approximately 70–80 percent of those who cycled between welfare and work or combined welfare with work[5] increased their income. However gains were more modest than those for the previous group (with only about one-third increasing their average monthly income by $350 or more).

Most women in our sample managed to make ends meet by combining a range of income sources, including formal-sector wage labor, network support, informal-sector work, and government income supports such as the EITC (earned income tax credit) and Food Stamps. This patchwork of income-generating strategies resulted in substantial income instability for many women in our sample. [See Scott et al. (2004) for our full analysis of these women's employment activity and income change in the first year of the Urban Change study.][6]

In our longitudinal, qualitative interviews, we documented substantial employment and income change, which allows us to examine how changes in maternal employment, family income, and other aspects of family life affected the women and their children and families. The longitudinal, qualitative data yielded contextualized accounts of women's experiences from their own point of view. These accounts do not provide the same kind of evidence as experiments about program impacts. They do, however, provide unique evidence on how policy changes are affecting women and their families, which can be used to complement and supplement evidence emerging from experimental evaluations of programs.

Quantitative Experimental Research Findings

I was working in the reception area. And I liked it. It was really nice. And it made me self-supporting and self-sufficient. I was able to come off public assistance through that job. And I've been supporting myself ever since. But, I'm still self-supporting [despite being laid off]. I'm not on public assistance in no way. Don't wish to go back on public assistance.

I enjoy working . . . And self-supporting. It made me—it made me feel much better about myself. You know, that I can—I was really productive, really a productive part of society.

> —Dorothy, a 38-year-old African American with
> one child under 18 years old, recently laid off
> from a job as a receptionist at a psychiatric facility.

I get less sleep . . . [lots of laughter]. . . I think I get less sleep, but I get more money, so it all weighs out . . . The six-year-old, like, he like, a lot of times I'm asleep, you know, you know, I'm asleep when he goes to school, I'm asleep when he come home. And, I jump up and I'm getting ready to go to work. So, he doesn't, he feel like he doesn't see me a lot.

> —Tamara, 41-year-old, African American, recently
> married mother of three children who worked
> the third shift doing laundry at a nursing home.

Despite considerable public support for policies that promote employment among welfare recipients, little is known about the effects of these transitions from welfare to employment for parenting and for children's development. As described earlier, arguments have been made on both sides about both the positive and negative effects of maternal employment for young children. Although reforms of welfare policy are likely to continue to keep maternal employment as a primary goal, understanding the effects on children of policies designed to promote such employment can help us to understand what families need as they make the transition from welfare to employment.

Increases in Employment without Income Gains

Effects on Parents' Well-Being and Parenting

In this section, we draw on the experimental findings of eight programs that increased employment but not income. In contrast to hypotheses about the increased self-esteem that might come with movements from welfare to employment, programs that increased employment but not income had few effects on parents' emotional well-being and parenting behavior two–four years after parents' entry into the programs (Bloom et al., 2000; Freedman et al., 2000; Hamilton et al., 2000; McGroder et al., 2000). None of the programs affected parents' risk for depression, and effects on parenting behaviors like warmth, harshness, and controlling discipline were relatively rare. In a few cases, effects were found on parents' reports of "feeling rushed" and on parents' reports of their knowledge of their children's activities and whereabouts, likely reflecting the time constraints faced by parents balancing work and parenting.

Effects on Children

While there has been considerable concern about children's well-being as mothers move from welfare to employment, our findings suggest that programs that increase maternal employment produce neither consistent harm nor consistent benefit for young children. In sum we find that two–four years after parents had started the programs, there were few effects on young children (children who were preschoolers at the beginning of the study and in elementary school when we interviewed their parents two–four years later; Bloom et al., 2000; Freedman, et al., 2000; Hamilton et al., 2000; McGroder et al., 2000). The scattered effects that were observed were as likely to be positive as negative. Moreover in the one study that assessed effects at two follow-up points, there continued to be few effects on children into the later follow-up point (Hamilton et al., 2001).

More specifically, at each of three sites testing two variants of mandatory employment services (Hamilton et al., 2000; McGroder et al., 2000) children were assessed with regard to their basic academic skills (using the Bracken Basic Concepts Test). There were few differences between the group subjected to the mandatory employment services and those in the control group across these six programs. Parents were also asked about children's internalizing and externalizing problem behavior, their positive social behavior, and how healthy children were. For these other aspects of children's well-being, parents in the program groups rated their young children similarly to parents in the control groups. The few effects that were found on child outcomes were mixed—sometimes positive and sometimes negative—in both the short- and long-terms. Similar measures were also assessed in two other programs that fit in this category—one was a mandatory program tested in Los Angeles, the other a time-limited welfare program tested in Florida. In both cases, effects on children were rare as well.[7]

Summary of Findings for Programs that Increase Employment Alone
Overall these results are consistent with research that has shown neutral effects of mother's employment under many circumstances (Zaslow et al., 1999). At the same time, one might have expected that *requiring* employment among mothers who had previously not been working might be more harmful to children than voluntary employment (Alvarez, 1985; Farel, 1980). As suggested by the qualitative studies described later, there may be countervailing influences. Specifically, the short-term stress of being mandated to move from welfare to work may be balanced by the benefits to families when mothers attain the positive status of worker.

Notably in the programs examined here, imposing a sanction for non-compliance with the participation mandate entailed reducing the family's monthly welfare grant by the adult portion of the grant and leaving the child portion unchanged (Hamilton et al., 2000; Freedman et al., 2000). These sanctions—known as partial family sanctions—typically reduced the welfare grant by 15–20 percent. The time limited policy that was tested examined the effects of a time limit bundled with a variety of services and supports to help families find and keep jobs, and did not result in income loss (Bloom et al., 2000). Transitions to employment in programs that include full family sanctions (i.e., fully eliminating the welfare grant for short periods of noncompliance) or those that impose time limits on welfare benefits without additional services, may result in such an income loss and thereby be more detrimental for both parents and children.

Simultaneous Increases in Employment and Income

In the previous section, we reported that effects on parents and children were few and mixed as mothers made the transition from welfare to employment. A very different view of the potential effects of welfare reforms on children stresses the role of family income and resources available to children. Proponents of welfare reform and the new work supports were optimistic that as parents moved into jobs, their future earnings (along with benefits for working poor families) would elevate family income above the level of welfare benefits.[8] In this section, we examine what is known from experimental research about how programs that increase both employment and income affect family and children's well-being (For details on these findings see: Huston et al., 2003, Knox et al., 2000; Michalopoulos et al., 2000; Morris and Michalopoulos, 2000).

Effects on Parents' Mental Health and Parenting

Five of the programs discussed earlier successfully increased both parents' employment and income by supplementing the earnings of welfare recipients who made the transition to employment. Although effects on parents' economic outcomes were similar across these five programs, effects on parents' well-being were few and inconsistent across programs, and effects on parenting behavior were extremely rare. More specifically three programs had no effects on parents' aggravation or depression, whereas effects in the other two programs were opposite in direction: One program reduced parental depression and another increased it. Only one of the programs assessed the stress levels of its participants, and although it found reductions in stress, it also found increases in time pressure.

Finally and surprisingly, measures of parenting behavior—one of the key ways in which increases in employment and income are expected to affect children—were not much affected by these programs. Across all five programs there were few differences in parenting behavior (including parental warmth, harshness, and control) between mothers in the program groups and those in the control groups. Nor were there any differences in measures of the quality of the home environment assessed in three programs.[9] Thus contrary to the hopes of many welfare reformers, work preparation or employment itself did little to improve mothers' mental health and parenting. Perhaps the continuing difficulty inherent in combining childrearing with employment—particularly within the context of single parenthood and economic hardship—does not confer any advantages over receiving welfare, even when income increases for families.

Short-Term Effects on Children

Despite limited impacts on parents' emotional well-being and parenting behavior, our analysis suggests that for young children, programs with earnings supplements resulted in consistently positive effects, particularly with respect to school achievement. These findings support the notion that policies that support parents' employment and improve their economic circumstances may improve children's well-being, and thereby help families cope as single parents make the transition into employment.

In four of the five different programs that all included generous earnings supplements, children who were preschool and early–school-age at the beginning of the studies, and in elementary school at follow-up two–three years later, showed improvements in achievement, either based on parental reports, teacher reports, or children's test scores. The effects were small, but noticeable, generally corresponding to effect sizes of .15. A .15 effect size corresponds to a movement from the twenty-fifth percentile (the level at which children typically were functioning in the control groups) to the thirtieth percentile on standardized tests. Pooling across these five programs and examining the pattern of effects across the childhood age span finds that these positive effects are most pronounced for the preschool children making the transition to elementary school during the follow-up period (the four–five-year-olds; Clark-Kauffman et al., 2003; Morris et al., in press). That effects are most pronounced for these children may be due to the increased sensitivity of points of transition in children's development to change. In terms of other aspects of children's development, the results were less consistent across the five programs, but the effects were either neutral or positive. In four of the five programs, there was also evidence of improvements in young children's behavior (either reducing children's problem behavior or increasing children's positive behavior). Two programs also improved children's health status, as reported by their mothers.

The results of earnings supplement programs are consistent with non-experimental research that reports positive associations between family income and children's well-being, particularly as reflected in cognitive performance and school achievement (Duncan and Brooks-Gunn, 1997). The fact that welfare programs with generous earnings supplements can lead to improvements in children's cognitive outcomes—improvements that are detected two–three years after their parents first enter the programs—holds important implications for policy and program design. It suggests that these policies may indeed help families cope with the transition from welfare to employment. Furthermore the consistency in the findings across the sites and studies considered here justifies greater confidence in the generalizability of the programs' effects.

Long-Term Effects on Children

In two of the five programs with earnings supplements, children were again assessed four–five years after parents enrolled in the study. In both of these programs, parents were eligible for a supplement to their earnings for only the first few years, so they were no longer eligible for this supplement at the time of the later follow-up. Although we found effects on employment and income were quite pronounced in the first few years, they had declined somewhat by the time of later follow-up. Effects on children's achievement in school began to decline, although not significantly so, by the later follow-up point (Morris, Gennetian and Duncan, 2005).

In sum this earnings supplement program appeared to benefit young children's achievement at least in the short-terms. These young children may have been set on a path of continued improvement in school performance based on earlier increases in family income. These effects appear to be particularly pronounced across the studies for those children at a transition point in their development—those children making the transition to elementary school over the follow-up period.

Summary of Quantitative Research Findings

Findings from the experimental studies reveal that impacts on children's well-being differ depending on the policy approach, and on subsequent changes in parents' economic outcomes. Programs that increased parents' employment and income benefited young children. Although small, the effects are consistent enough across differing program models and samples to lend confidence in their replicability. By contrast programs that simply moved mothers into employment did little to benefit young children. These findings point to the importance of these earnings supplement policies in increasing parents' income (as they increase employment), thereby benefiting children as their parents make the transition to work.

Although programs that support employment may help families cope by improving child well-being, they appear to have little effect on parents' own well-being, or the way they interact with their children. This finding runs counter to predictions by proponents of recent welfare reforms about the effects of moving mothers from welfare to employment. It also contradicts nonexperimental research findings about the link between economic conditions for families and parental well-being and parent–child interactions. Because experimental impacts are derived from the *difference* in functioning between children and parents in the program and control groups, these findings may reflect the fact that receiving welfare (as more parents in the control group are doing) and working (as more parents in the program group are doing) are equally stressful for parents. The advantages that employment may bring to parents may be outweighed by the stresses of balancing work and family. We explore these issues further in the qualitative analyses.

In the next section, we examine the effects of increases in employment—with and without increases in income—on parent and child well-being, as described by parents in qualitative interviews. These findings help us to better understand why we find few effects on parents and children from programs that increase employment but not income. They also help to explain how benefits to children (other than through changes in parenting behavior) occur in programs that increase income.

Findings from Qualitative Research

Increases in Employment without Income Gains

While the quantitative work suggests few negative effects on children as mothers make the transition to employment, the findings from the qualitative data suggest a somewhat less sanguine picture of single mothers' experiences. Moreover they provide insights into the potentially countervailing influences of maternal work on the well-being of mothers, children, and families. They also suggest how, in the absence of income gain, the negative consequences of maternal employment in the low-wage labor market may counterbalance or even sometimes outweigh the positive consequences of work. Here we present some of the qualitative data that illustrate parents' expectations about work, the benefits they felt they received despite the absence of income gain, as well as women's perceptions regarding the costs of work for them, their children, and their families when they were employed with no or little increase in their income.

Expectations about Work

At the beginning of the study, few of the respondents were working in the formal economy. At this time they said that they wanted to work and they anticipated employment would benefit them and their families. Their positive attitudes about work were based on the assumption that their future earnings would be quite high, and consequently the material well-being of the family would improve considerably. They also anticipated that work would enhance their self-esteem, as well as their children's sense of self-esteem. Mothers believed that their children would respect them more if they were engaged in wage labor and no longer reliant on cash benefits. Further they thought their work would provide appropriate role-modeling for their children.

However this optimism about work was tempered by concerns about how they would juggle their work and family obligations. They worried about the effect of their absence from the home on their children. They were concerned about finding adequate or affordable child care; where their children would go after school; who would help them with their homework and provide them moral guidance; and who would simply keep their children safe and on track in the face of their mothers' increased absence from the home.[10]

Perceptions of Family Well-Being

As women made the transition from welfare to work in the first year of the study, their overall material circumstances changed little, despite the fact that more than two-thirds of the women experienced some increase in their income. Most women remained below or very near the federal poverty threshold, which is consistent with the economic circumstances of the population from which they were selected. [See Brock et al. (2002) for more details from the Urban Change survey and ethnography about recent welfare leavers in Cleveland.] Nonetheless some respondents said they still benefited from work. Primarily they said they experienced psychosocial benefits, such as improved self-esteem and confidence, despite the general stasis in their overall material well-being.

Some respondents also spoke of the increased respect they received from their children as a consequence of their labor force participation. Occasionally respondents talked about the increased independence of their children, and the higher level of organization in the home, which resulted from their move from welfare to work. Because they felt better about themselves, many respondents still believed that work would improve their family's life—a view they had expressed earlier in the year during their baseline interview. Yet the gains were not as substantial as they had hoped, and most respondents talked extensively about the difficulties in meeting both their work and family obligations as single working parents (London et al., 2004).

Despite their initial optimism, most of the women we interviewed experienced more costs than benefits when they entered the labor force between the baseline and first main follow-up interview a year later. Most of the women were employed in low-wage, unstable jobs, and some seemed to be worse off than they were on welfare. Many worked second or third shifts, or did not have fixed hours, and some worked more than one job to try to make ends meet. Often respondents did not have child care that they believed was trustworthy, or they constantly had to juggle unstable care arrangements for their children (see Scott et al., 2005).

The stress levels of these single working parents increased, as did their exhaustion. Economic resources were still severely constrained, and women's increased absence from the household often contributed to greater disruption in family routines. Mothers worried that their absence from the home would negatively affect their children's development. In sum the women we interviewed spoke often of their experiences attempting to balance work and family responsibilities, and their concerns about the negative impact their entering the labor force was having on their children.[11]

Here we provide some examples to illustrate the benefits and costs of work perceived by the women in our sample. We examine two benefits: Improved maternal self-esteem and confidence, and children's increased independence. We also examine four costs: Increased exhaustion and disrupted family routines, children's problems in school, children's behavior problems, and finally, the more general problem of children and parents not seeing one another.

Improved Maternal Self-Esteem and Children's Independence
Even without substantial financial gains, the respondents in our sample talked about the positive effects of work on their sense of confidence and

self-esteem. Women said that they felt less isolated, more independent, and generally better about themselves. Olivia was 34 years old when our study began and had five school-aged children. She worked as a housekeeper in a hotel, and subsequently in a machine shop. In reflecting on the effects of her employment, she said:

> I just feel better, being out of the house instead of being in the house all of the time . . . It's busy. I'm working on my days off and everything. I try to take care of my house. I don't have a lot of time in the evenings. I get home, cook dinner . . . we just try to relax because my legs are so sore at the end of the day . . . It's like everything's in a rush any more. That's how it is all the time now . . .

Olivia thought that one of the unintended consequences of her employment was to push her children to become more independent:

> [The kids] seem to be getting a little bit more independent now that mom's not around twenty-four hours a day. They're learning to do things for themselves . . . So they're like more confident with themselves.

Flora, a 24-year-old woman with one child, said what she had gained was having "met a lot of people, gained a way of life, became more independent." Margie, a 38-year-old woman with three children, thought that the "life experience" she had gained from working as opposed to receiving welfare constituted an advantage. She said: "You get out, you get to meet people, you get a life of your own." In reflecting on her family life in the context of her employment, she said: "It [family life] got better. I got a life." Finally when Gayle, a 40-year-old mother of one child, was asked what she had gained from work, she stated quite simply, "self-respect."

These psychosocial benefits of work were commonly discussed, even among those respondents who realized little income gain from their employment. But the more frequent discussions about the costs of employment in the absence of income gain suggest that the effects of work may be countervailing. Women experienced positive individual effects, which they occasionally linked to their children's well-being. When discussing their children in the context of their newly acquired employment, women focused much more on the problems they encountered trying to manage work and family obligations, or the problems their children were having in school and at home. Their stories may illustrate some of the mechanisms for potential negative outcomes of work in low-wage single-parent families.

Exhaustion and Disrupted Family Routines

One of the most common concerns discussed as parents made the transition to employment was the exhaustion women felt and the disrupted routines that affected their family's well-being. The exhaustion was attributed to the unique conditions of the work of low-income women (i.e., working second and third shifts and juggling multiple jobs), and not simply a result of the more typical demands of balancing work and family [for a fuller analysis of these issues, see London et al. (2004)].

Marcia, a mother of two, tried to manage part-time work doing house-keeping, and full-time work as a personal care attendant. Despite the income gain she realized through these two jobs, she couldn't handle the exhaustion of the 60-hour work-week, and the care of her children:

> It was hard . . . work. I was [always] running late. I was late for the other job, for the one I had to resign from. So if I didn't quit, you know, they would have fired me. It was too much for me as far as getting home, cooking, cleaning. You know, when I get home late, stuff still needs to get done and I wind up going to bed at one, two o'clock in the morning 'cause I'm just finishing, and then trying to get up to get to work at eight a.m. Oh, I couldn't do it.

As a result, she quit the housekeeping job. Still she described the juggle of work and family as "chaos." She said her children were becoming "a little wilder, because I'm not home constantly watching them no more." She thought that working third shift made things difficult for her family. It was her belief that if she could get a job during standard work hours, it would be easier on her family, and thus would diminish some of the "wildness" she observed at home.

Toni, a mother of two, worked at a suburban McDonald's for five months between the beginning of the study and the first main follow-up interview. She stopped working because of exhaustion and the problems it was causing for her son:

> At first I started off in the morning time and I had somebody watching my children and they wasn't picking my son up on time from school and he was going to get put out of the program. So I switched to nighttime so that I could pick him up. And then I was making him late to school because I was so tired. I was getting in the house like 1:30–2:00 [A.M.]. . . And I couldn't get up in the morning to get him ready for school. And so I just tried to get back to [a] daytime [schedule] and they didn't have room and that was it.

Because she couldn't work out these conflicting demands, she ended up back on welfare.

Problems in School

Frequently discussions about the costs of being absent from the home centered around fears that children's grades would suffer if no one was monitoring homework. Even if children were not doing worse in school, mothers worried about this possibility. When they were doing worse, mothers often attributed it to their absence.

Karen spent several months between the baseline and first main follow-up interview working at a factory for $7.50 per hour. During that period she had only her wages and Food Stamps for income. By the time we interviewed her a second time, she was back on cash welfare because of health problems and because her employer was unwilling to give her time off during a short period of hospitalization. Subsequently Karen was diagnosed with multiple sclerosis and applied for SSI, but had not yet been notified whether she would receive aid by the time of our second interview with her. Because she had worked previously, and received the EITC between the baseline and second main interview, her monthly income increased by an average of $503, from $1,104 to $1,607.

Karen did not like working the second shift because it caused her to lose time with her children. She described her schedule:

Cause, like, when I'm going to work they, they're just now coming in from school, they haven't made it in yet, and when I get off work, it's like twelve midnight, then they in the bed, you know. So, I really didn't see 'em much, you know, except the weekends. So that's, that's what I lost. I would call home on a break and they [her children] keep telling me I need to find another job, you know, that's got better hours. 'Cause they barely see me.

In the course of this discussion, Karen blamed her work schedule for her children's failure in school (they were in sixth and seventh grades). When asked about what she thought her children's lives would be like in the future, Karen said:

I don't know. Cause they, they changed a lot since [last year]. . . They grades dropped and, you know, they fail. I don't know, I think it . . . kind of all depends on what I do, I guess. [If I don't have time for them, they don't do well.] So they both . . . failed, so they in summer school.

Similarly Debbie, who managed to find a good job relative to others in our sample and who felt quite good about her employment, was nonetheless worried that her absence from the home was affecting her son's performance in school. She said:

I've spoke to my older son's teacher a couple of times. He wasn't doing too well . . . in school . . .'cause I'm not home to stay on him, to keep his homework done, I mean sometimes he'll just have homework, he'll hurry up and rush through it, just to say when I come home from work, "I did it already. It's done, I already turned it in.". . . He really was doing that and getting away with it, for a lot of times. But he wasn't doing too well. I don't even know if he's passed to the next grade.

Behavior Problems

Respondents attributed emerging behavior problems to their work-related absences. Danielle faced substantial employment instability between the baseline and first follow-up interviews. During this period, she noted that her daughter had been acting out at school because she was not getting enough attention at home. She attributed this explanation to her daughter's principal.

Danielle spent most of the time between the initial interview and first main follow-up interview combining welfare and work. Initially she cleaned houses part-time for $7.50 an hour under the table and also received cash welfare. A month later, Danielle got a full-time telemarketing job paying $6.25 an hour, but still received cash benefits. After only a few months she was laid off, but found a job installing Hallmark displays in stores for $7 an hour. She enjoyed this job, but her hours were unstable and usually inadequate. She quit that job and took two under-the-table jobs, one delivering pizzas and another tending bar at a local pub—a job that took her away from home in the evenings. She no longer received cash benefits. Danielle's average monthly income increased by $406 between the first and second interviews (from $946 to $1,352); however she lost the child care subsidy she briefly received when she quit her part-time job and took the two under-the-table jobs.

Danielle said that work interfered with "family time" and her ability to parent her kids. She had no network assistance with child care. Consequently she wished she could afford to work less than full time:

> I like being at work, I like being around people. I just wish I didn't have to work [such] long [hours]. I wish I only had to work . . . maybe 4, 5 hours a day. That way I [would be] home . . . when my kids get out of school. [I think] I should be here with them. But I'm not. Who knows where my kids will grow up and go, you know, what way they're gonna turn.

At several points in the second interview, Danielle reported that her daughter was acting out and that she believed this was because she was not getting enough parental attention, but she also pointed out the conundrum she was in as a single working parent:

> [My daughter] was being bad at school. She does it or whatever 'cause it's a lack of attention [at home]. The principal told me that. [He said] "You gotta spend time with them." I'm like, how do you expect me to spend time with my kid when I gotta work? You tell me to spend time with my kid, welfare's telling me to go to work. They don't care if you leave your kid by herself, you gotta go to work.

Danielle told us she wanted to go back to school, but also said that given her concern about her daughter's behavior she was convinced that she could not do so while juggling work and family.

Eileen was another respondent who did not realize income gains from her work, and who felt the costs of her absence were becoming immediately evident. She worked at a laundromat and at times at Dunkin' Donuts. At the first main follow-up interview, Eileen expressed concern that her children "were picking up an attitude and having little problems here and there in school." Eileen said it had been harder raising her kids over the past year than it had been previously, "because I can't get them what I want and I am not home half the time." In response to a question about whether work was making a difference, Eileen said: "Yeah, they are having a very bad disposition about them." Later in the interview, Eileen indicated that she had a parent–teacher conference the next day because her "daughter has in-house arrest because she was lighting a match in school."

Just Missing One Another

Even when there weren't problems, mothers reported that they missed their kids and their kids missed them. Andrea planned to work some extra hours at her job in the laundry on a Saturday, but her kids said, "we miss you," so she just stayed home. Her schedule required her to leave before they left in the morning, and arrive home after 6 at night. With a bedtime of 8 P.M., her children barely saw their mom. The only way that Andrea was able to maintain this schedule was with the assistance of her mother and her children's father. Between them, they charged her $300 per month. They took turns getting the children ready for and to school, and picking them up and watching them after school. It was only with this support that Andrea felt she could sustain her employment.

Sarah reported that her full-time employment in retail was making her family life "kinda worse." She arrived home around 7 P.M., and felt depressed at not seeing her children. She also thought they were depressed:

> My three-year-old, he don't understand. He wants me here, and he does bad things to get my attention. My seven-year-old thinks I don't want to spend time with him.

For the mothers in our sample, missing their children and their children's expressions of longing for their mothers were very salient and caused them considerable worry.

The majority of respondents in the ethnographic sample did not experience stable work or sustained increases in income during the first year of the study. They struggled to make ends meet with income levels hovering around the federal poverty level. Juggling stressful jobs, irregular or part-time hours, and temporary employment, mothers worried a great deal about their children's well-being. Exhaustion, disrupted routines, and increased absence from the home due to employment meant that some mothers reported their children were doing worse overall, doing poorer at school, and exhibiting increased behavior problems. Additionally although perhaps less critical than these problems, the children missed their mothers.

Simultaneous Increases in Employment and Income

Consistent with the quantitative findings, the qualitative data suggest that when the welfare recipients in our sample moved from welfare to work *and* their incomes increased, they felt their families were benefiting. In the qualitative sample, drawn from the most disadvantaged neighborhoods in Cleveland and Philadelphia, there were only a few women who experienced substantial increases in income as a result of working.

Two other factors also appear to be critical to these families' success: (1) they had stable employment, and (2) they felt their child care arrangements were reliable and trustworthy.[12] Because these two factors tend to co-occur with work-related increases in income among the women in our sample, it is difficult to discern the relative contributions of maternal employment, the income increase that accompanied the transition to employment, or employment and child care stability to the improvements in their families' lives. Their stories, however, illustrate the benefits they perceived. We highlight two of these stories here.

Celeste

In the first year of the Urban Change study, Celeste, a mother of four, found a full-time position working three 16-hour days each week in a residential home for mentally disabled adults. Paid $9.00 per hour and working 48 hours a week, she was no longer eligible for cash assistance. However Celeste received Food Stamps and the EITC. Her average monthly income increased by $974, from a monthly average of $1,081 to $2,055. (Studies on those who have left the welfare system suggest that her earnings were unusually high; see, e.g., Polit et al., 2001.) She received medical benefits through her job, but was responsible for a co-payment of $17.00 every two weeks. As her earnings increased, she lost most of the $100 in income she received from informal sources in her social network.

Celeste felt that work had "definitely" improved her family life and her relationships with her children. However, in the beginning, Celeste said her children had difficulty adjusting. "They'd argue all the time, fightin', and I just didn't understand why, but they're getting better at it." She continued:

> I think they feel more proud of me, you know, working. [When I was on welfare] they come home from school [and] I'm there all of the time. Now, they're like, "Where's Mommy?" "Mommy at work." You know, they're more happy, and they get more things now, too. I think it's better.

Celeste believes, as she put it: "It pays to [work]. The income is much better, [the children] can get more . . . and I'm proud of myself." The most significant loss in her eyes was:

> time with my children. 'Cause I have to work by 5:00, so I leave at 4:00. When they come home from school, I'm right out the door. I just give them a kiss, and I don't have that time with them no more.

Three factors eased Celeste's transition from welfare to work: A schedule that allowed her to be home four days a week and working three long days; a boyfriend who, when she was at work, watched her children when he got home from his day job; and transportation assistance from her mother who owned a car and drove her to work, saving her time and money. Like most women we spoke with, Celeste mentioned the loss of time with her children as one of the costs of work, but she didn't worry about her children's well-being or safety while she was at work, an uncommon luxury for the women in our sample. Further since she had no additional work-related child care or transportation expenses, her disposable income increased substantially.

Linda

Linda, a 32-year-old woman with three children, found a job working full time for an employment training program. She received a relatively good salary of about $21,000 annually. She also received health insurance through her job and her children were enrolled in Healthy Start (Ohio's Child Health Insurance Program). Linda's husband received disability income, which was reduced when the family income increased with her employment. In the first year of the study, her husband continued to rely on Medicaid for his health care coverage.[13]

> Linda felt that her work had had positive effects on her self-esteem. She told us: Well, I've always liked to work. I never had a problem with that, you know, I did my volunteering with no qualms. I like working because I'm earning that money myself. It's good for the self-esteem. It's good for self-confidence. And . . . um . . . it just makes you feel better about yourself, that you're actually doing something for your family.

Furthermore she felt that she was providing a good role model for her children. Regarding her earnings, Linda reported: "I am naturally a little bit financially better off, but um . . . it's better. It's definitely better." She was pleased that she could buy more for her family now that she was working.

Her only concerns were that she was spending less time with her children. When asked if there were any disadvantages to working as opposed to receiving welfare, she said:

> Less time with your family. Um . . . feeling . . . feeling like basically just not being able to spend enough time with my family. That's really the only complaint I have. *[Interviewer: Ok. . . . and do you think working has improved your family life or made it more difficult?]* . . . Both. I think that it's made it better because I'm setting a good example for my children. Uh . . . I think it's . . . the disadvantage is not being able to be with my kids the way I used to . . . I got very used to being around my

children . . . being able to take them to the park and . . . play with them and I don't do that no more. Not like I used to.

Because Linda was married and her husband was home due to his disability, she did not worry about her children's care in the manner that some women in our sample did when they went to work. Linda was in a relatively unique position. She found employment with fairly good wages and health insurance coverage for herself; her children were covered under Healthy Start; and she felt confident that her children were well cared for in their own home. Although she missed being with them, she did not worry about their well-being.

Summary of Qualitative Findings

In the qualitative sample, the relatively small subgroup of women who left welfare for stable work, who felt good about their child care arrangements, and who also substantially increased their incomes, reported that they and their children were, for the most part, better off. Despite worrying some about their children when they were at work, and the greater stress and time pressures associated with juggling work and family, these women had experiences that came closer to the optimistic expectations of employment shared by most of the respondents.

Integrating the Quantitative and Qualitative Findings

In this section, we integrate the findings from the quantitative and qualitative studies to understand how transitions to employment, with and without increases in income, may be affecting families and children. Together these two lines of research help us develop a more nuanced understanding about (1) how families fare as single parents make the transition to employment, and (2) the conditions that aid families in coping with this transition.

Increases in Employment without Income Gains

The qualitative findings present a slightly different account of the way in which changes in maternal employment—without increases in income—may be affecting families and children, as compared to the quantitative data. In the quantitative data, few effects were observed when programs increased parents' employment but not their income. In contrast, the qualitative findings demonstrate more costs than benefits of maternal employment for families.

Perhaps these differences are due to the different contexts for the two studies. One examines the effects of transitions to employment under mandatory employment programs and cautious time limited policies, whereas the other does so under time limits implemented with fewer supports.

Moreover the qualitative data suggest that the few effects observed on parents' well-being and parenting may be a result of countervailing influences reflecting both gains and costs of maternal employment. At the same time, parents in the qualitative interviews are clearer about the negative effects of their transition to employment for their children. Here we discuss some possible explanations for these differences in findings.

As has been found in previous nonexperimental research (Moore and Driscoll, 1997; Parcel and Meneghan, 1994, 1997), some conditions of employment, such as long and irregular hours, may negatively affect parents and their children. Moreover research has suggested that mandatory, rather than voluntary, employment may play out more negatively for families and children (Alvarez, 1985; Farel, 1980). Perhaps the fact that respondents in the qualitative study were faced with welfare time limits with few additional supports pressured parents to move from welfare to employment with some urgency, and increased the need to balance multiple jobs. This stress is clearly demonstrated in the qualitative work (see also London et al., 2004). In the quantitative study with the exception of parents in one program studied, parents were faced with mandates to participate in employment without time limits. Being faced with partial family sanctions may not result in the same pressure to find and keep employment as being faced with time limits on welfare benefits. And, the single program with time limits studied bundled time limits with services to families, potentially mitigating any negative effects.

More salient is the fact that the qualitative findings suggest important countervailing influences on parents of mothers' employment not detected in the quantitative work. Predictions about the benefits of maternal employment, by enhancing maternal self-esteem and increasing the regularity of routines, receive virtually no support from the quantitative data. However the qualitative work suggests that these benefits may have indeed been part of the experience of single mothers making the transition to employment. Single mothers in the qualitative work did mention increased self-esteem for themselves and increased independence for their children. At the same time, however, these parents describe increased stress, disrupted routines, and exhaustion, which may counterbalance these positive aspects of employment. Although the net result may be the same, understanding the effects on families as counterbalancing effects rather than neutral effects has very different policy implications.

Unlike the quantitative findings, the qualitative findings point to more costs than benefits of increases in maternal employment for children's well-being, in particular, even while the effects on parents are more mixed. What is unclear is whether such negative effects are due to differences in children's behavior that emerge over time, or real differences between groups that are attributable to differences in their employment status. In the quantitative studies, both program and control group families make the transition to employment—it is simply that a slightly greater proportion of program group members make this transition. One possible explanation is that effects among the small proportion of families who were induced by the program to make the transition to employment were too small to find differences when all families are examined together. Alternatively if the transition to employment is as stressful as remaining on welfare, no differences between groups may emerge in the quantitative data even though children may respond negatively to the transition to employment.

In effect both groups of children may be having difficulties—it may be equally difficult for children whether parents are poor and receiving welfare (and perhaps looking for work) or are working and struggling with the demands of low-wage work. Finally parents struggling with work and family may be especially sensitive to any changes in their children's behavior, and may attribute any problems they observe to employment, rather than to other changes in their lives or developmental changes on the part of the children.

The qualitative findings do point, however, to the high levels of difficulties generally facing children and families in these studies. Although not a focus of the impact estimates presented in the quantitative studies, such high levels of problems are also observed in the quantitative data. Parents in both studies report high levels of depression and stress, and children are at risk of long-term difficulties. For example, about one-third of parents report levels of depressive symptoms, which put them at risk of clinical depression, and children are performing on average at the twenty-fifth percentile on standardized tests. Even in programs that increase employment and income and benefit children, levels of problems are still high—even after accounting for the improvements in children's well-being observed in these programs.

Increases in Employment and Income

The qualitative findings regarding the work–family tradeoffs women faced when they moved from welfare to work, and how such transitions affected children, are broadly consistent with the experimental findings. These showed that programs that increased maternal employment *and* income through earnings supplements improved outcomes for young children. From the qualitative data it is clear that when considering employment, income, and family well-being, we must consider a host of interacting factors. Income increases must be substantial and not offset by work expenditures; employment and income must be stable; and children must be in reliable care that is trusted by their mothers.

Proponents of changes in welfare policy had suggested that one way maternal employment may benefit children is that it would increase the regularity of family routines. These findings suggest that employment itself does not necessarily lead to such regularity. But employment increases that are accompanied by increases in income, perhaps because they are accompanied by increases in stable employment and child care, are more likely to result in such benefits for family life, and, in turn, children's development.

The qualitative findings point to the role of employment stability as an important component of the benefits of increased employment and income for young children. Interestingly employment stability may indeed be responsible for some of the benefits of the experimental programs that increase both employment and income. The findings suggest that earnings supplement programs do indeed increase employment stability as they increase the proportion of families working. While some of these programs increased the number of jobs or spells of employment experienced by program group members (indicating a greater number of employment transitions), they all increased the length of employment spells. More specifically, the programs that increased employment and income also typically increased the length of employment spells, either as measured by the length of the longest job spell, or as measured by the proportion of families whose first spell lasted 13 or more months (as in the other three programs). It appears that at least some of the increase in employment generated by these programs was in stable employment. As indicated by the qualitative research, this may have added some stability to these families' lives and led to some of the benefits for children.

The qualitative findings point to the role of stable and reliable child care as a key intervening mechanism in the benefits of increased employment and income (also, see Scott et al., 2005). Interestingly the quantitative studies also find evidence that programs that increase employment and income may increase formal child care and participation in after-school programs, but particularly when they include some form of direct child care assistance. [See Gennetian et al. (2002) for greater detail on the effects of experimental programs on children's care arrangements.] Thus child care, at least formal child care, may play a role in the benefits to children of earnings supplement programs.

These findings stand in contrast to those previously discussed regarding impacts of these earnings supplement programs on measures of parenting behavior, which were not much affected by these programs. Both the quantitative and qualitative findings suggest the important role child care may be playing in helping families cope with the transition to employment, and in conferring benefits to children.

Conclusion and Policy Implications

Together these findings point to the benefits to children when welfare-reliant parents increase both their employment *and* their income. Based on the quantitative findings from experimental evaluations, consistent benefits to young children's achievement were observed in programs that resulted in increases in income and employment. Qualitative findings suggest that increases in employment and income may benefit families in part because they are accompanied by stability of employment and child care arrangements. By contrast few benefits, and perhaps countervailing effects, were observed when parents increased their employment but not their income, or when income increases were not enough to move families substantially above the poverty threshold.

These findings point to the importance of policies that provide low-income families with supports for employment. With the continuing evolution of welfare policy at the state and federal levels, and the renewed focus on child well-being as a key goal of welfare policy, this research provides some critical information to inform policy makers' decisions. The research here suggests that policies that supplement the earnings of low-income workers may help families cope with the transition from welfare to employment by improving outcomes for their young children.

Policies to support work include increasing funding for child care for low-income working families, expanding coverage and take-up of health insurance, and expanding the EITC. In several of the experimental studies described here, improvements in children's achievement were found in the context of benefits like those that were available to both the program and control groups. This implies that even if the EITC and other supports for employment currently in effect do have some similar positive effects on children, there is room for further improvement for families through additional work supports or through expansion of existing programs.

In addition to expanding current supports for work at the state and federal levels, states can redesign their welfare programs so that they more effectively support employment among welfare recipients. For example, many state welfare programs currently couple time limits and earnings supplements, although it is unclear whether such policies will benefit children in the same way as policies that include earnings supplements without time limits. Time limits encourage people to leave welfare quickly and save their remaining months of welfare eligibility for a period of crisis. In contrast, earnings supplements—when provided within the welfare system—encourage families to continue to receive welfare benefits while they are working.

Studies of the effects of programs that combine these two policy components suggest that the effects on family income are likely to be smaller and effects on children more limited, than in programs that provide earnings supplements without imposing time limits (Bloom and Michalopoulos, 2001; Bloom et al., 2002; Gennetian and Morris, 2003). States might consider providing supports to working families that are not time limited,[14] in order to ease parents' transition from welfare to employment and simultaneously increase benefits to children.

These findings provide information critical to policy makers to make informed choices about how to help low-income families cope with the transition from welfare to employment. Welfare and employment policies that result in stable employment and increases in income can be another route to improving the well-being of children.

Notes

This chapter was completed as part of the Next Generation project, which examines the effects of welfare, antipovery, and employment policies on children and families. This paper was funded by: The David and Lucile Packard Foundation, William T. Grant Foundation, the John D. and

Catherine T. MacArthur Foundation, and the Annie E. Casey Foundation. We thank the original sponsors of the studies for permitting reanalyses of the data.

1. Findings on the effects of welfare and employment policies for parents on their adolescent children have been less positive than the findings for the younger age group of children. In brief, small negative effects of welfare policies have been observed for these older children. We do not focus on this older age group here, since the findings are less directly linked to the *type* of welfare policy, and so the policy implications for older children are less clear. See Gennetian et al. (2002), and Gennetian et al. (2004) for a detailed description of the findings for this older age group.

2. The following studies were included in this analysis: Connecticut Jobs-First (Bloom et al., 2002), Florida's Family Transition Program (Bloom et al., 2000), Los Angeles Jobs First GAIN (Freedman et al., 2000), Minnesota Family Investment Program (MFIP; testing the effects of two programs, Full MFIP and MFIP Incentives Only; Gennetian and Miller, 2000; Knox et al., 2000), National Evaluation of Welfare-to-Work Strategies (testing the effects of six programs in three sites across two follow-up points; Hamilton et al., 2000; Hamilton et al., 2001; McGroder et al., 2000), New Hope (testing the effects of one program at two follow-up points; Bos et al., 1999; Huston et al., 2003), and the Canadian Self-Sufficiency Project (testing the effects of one program at two follow-up points; Michalopoulos et al., 2000; Michalopoulos et al., 2002; Morris and Michalopoulos, 2000).

3. Although we focus on preschool-aged and early–school-aged children in many of the analyses in this chapter, the age groups are not identical across the 13 programs discussed. In some cases, the age range is more restricted (e.g., including only children aged 3–5 years at random assignment); in one case, the age range is larger. Analyses have been conducted on common samples, and results are consistent with those presented here (see Morris et al., 2001; Morris et al., in press).

4. Wilson (1987) and Massey et al. (1994) define neighborhoods of concentrated poverty as those where 20 percent or more of the residents live below the poverty threshold. We chose a higher threshold of poverty strategically to target the most disadvantaged neighborhoods where the impact of welfare reform is likely to be most evident.

5. Women in the *cycling* category had stopped receiving cash benefits for some period of time during the year because they were working, but had either re-enrolled or hadn't worked long enough (at least 6 months) to meet our criteria for the work-only category. Women we classified as *combiners* worked formally at some point during the year, but continued to receive cash welfare benefits.

6. Notably some families who did not work also increased their income level. Approximately 50 percent of women who remained reliant on welfare with no formal-sector work increased their average monthly income through other means; 13 percent experienced an increase of $350 or more.

7. For more details concerning these findings, see Bloom et al. (2000), Freedman et al. (2000), Hamilton et al. (2001), and Morris et al. (2001).

8. At the same time, armed with forecasts of dramatic increases in child poverty, critics of welfare reform focused on the likely detrimental effects on children's well-being of families losing welfare benefits. Unfortunately these data are too limited to examine how children fare when they experience decreases in their income level, even while parents transition to employment.

9. While the measures are primarily parental reports of parenting behavior, they are associated with children's outcomes in predictable ways (see Huston and Gennetian, 2001). However, it is still possible that the lack of program effects on these measures of parenting are due to a lack of validity.

10. See Scott et al. (2001) for more discussion of women's expectations about employment as they were initially responding to welfare reform's work requirements and time limits on the receipt of cash benefits.

11. In this first year of the study, the intense difficulty some women experienced trying to juggle work and family responsibilities may reflect the initial transition from welfare to work more than some enduring family pattern. For some women, the stress of juggling work and family may ease as they find a new balance, as their children age, or as other circumstances in their lives change. It is, however, possible that new or different circumstances that disrupt established balances will emerge. It is well documented in the literature that work–family conflicts are enduring and dynamic across the income distribution. Thus it is likely that the women we interviewed, most of whom are single parents working in low-wage jobs, will continue to face difficulties managing their work and family responsibilities.

12. Most of the families in our sample defined "trustworthy care" (rightly or wrongly) as kin-care (Scott et al., 2005).

13. We know from subsequent interviews that later he lost his Medicaid insurance because the family income was too high. Linda tried to add him to her policy through her employer, but his preexisting

medical condition made the cost prohibitive. Linda and her husband resorted to paying for his medication out of their pockets.

14. For example, states may be allowed to define supplements provided to working families as "nonassistance." If defined as such, these supplements would not be subject to welfare time limits.

References

Alvarez, W. (1985). The meaning of maternal employment for mothers and the perceptions of their three-year-old children. *Child Development, 56*, 350–360.

Bloom, D. and Michalopoulos, C. (2001). *How welfare and work policies affect employment and income: A synthesis of research.* New York: Manpower Demonstration Research Corporation.

Bloom, D., Kemple, J. J., Morris, P., Scrivener, S.,Verma, N., and Hendra, R. (2000). *The family transition program: Final report on Florida's initial time-limited welfare program.* New York: MDRC.

Bloom, D., Scrivener, S., Michalopoulos, C., Morris, P., Hendra, R., Adams-Ciardullo, D., and Walter, J. (2002). *Jobs first: Final report on Connecticut's welfare reform initiative.* New York: MDRC.

Bolger, K. E., Patterson, C. J., Thompson, W. W., and Kupersmidt, J. B. (1995). Psychosocial adjustment among children experiencing persistent and intermittent family economic hardship. *Child Development, 66*, 1107–1129.

Bos, J., Huston, A., Granger, R., Duncan, G., Brock, T., and McLoyd, V. (1999). *New hope for people with low incomes: Two-year results of a program to reduce poverty and reform welfare.* New York: MDRC.

Bradley, R. H. and Caldwell, B. M. (1984). 174 children: A study of the relation between the home environment and early cognitive development in the first 5 years. In A. Gottfried (ed.), *The home environment and early cognitive development* (pp. 5–56). Orlando, FL: Academic Press.

Brock, T., Coulton, C., London, A., Polit, D., Richburg-Hayes, L., Scott, E. and Verma, N. (2002). *Welfare reform in Cleveland: Implementation, effects, and experiences of poor families and neighborhoods.* New York: MDRC.

Clark-Kauffman, E., Duncan, G., and Morris, P. (2003). How welfare polices affect child and adolescent achievement. *Papers and Proceedings of the American Economics Association, 93*(2), 299–303.

Conger, R. D., Conger, K. J., and Elder, G. H. (1997). Family economic hardship and adolescent adjustment: Mediating and moderating processes. In G. J. Duncan & J. Brooks-Gunn (eds.), *Consequences of growing up poor* (pp. 288–310). New York: Russell Sage Foundation.

Duncan, G.J. and Brooks-Gunn, J. (1997). *Consequences of growing up poor.* New York: The Russell Sage Foundation.

Duncan, G. J., Brooks-Gunn, J., and Klebanov, P. K. (1994). Economic deprivation and early childhood development. *Child Development, 65*, 296–318.

Edin, K. and Lein, L. (1997). *Making Ends Meet. How single mothers survive welfare and low-wage work.* New York: Russell Sage Foundation press.

Elder, G. (1974). *Children of the great depression.* Chicago: University of Chicago Press.

Elder, G. (1979). Historical change in life patterns and personality. In P. Bates and O. Brim (eds.), *Life span development and behavior* (pp. 117–159). New York: Academic Press.

Elder, G., Liker, J., and Cross, C. (1984). Parent–child behavior in the great depression: Life course and intergenerational influences. In P. Bates and O. Brim (eds.), *Life span development and behavior* (pp. 109–158). Orlando, FL: Academic Press.

Farel, A. M. (1980). Effects of preferred maternal roles, maternal employment, and sociodemographic status on school adjustment and competence. *Child Development, 51*, 1179–1196.

Freedman, S., Knab, J., Gennetian, L.A., and Navarro, D. (2000). *The Los Angeles jobs-first GAIN evaluation: Final report on a work first program in a major urban center.* New York: MDRC.

Freedman, S., Friedlander, D., Hamilton, G., Rock, J., Mitchell, M., Nudelman, J., Schweder, A., and Storto. L. (2000). *Evaluating alternative welfare-to-work approaches: Two-year impacts for eleven programs.* National Evaluation of Welfare-to-Work Strategies. Washington, DC: U.S. Department of Health and Human Services, Administration for Children and Families and Office of the Assistant Secretary for Planning and Evaluation; U.S. Department of Education, Office of the Under Secretary and Office of Vocational and Adult Education.

Gennetian, L. and Miller, C. (2000). *Reforming and rewarding work: Final report on the Minnesota Family Investment Program, Vol. 2, Effects on children.* New York: MDRC.

Gennetian, L. and Morris, P. (2003). How time limits and make work pay strategies affect the well-being of children: Experimental evidence from two welfare reform programs. *Children and Youth Services Review*, 25(1/2), 17–54.

Gennetian, L., Huston, A., Crosby, D., Chang, Y., Lowe, E., and Weisner, T. (2002). *Making child care choices: How welfare and work policies affect parents' decisions.* New York: MDRC.

Gennetian, L. A., Duncan, G., Knox, V., Vargas, W., Clark-Kauffman, E., and London, A. S. (2004). How welfare policies can affect adolescents. *Journal of Research on Adolescents*, 14(4), 399–423.

Hamilton, G. (2000). Do mandatory welfare-to-work programs affect the well-being of children? A synthesis of child research conducted as part of the National Evaluation of Welfare-to-Work Strategies. Washington, DC: U.S. Department of Health and Human Services, Administration for Children and Families and Office of the Assistant Secretary for Planning and Evaluation; and U.S. Department of Education, Office of the Under Secretary and Office of Vocational and Adult Education.

Hamilton, G., Freedman, S., Gennetian, L., Michalopoulos., C., Walter, J., Adams-Ciardullo, D., Gassman-Pines, A., McGroder, S., Zaslow, M., Brooks, J., and Ahuluwalia, S. (2001). How effective are different welfare-to-work approaches? Five-year adult and child impacts for eleven programs. Washington, DC: U.S. Department of Health and Human Services, Administration for Children and Families and Office of the Assistant Secretary for Planning and Evaluation; and U.S. Department of Education, Office of the Deputy Secretary, Planning and Evaluation Service and Office of Vocational and Adult Education.

Harvey, E. (1999). Short-term and long-term effects of early parental employment on children of the National Longitudinal Survey of Youth. *Journal of Economic Literature*, 33(4), 1829–1878.

Huston, A. C. and Gennetian, L. A. (2001). Parents' Coping Strategies and Child Well-being. Paper presented at Conference on Coping Strategies in Working Poor Families sponsored by Office of the Assistant Secretary for Planning and Evaluation, Health and Human Services and Chapin Hall Center for Children, Washington, DC.

Huston, A., Miller, C., Richburg-Hayes, L., Duncan, G., Eldred, C., Weisner, T., Lowe, E., McLoyd, V., Crosby, D., Ripke, M., and Redcross, C. (2003). *New hope for families and children: Five-year results of a program to reduce poverty and reform welfare.* New York: MDRC.

Klerman, L. (1991). The health of poor children: Problems and programs. In A. Huston (ed.), *Children and poverty.* New York: Cambridge University Press.

Knox, V., Miller, C., and Gennetian, L. (2000). *Reforming welfare and rewarding work: A summary of the final report on the Minnesota Family Investment Program.* New York: MDRC.

Korenman, S. and Miller, J. E. (1997). Effects of long-term poverty on physical health of children in the National Longitudinal Survey of Youth. In G. J. Duncan and J. Brooks-Gunn (eds.), *Consequences of growing up poor* (pp. 70–99). New York: Russell Sage Foundation.

London, A. S., Scott, E. K., Edin, K., and Hunter, V. (2004). Welfare reform, work-family tradeoffs, and child well-being. *Family Relations*, 53(2), 148–158.

Massey, D. S., Gross A. B., and Shibuya, K. (1994). Migration, segregation, and the geographic concentration of poverty. *American Sociological Review*, 59, 425–445.

Mayer, S. E. (1997). *What money can't buy: Family income and children's life chances.* Cambridge, MA: Harvard University Press.

McGroder, S. M., Zaslow, M. J., Moore, K. A., and LeMenestrel, S. M. (2000). *Impacts on young children and their families two years after enrollment: Findings from the Child Outcomes Study.* National Evaluation of Welfare-to-Work Strategies. Washington, DC: U.S. Department of Health and Human Services, Office of the Assistant Secretary for Planning and Evaluation and Administration for Children and Families; and U.S. Department of Education, Office of the Under Secretary and Office of Vocational and Adult Education.

McLoyd, V. (1990). The impact of economic hardship on Black families and children: Psychological distress, parenting and socioemotional development. *Child Development*, 61, 311–346.

McLoyd, V. (1998). Children in poverty, development, public policy, and practice. In I. E. Siegel and K. A. Renninger (eds.), *Handbook of child psychology* (4th ed.). New York: Wiley.

McLoyd, V. C., Jayartne, T. E., Ceballo, R., and Borquez, J. (1994). Unemployment and work interruption among African-American single mothers, effects on parenting and adolescent socioemotional functioning. *Child Development*, 65, 562–589.

Michalopoulos, C., Card, D., Gennetian, L., Harknett, K., and Robins, P. K. (2000). *The Self-Sufficiency Project at 36 months: Effects of a financial work incentive on employment and income.* Ottawa: Social Research and Demonstration Corporation.

Michalopoulos, C., Tattrie, D., Miller, C., Robins, P., Morris, P., Gyarmarti, D., Redcross, C., Foley, K., and Ford, R. (2002). *Making work pay: Final report on the Self-Sufficiency Project for long-term welfare recipients.* Ottawa: Social Research and Demonstration Corporation.

Moore, K. and Driscoll, A. (1997). Low-wage maternal employment and outcomes for children: A study. *Future of Children,* 7(1), 122–127.

Morris, P. and Michalopoulos, C. (2000). *The Self-Sufficiency Project at 36 months: Effects on children of a program that increased employment and income.* Ottawa: Social Research and Demonstration Corporation.

Morris, P., Duncan, G., and Clark-Kauffman, E. (in press). Child well-being in an era of welfare reform: The sensitivity of transitions in development to policy change. *Developmental Psychology.*

Morris, P., Gennetian, L., and Duncan, G. (2005). Effects of welfare and employment policies on young children: New findings on policy experiments conducted in the early 1990's. *Social Policy Report, Society for Research in Child Development Vol. XIX* (2), 3–14.

Morris, P. A., Huston, A. C., Duncan, G. J., Crosby, D. A., and Bos, J. M. (2001). *How welfare and work policies affect children: A synthesis of research.* New York: MDRC.

Parcel, T. L. and Menaghan, E. G. (1994). *Parent's jobs and children's lives.* New York: Aldine de Gruyter.

Parcel, T. L. and Menaghan, E. G. (1997). Effects of low-wage employment on family well-being. *Future of Children,* 7(1), 116–121.

Polit, D. F., Widom, R., Edin, K., Bowie, S., London, A. S., Scott, E. K., and Valenzuela, A. (2001). *The Project on Devolution and Urban Change: Is work enough? The experience of current and former welfare mothers who work.* New York: MDRC.

Quint, J., Edin, K., Buck, M. L., Fink, B., Padilla, Y. C., Simmons-Hewitt, O., and Valmont, M. E. (1999). *Big cities and welfare reform: Early implementation and ethnographic findings from the Project on Devolution and Urban Change.* New York: MDRC.

Scott, E. K., Edin, K., London, A. S., and Kissane, R. J. (2004). Unstable work, unstable income: Implications for family well-being in the era of time-limited welfare. *Journal of Poverty,* 8(1), 61–88.

Scott, E. K., Edin, K., London, A. S., and Mazelis, J. (2001). My children come first: Welfare-reliant women's post-TANF views of work-family tradeoffs and marriage. In G. J. Duncan and P. L. Chase-Lansdale (eds.), *For better and for worse: Welfare reform and the well-being of children and families.* New York: Russell Sage Press.

Scott, E. K., London, A. S., and Hurst, A. (2005). Out of their hands: Patching together care for children when parents move from welfare to work. *Journal of Marriage and the Family,* 67(2), 369–385.

Smith, J. R., Brooks-Gunn, J., and Klebanov, P. K. (1997). Consequences of living in poverty for young children's cognitive and verbal ability and early school achievement. In G. J. Duncan and J. Brooks-Gunn (eds.), *Consequences of growing up poor.* New York: Russell Sage Foundation.

Sugland, B. W., Zaslow, M., Smith, J. R., Brooks-Gunn, J., Moore, K. A., Blumenthal, C., Griffin, T., and Bradley, R. (1995). The early childhood HOME Inventory and HOME Short Form in differing sociocultural groups: Are there differences in underlying structure, internal consistency of subscales, and patterns of prediction? *Journal of Family Issues,* 16(5), 632–663.

Vandell, D. L. and Ramanan, J. (1992). Effects of early and recent maternal employment on children from low-income families. *Child Development,* 63(4), 938–949.

Wilson, W. J. (1987). *The truly disadvantaged.* Chicago, IL: The University of Chicago Press.

Yoshikawa, H. and Hsueh, J. (2001). Child development and public policy: Towards a dynamic systems perpective. *Child Development,* 72, 1887–1903.

Zaslow, M. J. and Emig, C. A. (1997). When low-income mothers go to work: Implications for children. *Future of Children,* 7(1), 110–115.

Zaslow, M. J., McGroder, S., Cave, G., and Mariner, C. (1999). Maternal employment and measures of children's health and development among families with some history of welfare receipt. *Research in the Sociology of Work,* 7, 233–259.

CHAPTER FIVE

Parenting in a Changing Welfare Policy Landscape: What Does It Mean for Young Children?

KARIE FRASCH

Welfare reform reflected a substantial shift in government welfare policy. It ended the entitlement to cash and in-kind assistance for poor families, and shifted policy into a new arena, namely influencing the behavior and private lives of parents. In particular, strong government messages pushed poor women with children into the labor market, and imposed time limits on the receipt of cash aid and sanctions for noncompliance. These changes were grounded in nearly two decades of smaller reforms involving experiments with work inducements and new program requirements for welfare recipients.

Debates concerning reauthorization of the current welfare law focus on a continuation of the central tenets of PRWORA. Although the majority of welfare recipients are children, and the government safety net prior to PRWORA provided a marginal cushion of protection to all poor children, current welfare policy continues to focus primarily on the behavior of parents. Proponents of this policy believe that children will benefit from the increased financial resources afforded by parents' employment and the positive role modeling work provides. Opponents, on the other hand, believe that families supported by work will not necessarily be any better off financially than while on welfare, children will receive less supervision and quality time with their parents, and parents will experience more stress (Blank & Haskins, 2002).

A body of research has begun to illuminate the effects of the welfare law, specifically on children (see chapter 4), despite the fact that child well-being is a lesser priority under the law than parental self-sufficiency. The vast majority of these studies have been large-scale quantitative endeavors focused on determining average effects for particular groups—an important and necessary step. However the information learned from quantitative research does not highlight important subgroups of families; nor does it differentiate between children with different experiences, such as those succeeding beyond expectations, being affected more adversely than predicted, or not being affected at all.

Qualitative research, involving the voices of the women and children themselves, can provide information about the diversity of adaptation to poverty and welfare reform. Such research conveys in-depth information about how parents understand and respond to a rapidly shifting policy environment and the new messages of welfare reform, and, in turn, how their responses impact the well-being of their children. This study was undertaken with the goal of contributing to our understanding of the specific mechanisms and processes through which poverty and welfare changes affect poor women and young children, using qualitative methods. Information of this kind is important to take into account when developing policies for a diverse population.

Poverty and Welfare

The well-being of millions of children in the United States is severely compromised by poverty, a condition of relative deprivation. Nearly 40 percent of all children live in low-income families (below 200 percent of the federal poverty line), with 16 percent living in families with incomes below the official federal poverty level (NCCP, 2003). Those with particular characteristics—living in single-mother families, being very young, or belonging to a racial or ethnic minority group—represent a disproportionate share of the poor (U.S. Bureau of the Census, 2000). Families living in poverty for long periods of time lead a precarious existence, often one step removed from total destitution, and most at-risk for adverse outcomes.

For some children, the mere accumulation of negative circumstances and family characteristics seems to affect their well-being. For others, the functioning of their parents and family largely mediates the influences of low income. And for still others, the pathways are more complex (McLoyd, 1990; Sameroff et al., 1987). As a multidimensional phenomenon, poverty affects many facets of children lives, including the neighborhoods their families can afford to live in, the quality of the schools they attend, the environment of their home, and their parents' ability to provide them with consistent care. Overall children raised in poor families have worse physical development and greater likelihood for accidents and injuries, lower cognitive achievement and rates of school completion, and more socioemotional difficulties in the form of difficult relationships, behavior problems, and depressive symptomatology (Brooks-Gunn and Duncan, 1997; Duncan and Brooks-Gunn, 2000; Klerman, 1991; Korenman and Miller, 1997; Korenman et al., 1995; McLoyd et al., 1997). Children who, beginning early in life, are very poor for a number of years, have the most compromised outcomes. However, despite formidable challenges, some poor children exhibit positive adaptation in these circumstances.

Many poor children live in families where a parent works part-time or full time, whereas others live in families that rely partially or completely on government cash assistance and in-kind benefits to survive. Of the children and families who are poor, a significant proportion relies on welfare to make ends meet. Children's developmental outcomes, however, are related more to the total level of their family's financial resources than to whether a parent is employed or relies on government assistance (Zill et al., 1991).

A particular group of welfare recipients—children on long-term welfare—have more significant negative developmental outcomes than children in families who receive welfare for short periods of time. The adults in these long-term recipient families are also more disadvantaged. As a group, they are more likely to have significant barriers to economic self-sufficiency, more signs of depression, and less ability to provide intellectual stimulation and emotional support to their children (Zaslow et al., 1998).

Have Children's Lives Improved under the New Policy Frameworks?

We know a good bit about the effects on children and families of living in poverty and depending on welfare over extended periods of time. What isn't known is how children's well-being is directly or indirectly being affected by the new welfare laws. It is still too soon to know what the *long-term* effects of these changes are because they are relatively recent, and also because the economic environment has changed drastically since the passage of PRWORA.

In the early and mid-1990s, prior to PRWORA and TANF (Temporary Assistance to Needy Families), many individual states petitioned the government to obtain waivers of the AFDC (Aid to Families with Dependent Children) requirements, in order to conduct experimental projects aimed at reducing the welfare rolls and increasing self-sufficiency. Waivers were granted for such things as introducing stricter work requirements, time limits to the receipt of aid, changes in grant amounts, and sanctions for various rule disallowances (Klerman et al., 2000). A proliferation of evaluations of the state waiver programs followed their inception, some of which incorporated child outcome measures. Many of the state waiver evaluations were focused on the effects of particular components, which were later included in the provisions of PRWORA. However most did not publish results until well after the passage of the PRWORA legislation.[1] Although it is useful to review the findings from these studies, none of the programs had approaches and requirements that truly mirrored the ones in place now; most programs were more generous in providing support services than are currently offered under PRWORA.

Using a combination of earnings supplements, earnings disregards, mandatory employment, or support services, the state waiver evaluation programs demonstrated higher levels of parental employment and increased family financial resources among program group participants, as opposed to control group participants. A synthesis of welfare waiver evaluations and their effects on the well-being of children indicates mixed findings (Morris et al., 2001). For example, programs with earnings supplements generally resulted in higher school achievement among elementary school-age children, and, in some cases, led to fewer behavior problems, more positive social behavior, and better overall health. These effects were most pronounced for children of long-term welfare recipients. Programs with mandatory employment provisions but no earnings supplements or with time limits to the receipt of aid had few effects on children (Morris et al., 2001).

A rigorous but nonexperimental study published in *Science* by Chase-Lansdale and colleagues with the Three-City Study provides longitudinal, post-welfare reform findings from 2,402 low-income preschool and adolescent children and mothers (Chase-Lansdale et al., 2003). The data for the study were collected in 1999 and 2001, during the economic boom of that time. Findings indicate that for preschool-age children, mothers' welfare and employment transitions had no effect on them either positively or negatively. Adolescents of mothers entering employment showed an improvement in mental health, whereas those whose mothers became unemployed showed an increase in behavior problems. The lack of statistically significant findings related to young children, and few associations found for adolescents suggests that capturing the complexity and variability within welfare populations may, in some cases, be better suited to the use of alternative methodologies, such as qualitative analyses.

Assessing the Effects of Welfare Reform on Families with Young Children

This study addressed a number of the major gaps in current knowledge about the effects of welfare reform on children. It was initiated to examine the relationship between family economic status and children's development, and the specific mechanisms and processes through which poverty and welfare reform affect children's well-being. Particular attention was paid to the relative influence of factors related to welfare reform, family financial resources, and characteristics associated with parent, child, and family functioning.

The overall study used an integrated mixed-methods approach, employing both quantitative and qualitative methods simultaneously.[2] The quantitative component involved analyses of cross-sectional telephone survey data collected in 2000 of a total of 546 long-term welfare recipients in Alameda and Los Angeles counties. These recipients were also surveyed in the early and mid-1990s as part of the California Work Pays Demonstration Evaluation (CWPD), which examined changes in California's welfare rules [see Brady (1997) for information published on this data set]. Therefore the recipients in the study represent a population of long-term welfare recipient families.

Analyses were completed with 186 families that had at least one child under the age of 12. The data include information on parental characteristics, family employment history, health insurance, housing, transportation, social support, financial resources, parental psychological well-being, parenting quality, and child well-being.

The qualitative component involved an in-depth examination of six families on long-term welfare in Alameda County, over the course of an 18-month period. The purpose of following a small number of families intensively was to focus on the lived experience of adaptation to welfare reform and poverty. This provided the advantage of gaining insights into and an appreciation for the ways in which families hear and respond to government messages in their daily lives, and over the course of time.

The research design falls under the template approach, which involves entering the field with clearly defined research questions and a guiding framework, rather than entering the field and allowing the aims and framework to emerge over time (Crabtree and Miller, 1992; Miles and Huberman, 1994; Tesch, 1990). In terms of data collection and analysis, using a template approach involves a combination of a priori defined interview guides and questions, and codes for analysis, while remaining flexible to changes and interpretations that occur in the field and through readings of the text.

The qualitative study sample was drawn from the CWPD study population. The sampling plan used a combination of random and purposive sampling to select a sample of six participants who had a range of factors known to denote risk for young children, such as long-term receipt of AFDC/TANF with little reported earned income, female-headed family, large family size, poor parental health, homelessness, and lack of access to child care. Based on past interview data and initial discussions, a sample of six single, female adults who appeared to be sufficiently articulate about their experiences to participate in an ongoing study were chosen for the sample. Articulate did not refer to level of education, but instead to an interest in conversing about their life experiences.

Each family was on welfare for a minimum of seven years, and had at least one child under the age of 6 in 1999. Four of the six women did not complete high school, and only two of them had a history of sustained employment. They ranged in age from 24 to 36 years at the beginning of the interview period, and all were either African American or Latino. Family size ranged from two to four children, with four of the six women raising three children. Finally, four of the six women had some kind of health-related problem, only one family used formal group child care, and all of the families had either subsidized housing or lived with family members.

The qualitative component involved the use of a theoretically based conceptual framework as a guide. The framework, developed by the researcher, is an ecological/transactional model of the effects of poverty and welfare reform on young children's well-being. It is based in part on the family functioning model of McLoyd (McLoyd, 1990), aspects of cumulative risk models (Sameroff et al., 1987), components of resiliency theory

(Baldwin et al., 1990; Werner and Smith, 1989), and research that has combined those approaches (Bolger et al., 1995; Egeland et al., 1993).

This framework serves as a way to both qualitatively and quantitatively examine the major pathways through which poverty and other environmental factors affect children, both positively and negatively. The model is specific to single-mother families rather than married-couple families, long-term poverty and welfare use rather than income loss, young children rather than school-age children or adolescents, and well-being in terms of both positive and negative adaptation. Additionally this model is intended to examine child well-being at a period in time rather than as an outcome per se. In this way it recognizes the transactional nature of development, the bidirectional influence of factors, the possibility for both continuity and discontinuity, and the dynamic interplay between the child's well-being and other proximal and distal factors. Figure 5.1 illustrates the model.

Qualitative data were collected through face-to-face, semi-structured interviews and observation, approximately monthly for one–three hours, over the course of one year. An additional follow-up was conducted six months after the last interview. Data collection also included an interview with the focal child's grandparent, and numerous play sessions with the focal child. Interviews took place primarily in families' homes, but also in the car on the way to baseball practice, on the back porch, and at fast-food restaurants. Data collection sessions were loosely organized around the key factors in the conceptual framework: Social support, environmental factors, parental characteristics, total financial resources, parental psychological well-being, parenting quality, child characteristics, and child well-being.

Participant observation was used to assess the focal child within the family (identified child under the age of six), and to observe interactions between all family members. Additionally informal play sessions occurred in

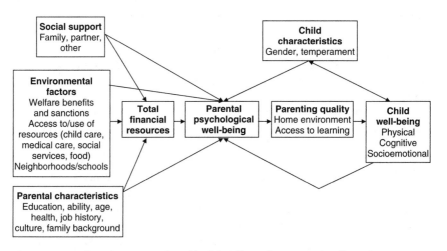

Figure 5.1 Ecological/transactional model of the effects of poverty and welfare reform on young children's well-being.

the home and were tailored to the developmental level of the child. The researcher referred to normative developmental scales, observation, and interviews with parent and grandparent to assess child cognitive, social–emotional, and physical development.

Data analysis began following the first interview and continued until well after the end of the data collection period. All interviews were audiotaped and transcribed verbatim, resulting in an average of 40 pages of single-spaced text for each interview. Data also included field notes, memos, and team meeting notes. The qualitative analysis software package Atlas.*ti* was used to manage and analyze the data, which consisted of a total of 103 primary documents (63 transcribed interviews and 40 separate field note files).

The data analysis process followed the template approach, which is both deductive and inductive (Crabtree and Miller, 1992; Miles and Huberman, 1994), and involved the following steps: (1) Development of a template of a priori codes based on the conceptual framework, prior theory, and emerging patterns from the interviews; (2) reading and partial "open coding" of the texts; (3) refinement and revisal of the template of codes; (4) continued coding, refinement, sorting of codes into "code families" or themes, and reinterpretation of the data within and between subjects; and (5) final review of coded text segments and text memos to verify interpretations, extract subject narrations, and create thematic descriptions and discussions.

Although it would be impossible to guard against all possibility of bias in the data, several strategies were employed in this study to reduce the threat (Padgett, 1998). First interviews and participant observation were conducted over a relatively long period of time rather than relying on a single interview session. Second triangulation was used as a method for increasing confidence in interpretations about child well-being—interpretations were based on personal observation, interviews with parents, discussions with grandparents, and the interpretations of colleagues not involved with the study. Third regular team meetings helped to minimize bias. Finally member checking was done throughout the study by regularly engaging the subjects in discussion.

What Makes a Difference for Young Children's Well-Being

Analyses of the qualitative interview and field note data revealed a number of overall study themes. Prior to the discussion of two case examples, a summary of these findings is presented.

Income has Both a Direct and Indirect Effect on Children's Well-Being. The ways that income, or total family financial resources, affects children's well-being is based on three major pathways. First parents' subjective experience of financial strain, and the way they directly or indirectly communicate that experience to their children, is as important as the actual amount of money available to support them each month. Second income affects the children in this sample through reduced learning opportunities and a lower-quality home environment. Finally financial strain affects parents' well-being by increasing stress and anxiety, and decreasing life satisfaction. These feelings in turn influence the quality of parenting provided to children in the home.

The Effects of Welfare Reform Depend on Family Characteristics and Circumstances. There were several family responses to welfare reform: (1) The changes had no major impact because of increased earnings through already held employment or a shift to a different income source such as SSI; (2) the potential for the profound impact of reduced income was avoided through the use of "income packaging," such as sharing housing, utility, or food resources with others; or (3) lack of compliance with CalWORKs (California's version of TANF's welfare-to-work program) resulted in a sanction of the adult portion of the monthly welfare grant, and subsequent lower overall family financial resources.

Work in and of Itself Does not Predict Positive or Negative Child Well-Being. The findings from this study provide a mixed picture. On the one hand, working predicts significantly more monthly financial resources compared to not working. However working does not always have a positive influence on the psychological well-being of parents or the well-being of children. It may be that work has a more beneficial effect on families on short-term welfare—those who dip in and out of poverty temporarily—as compared to the population of long-term welfare recipients.

Social Support Makes a Significant Difference for Children. Social support can take many forms, such as moral support, financial assistance, or involvement with formal services, and can be both a direct or indirect influence on children and their families. Overall social support plays a crucial role in predicting positive child well-being in the face of adversity, although the type matters less than the quality of the support. Social isolation, on the other hand, detracts from child well-being through lack of financial support, increased parental depression or lower self-esteem, or a lack of beneficial relationships.

Parental Characteristics and the Family Environment are Significant Predictors of Children's Well-Being. In this study, parental characteristics are a major pathway to child well-being but seem to operate more as an influence on parental well-being and parenting quality, rather than directly on the child. In the sense that they do directly impact the child, it is through cumulative risks rather than particular, specific factors. Parental psychological well-being and parenting quality is clearly and directly predictive of children's well-being. A developmentally appropriate, consistent home environment combined with a healthy attachment relationship with a primary caregiver is associated with more resilient outcomes for children.

Overall these themes indicate that the presence or absence of four pivotal factors or processes—financial strain, social support, specific parental characteristics, and the family and home environment—is most associated with resilient or problematic children in these long-term welfare recipient families. The following two case examples provide in-depth illustrations of the challenges associated with living in poverty, as well as the ways in which parents interpret and respond to government messages about welfare and work.

Gloria and Hope: Divergent Pathways of Adaptation to Poverty and Welfare Reform

Case #1. Gloria and Ben: High Risk, High Conflict

Gloria is a 30-year-old mother of four children, ages 11, 9, 3, and 1. Gloria's partner for most of the last five years, Robert, is the father of Ben (age three) and his 1-year-old sister. Ben is the focal child of this discussion. The six of them live together in a federally subsidized, small two-bedroom apartment in an impoverished, high-crime urban neighborhood. Gloria has received welfare assistance for over ten years and has very limited employment experience. Robert works sporadically as a laborer and therefore contributes to the household expenses some of the time.

Ben is tall and heavy for his age, so at first glance he appears much older than he is. He has a bright smile and a noticeable exuberance. Although he is active and strong, his physical development suffers from undertreated asthma and very poor nutrition. During one two-hour interview, for example, Ben was observed guzzling kool-aid from a gallon jug several times, squirting large amounts of canned whipped cream directly in his mouth, and eating several Popsicles; eating behavior with no limits observed on numerous occasions during the study period.

In terms of cognitive development, he has a fairly significant language delay, has not received any preparation for learning other than what he sees on television, and has an extremely difficult time concentrating or focusing on any one task for more than a couple of minutes. Most significantly Ben has serious behavior problems—he throws tantrums regularly, is aggressive, defiant, intensely active, and is seemingly unable to control himself. He spends a lot of time receiving negative attention from Gloria or his sisters. Occasionally he is observed having positive interactions with his family, but these tend to be fleeting compared to his generally disturbing behavior.

Gloria: Cumulative Risks

Gloria's own childhood was characterized by marked instability and poverty. Her father was an alcoholic who physically abused Gloria's mother, and was killed when Gloria was a young child. In subsequent years, her mother had relationships with other men, most who were reportedly abusive or alcoholic. During her childhood, Gloria lived for periods of time with various relatives or family friends. She always had a difficult time in school and was recognized as having a learning disability, but failed to receive sustained help. By the seventh grade, Gloria was smoking cigarettes, and, by the ninth grade, was taking drugs, including cocaine, on a regular basis.

Her first daughter was born when she was 17 years old, at which time she dropped out of school and became reliant on AFDC. She had a series of abusive relationships, had a second daughter, and never had sustained employment. In 1995, the baby she was pregnant with was stillborn because of her cocaine use. She enrolled in an outpatient drug treatment program in lieu of having her children removed from her care. However less than a year later and while still in the program, Ben was born exposed to cocaine.

> I was still goin' through the program, and I got pregnant with Ben. An' he was—when he was born, he was tested with it an' it was like, look, "enough is enough. You goin' through the program, why can't you stop?". . . They said "this is the last straw. We are gonna take this child from you." Oh, I beg and plead and beg and plead.

She has been clean and sober since his birth, with the support of a weekly home-visiting program, and the threat of going to jail if she tested positive for drugs in her urine.

Gloria's Current Well-Being, the Home Environment, and Parenting

Gloria's psychological and emotional development was understandably impacted by her difficult family background, drug use, teen parenthood, and volatile relationships with men. As an adult, she is in many ways dissatisfied with her life. She has a poor sense of self, suffers from depressive symptoms and mild but chronic physical problems, and has low self-efficacy. She feels trapped by her life as a parent and is often resentful of her children's needs and of her partner.

> No one was appreciating—no one appreciate anything. An' I have to fight to get a glass of water. I have to fight to—actually it takes them a long time to get me some water, to go to the store for me. Just to do anything. I got to the point where I started picking up—I would go to the store. I leave them in the house and go to the store. Come back, "but mama can I have some?" "No." I can't have—I don' have any reading time to myself. I don't have mommy time to myself. I don' have Gloria time to myself. I was like, "This is mine." It's like, "hey you guys." Like they go to the store and get something' it's with attitude. And say, "no, that's mine, no." So when I go to the store I get what I want. An', it's mine, I don' have to share. That's why when I go to the store and get something I always get somethin' that they can't eat.

Additionally she has few relationships or social support other than her mother and Robert. "I can't—that's about all the people—that's about all because I really can't trust anybody, you know."

Environmental factors, involvement with the social services department, and living in a dangerous, impoverished neighborhood have all impacted Gloria's psychological well-being, as has the family's total financial resources. Social support from her mother, family, and partner serve to buffer, slightly, the impact of other circumstances in Gloria's life. However her background and personal characteristics most influence how she feels about herself, how she functions on a daily basis, and what she imagines is possible for herself. This in turn contributes directly to the way she parents, and the home environment in which she raises her children.

The home environment is chaotic, disorganized, and filthy with stains, spilled food, broken toys, and small appliances, and many items that are hazardous for young children. The dynamics of relating to each other in the home environment mirror the chaos of the physical surroundings. Gloria's demeanor with the children ranges from flat to aggravated, with little room in between. Gloria's own neediness is apparent in reference to Ben:

> He just wants me all of the time, and then when he gets me, he leaves me . . . Ben gets up, comes over, and starts harassing me. So I get up and make him his oatmeal. He can't just have oatmeal, no, he also have to have his little eggs.

Making Ends Meet

Gloria survives financially through a variety of income sources, although the combined amount fluctuates considerably each month, and as a consequence she experiences significant financial strain. She receives a small TANF grant, a Social Security payment (her daughters' father died of a drug overdose a number of years ago), Food Stamps, MediCal, a housing subsidy, and her partner's employment (his income as a day laborer varies from nothing up to about $800 per month and is mostly not reported to the welfare department). Because of the family cap she does not receive any benefits for her youngest daughter.

Given the family's precarious financial situation, the welfare department plays a fairly central role in their lives. Gloria feels a sense of entitlement to welfare, and refers to her cash grant as her "paycheck" or "guaranteed income." She was angry when CalWORKs was implemented in Alameda County and she was required to attend the four-week Job Club; she quit after the first day. She said,

> An' it's like where you—first of all, they have you come sit in this room for three to four hours . . . Tell you how to fill out applications . . . I went once but I didn't go back because I'm sittin' in a room with like 12 other people filling out applications. They don't tell you how—they're supposed to tell you how to go about getting a job. They don't just say

you fill this paper out . . . An' then you can go out there and apply for
these jobs. No, it's not that easy.

Although the government message about welfare reform is clearly one of
work-first, Gloria misunderstood the meaning, thinking that there wouldn't
be any negative repercussions for not participating. After her dissatisfying
experience at Job Club, Gloria met with a CalWORKs worker and told her
that she wanted to go back to school to get her GED instead of getting a
job right away. She was approved for this activity but told that she would
have to pay for the books herself and so she decided not to do it. She was
then surprised to receive a sanction of the adult portion of her grant for
noncompliance.

The changes in welfare brought stricter rules but a more anonymous mes-
senger. Gloria was very frustrated with some of these changes in the welfare
department, particularly the fact that her case was moved to "transfer desk,"
a term used to denote the lack of a specific worker assigned to her case. She
wanted to know who was sending her the sanction letters, and who was
involved with her case. On one occasion a letter arrived with a first initial
and last name written and then whited-out in the top corner of the page.
Gloria spent the next hour erasing and uncovering the name and then calling the welfare office to ask for the person. Reportedly when the worker
answered and Gloria confronted her, the worker wanted to know where she
had gotten her name. Gloria simply replied, "Oh, I have my ways."

A number of months later, Gloria received another letter requesting her
participation in CalWORKs. This letter reportedly threatened to cut off
all support, including Food Stamps, although in California sanctions are
officially only given for the adult portion of the cash grant. Given this ultima-
tum, she signed up for Job Club and was assigned to an employment center
where she was one of a small number of recipients in the program. There she
received personal, one-on-one attention. The welfare message was the same,
but unlike her previous experience, she felt that the staff made it fun and really
cared about her success. She was therefore more willing to participate.

Staff brought in applications from the community and helped Gloria fill
them out. By the end of the four weeks, Gloria had shifted from feeling
antagonistic toward the welfare department to being excited about her
ability to do well. She got a full-time job cleaning houses for $7/hour, or
about $1,000 gross per month. Although the hourly rate was relatively low,
it was moderately higher than the minimum wage at the time and allowed
her to exit the welfare program. No longer a TANF recipient, she continues
to get a modest Food Stamp benefit, and she and Ben receive MediCal.

While Gloria has complaints about the work, at our last contact she had
kept the job for over six months and was planning to stay until she found
something she liked more.

I'm sticking to this until I find another job. Then when I find another
job, they call—that other job call me—whatever it is—call me back

and I'll say, "Well, I'm going to need two weeks." Cause I do have to give them two weeks.

Participating in work outside the home gave Gloria a new enthusiasm and confidence in herself. She no longer spent every day in her apartment. When talking about her job, she had energy not present before. "And then everybody be saying, 'we missed you, Gloria. Why—where you at?' Everybody seen that I was working . . . And it shocked a lot of people."

Having time away from her children improved Gloria's well-being and lessened her aggravation toward them, though she often felt exhausted at the end of her workday. Additionally Robert began to be more involved with the family and to help with the children. When Gloria began work, she enrolled Ben in Head Start and day care, and his younger sister in day care, both paid for by the welfare department. This represented a significant, positive change for the children, who were exposed to other models of caregiving, nutritious meals, other children, and structure. Ben's behavior was reportedly somewhat improved, and he demonstrated less aggressiveness and defiance.

In summary, despite not escaping poverty, the pathways for change in this family included an increase in family financial resources, a change in the mother's psychological well-being and parenting quality, access to support services in the form of education and day care, and a change in the children's well-being. Despite multiple barriers to employment, Gloria was able to move toward self-sufficiency, and her children were affected in an indirect but positive way. However the reason she was successful is due in large part to the individually responsive program she participated in. While the government message of "work-first and delay childbearing" was originally misinterpreted and destabilizing, at least in the short-term it made a positive difference for this family.

Case #2. Hope and Kamila: Chronic Parental Illness, Child Behavior Problems

In contrast to the case of Gloria, the case of Hope provides an example of how multiple barriers can impede the ability to succeed in the current welfare environment, and negatively affect children's well-being.

Hope is a 34-year-old single mother of three children, ages 15, 12, and 2. The family lives in a refurbished public housing complex in a high-crime inner-city neighborhood of a large city. They moved there from a more dilapidated building a few years ago when the complex remodeling was complete. Although there has been major revitalization work in the surrounding community and less crime in recent years, drugs and gangs are still a problem. Hope's two older children are at school all day, and sometimes into the early evening when they attend after-school activities. Kamila, age 2, spends her days at home with Hope.

Kamila (the focus child of this case) is a vibrant, healthy girl with cute features and a warm laugh. She is tall and slender for her age, and, although slow to warm up, is affectionate and playful. She is physically healthy and eats a nutritious diet, though she is given few opportunities for large motor development such as running, jumping, and climbing. She is not allowed to play in the housing complex playground because Hope does not feel it is safe there, and so she sometimes runs and rides her tricycle in the small apartment. Kamila's language development is somewhat delayed, although as is true with children her age, her recognition surpasses her ability to communicate. The home environment is noticeably absent of cognitively stimulating toys or activities. Much of her time is spent watching television rather than having other learning opportunities. Although Kamila is often happy and content, she also has behavior problems, including serious aggressiveness, tantrums, defiance, and a very short attention span. She also exhibits significant anxiety, especially concerning separation from her mother.

Hope: Little Job Experience and Chronic Illness

Hope grew up in a large, religious working-class family. She dropped out of high school in the twelfth grade, reportedly because of the way she was treated by other students, a decision she now considers to be one of her "biggest mistakes." After leaving high school, Hope worked at two different service sector jobs for a total of about nine months. Her first child was born when she was 19 years old and her second three years later. During the ten-year span between the birth of her second daughter and Kamila, Hope spent most of her time raising her children. She has not worked in over fifteen years, and has been on welfare this entire time.

Hope is uncomfortable with her lack of work experience. She wishes that she had gotten her GED, and says that someday she would like to get training so that she can work in a medical office. Hope is clearly anxious about her ability to work after so many years. When asked about her most recent job, she initially indicated that it was "about five years ago." It wasn't until many months later that she felt comfortable revealing the true length of time. In 1993, Hope was diagnosed with Type II diabetes. She is also obese and struggles with back pain, foot pain, and headaches. Despite these health concerns she unintentionally became pregnant with Kamila in 1997. The decision to continue with the pregnancy and raise a third child by herself was difficult for Hope.

> An' I got these two that I'm trying to—I'm struggling with them an' . . . the lady asked me what do I wanna do—was I gonna keep the baby or did I wanna have an abortion. So I said, um, I'm not gonna have an abortion. I'm gonna keep the baby . . . I—everything was going through my head. I knew—I said this is gonna be—I knew it was gonna be hard 'cause I was thinking of diapers an' clothes—I don' have a dime nowhere an' what am I gonna do an' all this an' that but I—I still decided just to keep her. I figure I'll make it some kinda way.

Kamila was born one month before the enforcement of the family cap rule, allowing Hope to receive government benefits for her daughter, though she was unaware of this policy at the time.

Holding It together: Financial Strain

Hope struggles to make ends meet each month, although she does an extraordinary job of budgeting.

> It's really not enough money to really—with necessities when you have—I think when the child is smaller, it's kinda okay but as the kids start getting older . . . they take more money 'cause they eat more an' . . . then the clothes an' then it's different stuff come up at school. Lotta time you might not even have the money for your child to, you know, maybe participate in something.

Unlike many welfare recipients, she relies completely on government support, rather than supplementing her resources with under-the-table work or family support. She receives TANF (including $9 extra per month because of her Type II diabetes), Food Stamps, a housing subsidy (she pays only $109 per month after being on a waiting list for eight years), food from WIC for Kamila, free breakfast and lunch for her older children, and MediCal health insurance. Hope's total yearly resources are barely over 50 percent of the poverty line for a family of her size. She therefore regularly uses services that provide free food and supplies, such as food pantries, in order to make ends meet each month.

Hope: Focus on Illness, Lack of Self-Esteem

Hope's strong desire to be responsible for her children's well-being gives her a sense of purpose in the world. Her primary identification is as a parent, and not as her own person with unique interests and needs. For all of her adult years, she has focused on parenting, and has had few close relationships other than with her mother and some of her siblings. Her affect and demeanor suggest that she is depressed, and she generally has low self-esteem. Other than her parenting role, Hope is preoccupied with her health and body. She spends a great deal of time thinking, talking, and worrying about it. Many discussions are focused on her doctor appointments, physical symptoms, or fears. Although she hasn't yet had any serious complications related to her diabetes, she uses the illness as a justification for not being able to meet the requirements of a job. Between her morning and evening blood sugar testing and insulin regimen, and her need to frequently eat during the day, she feels that she would have a hard time keeping to a work schedule.

Welfare Reform

Hope correctly heard the government messages about welfare reform before the changes even began taking place in her county. While she was pregnant with Kamila, she received an information pamphlet in the mail that discussed CalWORKs and work requirements. Hope was anxious about getting involved in the program after hearing stories from other women who went through Job Club. She worried that if she wasn't able to succeed with welfare reform and be self-sufficient within five years, she and her children would become homeless. With so few resources, and no back-up support in case of emergencies, Hope survives by keeping her family's lives extremely contained. Not surprisingly she greatly fears the changes in welfare policies.

Hope contacted the welfare office to speak to someone when her daughter was about one year old. As was true with Gloria, Hope's case is officially on "transfer desk," so she spoke with whoever answered the phone that day. The man told her that she would receive a letter in the mail soon to tell her where and when to sign up for CalWORKs. Hope waited but never received any information. Many months later a woman from the county came to her health center to tell people about the program. She suggested that they contact the welfare office rather than wait to receive a notice or a telephone call. "Don't wait for them to call you, you call them so you can go on into the program before the money run out." Since Hope had already called, she decided to wait. After nearly three more months she finally received a telephone call from a worker telling her how to sign up for Job Club.

At the Job Club orientation, Hope was given a medical exemption form to get filled out and signed by her doctor when she told the orientation staff that she had diabetes and was having symptoms related to her illness. Her doctor signed the form, giving her a three-month exemption from CalWORKs activities. Hope was told, however, that her five-year lifetime "clock" was still running. At that time, Hope expressed a desire to participate in CalWORKs and to be assisted with training and child care. She interpreted the exemption as helpful support.

> But it ain't really like I want to be exempted, . . . but I mean—I really didn't wanna be exempt anyway. I wanted to go along an' do, um, the program and then get her childcare, 'cause I'm not—like right now, I couldn't pay for childcare for her an' Deanne. 'Cause you know how high that'd be. An' then I do wanna have my own job, an' have my own money an' everything because I don't—I won't—I'm tired of Social Service anyway.

Over time it became clear that Hope actually had significant anxiety about really participating in the program, getting hired by an employer, and working. Sometimes she indicated that she could probably get a job, just not one that she would want to have, and other times she was concerned that she might not be able to get one at all.

> I've had a couple (jobs) but I haven't had just a whole bunch. So even for me with the little bit of experience that I do have, it's still probably

gonna be hard for me because I don' have a whole—whole bunch of experience in a lotta different stuff.

Getting a medical exemption appeared to be a way of stalling from the inevitable need to deal with the welfare changes.

The same month that Hope's three-month medical exemption was over, she had to go to the welfare office for her yearly recertification. While there, she inquired about her status for Job Club.

> So I had went and then when the lady called me up to the window, you know, to bring my papers and everything, and then they had a little form on there about the job thing, asking questions about job and do you need child care, this and that? An' so then the lady asked me was I—was this the baby and I said yes, and she asked me how old and I said two. An' then she said—I said, "Are they going to call me for this job thing?" An' then she said, "I doubt it 'cause the baby's only two. I think it's like when they're three."

Hope knew enough to realize that this information was incorrect, but she didn't pursue the issue further with the woman. Three months later, Hope received her Job Club letter in the mail and went to the orientation. She participated in the four-week program and had a fairly positive experience; by the end, she expressed more confidence about the idea of doing interviews, but not necessarily getting a job. Hope did, however, find it stressful and exhausting to get up so early each day and be out of the apartment for the entire day, including a one-hour bus ride each way. She brought Kamila with her for the first week because it was too short notice to arrange care, and then began leaving her with her mother, who took time off from her low-income job to care for the girl. This transition was difficult for both Hope and Kamila.

After completing Job Club, but before Hope began the actual job search process, she became sick and was given another medical exemption. Initially she thought it was related to her diabetes but then discovered that she had a large cyst that needed to be removed. A month later, she underwent surgery, was in the hospital for several days, and spent the next several months recovering from the operation. Six months later, Hope applied for SSI but was denied, and at that point was unsure what she would do when her exemption was up. She did not feel that she would be able to succeed in the job market, but was also afraid that she wouldn't qualify for SSI if she applied again.

Hope's experience of CalWORKs and her anticipation of participating caused her a great deal of stress. In terms of pathways from welfare to her child's well-being, Hope's experience affected her own psychological well-being by exaggerating her physical and depressive symptoms, and increasing her feelings of low self-efficacy. As a result, over the course of nearly a year, her parenting was also detrimentally affected. Although she continued to maintain regular routines for Kamila, she was often short with her and felt aggravated.

From the initial months of the interview period, Kamila had a very difficult time when she felt she had to compete for her mother's attention. She began interview sessions cheerful and happy, but slowly began to get negative attention by playing with things that were off-limits. When she was not redirected toward positive activities, she became defiant and angry, and often threw aggressive tantrums. Hope responded with annoyance, aggravation, and threats that she never followed through with. A common litany was, "Stop, Kamila, stop! You actin' up. Why you actin' up? What do you want? I don' know why she actin' up. Stop!" Therefore while Hope experienced changes associated with welfare reform, and suffered from significant financial strain, it was the changes to her fragile psychological well-being that had the most impact on Kamila's development.

Hope is someone for whom the current work-first message is not likely to be successful. Although she would like to be self-sufficient, she would benefit from support that helps her build skills in an individually responsive training program, or to receive help in gradually transitioning into the labor market. Her significant barriers—poor physical health, low education, lack of job history, and depressive symptoms—would likely prevent her from becoming entirely self-sufficient even if she were to secure a minimum-wage job.

Parenting in a Changing Welfare Policy Landscape

The stated purposes of TANF are to provide assistance to needy families, end government dependency of needy parents, reduce the incidence of out-of-wedlock births, and promote the formation and maintenance of two-parent families. In practice, the program is largely related to the second purpose: Reducing the welfare caseloads by moving recipients from welfare to work. Although the current welfare policy addresses children's needs to some extent, such as by requiring up-to-date immunizations and school attendance, there is an overall lack of attention given to children's development and well-being.

Research findings are clear in indicating that poverty, especially when experienced for multiple years in young childhood, leads to poor developmental outcomes. Therefore the reduction of family poverty as a program goal, rather than parental employment alone, would have a much greater positive effect on children's long-term well-being. The findings also show that more attention needs to be paid to parental psychological well-being and caregiving in long-term welfare recipient families. This may require expanding the availability of mental health and parenting services and supports.

Unfortunately most existing welfare programs meant to move adults toward self-sufficiency are not likely to have significant immediate effects on young children during the time they are most vulnerable to detrimental impacts. If the well-being of young children of long-term recipients is a priority, then it may be appropriate to offer services that contain the following elements: Developmentally stimulating and appropriate experiences for young children; regular emotional and physical parental support; parental assistance in enrolling in education or training programs to improve job skills; parenting guidance and involvement in a center-based program; and a practical approach toward financial issues through budgeting support and connection to other community support agencies.

There also may be limitations to the work-first approach, especially for long-term recipient families, who are more likely to have significant barriers to self-sufficiency. A different standard of welfare success may make sense for people such as Hope, for whom the current expectations are too high. For those recipients identified as unlikely to become self-sufficient, support toward consistent half-time work with a reduced TANF grant may be considered successful. Although Gloria "succeeded" through an individualized approach within the work-first framework, she too would not be considered self-sufficient by current welfare program standards.

Supports aimed at addressing parental characteristics such as educational background, job history, ability, or health would also significantly improve families' situations. For example, the expanded availability of non–income related supports, such as quality child care and transportation, and education and training can make all the difference in whether long-term recipients succeed in transitioning from welfare to work.

Additionally removing the family cap in families where it has been applied would improve children's well-being. As a case in point, Hope did not plan to get pregnant or plan her family based on the government message about fertility. She simply lucked out by giving birth to her daughter one month before the cut-off date. When a California grant is about $800 per month for a family of four,[3] imposing a reduction of almost $150 per month as a penalty for the birth of a new baby is likely to make a significant difference in the well-being of the entire family.

A lifetime limit of five years may also be problematic for a sizeable number of families who become partially self-sufficient, but continue to rely on the government for Food Stamps and health insurance to make up for minimum wage work. These same families likely will need support off and on for many years, especially during economic downturns or recessions. Reduced financial resources as a result of the five-year limit (and considerably shorter in some states) will likely cause increased hardship and poor developmental outcomes for children.

Finally no matter what the ultimate requirements and emphases in federal policy, there exists room for improvement in service provision at the local level. Although many welfare recipients—particularly the ones who have been reliant on aid for many years—may experience welfare reform as simply another change in rules, the new expectations have serious implications for the functioning of entire families. Social workers who are considerate and sympathetic about communicating the new messages of policy reform may help parents succeed in the long run. The cases of Gloria and Hope demonstrate the extent to which personal and caring interactions can make the difference between becoming self-sufficient or giving up. The children in these families stand the most to lose if the focus remains primarily on workforce participation without a concomitant emphasis on child well-being.

Notes

Funding for this study was provided by the California Social Work Education Center (CalSWEC) and the Stuart Foundations.

1. The most rigorous of the evaluations include the New Chance Demonstration, the New Hope Project, Minnesota's Family Investment Program Evaluation, Florida's Family Transition Program, and the National Evaluation of Welfare-to-Work Strategies.
2. Results from the quantitative study are reported elsewhere (Frasch, 2001).
3. Based upon estimates in 2000.

References

Baldwin, A. L., Baldwin, C., and Cole, R. E. (1990). Stress-resistant families and stress-resistant children. In J. E. Rolf, A. S. Masten, D. Cicchetti, K. H. Nuechterlein, and S. Weintraub (eds.), *Risk and protective factors in the development of psychopathology* (pp. 257–280). Cambridge, MA: Cambridge University Press.

Blank, R. and Haskins, R. (2002). *The new world of welfare.* Washington, DC.: Brookings Institution Press.

Bolger, K. E., Patterson, C. J., Thompson, W. W., and Kupersmidt, J. B. (1995). Psychosocial adjustment among children experiencing persistent and intermittent family economic hardship. *Child Development, 66,* 1107–1129.

Brady, H. (1997). *Recommendations for research priorities and data sources for monitoring and evaluating welfare reform: Results of two surveys and a discussion on March 7, 1997.* Berkeley, CA: California Policy Seminar Report.

Brooks-Gunn, J. and Duncan, G. J. (1997). The effects of poverty on children. *Future of Children, 7*(2), 55–71.

Chase-Lansdale, P. L., Moffitt, R. A., Lohman, B. J., Cherlin, A. J., Coley, R. L., Pittman, L. D., Roff, J., and Votruba-Drzal, E. (2003). Mother's transitions from welfare to work and the well-being of preschoolers and adolescents. *Science, 299,* 1548–1552.

Crabtree, B. and Miller, W. (eds.), (1992). *Doing qualitative research.* Thousand Oaks, CA: Sage Publications.

Duncan, G. J. and Brooks-Gunn, J. (2000). Family poverty, welfare reform, and child development. *Child Development, 71*(1), 188–196.

Egeland, B., Carlson, E., and Sroufe, L. A. (1993). Resilience as process. *Development and Psychopathology, 5,* 517–528.

Frasch, K. M. (2001). Precarious families: Divergent pathways of adaptation to poverty and welfare reform. Unpublished dissertation. Berkeley, CA: University of California at Berkeley.

Klerman, J. A., Zellman, G. L., Chun, T., Humphrey, N., Reardon, E., Farley, D., Ebener, P. A., and Steinberg, P. (2000). *Welfare reform in California: State and county implementation of CalWORKs in the second year.* Sacramento, CA: RAND Statewide CalWORKs Evaluation, California Department of Social Services.

Klerman, L. V. (1991). The health of poor children: Problems and programs. In A. C. Huston (ed.), *Children in poverty: Child development and public policy.* Cambridge: Cambridge University.

Korenman, S. and Miller, J. E. (1997). Effects of long-term poverty on physical health of children in the National Longitudinal Survey of Youth. In G. J. Duncan and J. Brooks-Gunn (eds.), *Consequences of growing up poor*. New York: The Russell Sage Foundation.

Korenman, S., Miller, J. E., and Sjaastad, J. E. (1995). Long-term poverty and child development in the United States: Results from the NLSY. *Children and Youth Services Review, 17*(1/2), 127–155.

McLoyd, V. C. (1990). The impact of economic hardship on Black families and children: Psychological distress, parenting, and socioemotional development. *Child Development, 61*, 311–346.

McLoyd, V. C., Ceballo, R., and Mangelsdorf, S. C. (1997). The effects of poverty on children's socioe-motional development. In S. Greenspan, S. Wieder, and J. Osofsky (eds.), *Handbook of Child and Adolescent Psychiatry, Vol. 1*. New York: J. Wiley and Sons.

Miles, M. B. and Huberman, A. M. (1994). *Qualitative data analysis* (2nd ed.). Thousand Oaks, CA: Sage Publications.

Morris, P. A., Huston, A. C., Duncan, G. J., Crosby, D. A., and Bos, J. M. (2001). *How welfare and work policies affect children: A synthesis of research*. New York, NY: The Next Generation, MRDC.

National Center for Children in Poverty (2003). *Low-income children in the United States: A brief demographic profile*. New York: Columbia University School of Public Health.

Padgett, D. K. (1998). *Qualitative methods in social work research: Challenges and rewards*. Thousand Oaks, CA: Sage Publications.

Sameroff, A. J., Seifer, R., Zax, M., and Barocas, R. (1987). Early indicators of developmental risk: The Rochester Longitudinal Study. *Schizophrenia Bulletin, 13*, 383–393.

Tesch, R. (1990). *Qualitative research: Analysis types and software tools*. New York: Falmer.

U.S. Bureau of the Census. (2000). *Census of population and housing*. Washington, DC: U.S. Bureau of the Census.

Werner, E. E. and Smith, R. S. (1989). *Vulnerable but invincible: A longitudinal study of resilient children and youth*. New York: Adams-Bannister-Cox.

Zaslow, M., Tout, K., Botsko, C., and Moore, K. (1998). *Welfare reform and children: Potential implications (Report number A-23)*. Washington, DC: The Urban Institute.

Zill, N., Moore, K., Smith, E., Stief, T., and Coiro, M. J. (1991). *The life circumstances and development of children in welfare families: A profile based on national survey data*. Washington, DC: Child Trends.

SECTION III

The Good Father

CHAPTER SIX

How Mothers See Fathers

ALLISON ZIPPAY AND ANU RANGARAJAN

Eager to promote involved fathers in the lives of families headed by unwed mothers, the 1996 welfare reform legislation strengthened paternity establishment and child support enforcement, and increased benefits for two-parent families (Kobell and Principe, 2002; Personal Responsibility and Work Opportunity Act, 1996). Spurred in part by an economic motive to decrease welfare dependency among female-headed households, one of the goals of the legislation is "the formation and maintenance of two-parent families."

In response, policy makers are pushing a series of initiatives aimed at promoting healthy marriages among poor families (Horn and Bush, 1997; Lerman, 2002; Mincy and Dupree, 2001). In addition, the U.S. Department of Health and Human Services (DHHS) has approved several state demonstration projects aimed at enhancing unmarried fathers' capacities for financial and emotional support of their children (Carlson and McLanahan, 2002).

These early initiatives are receiving support among many politicians and family advocates (Lerman, 2002). Underlying this enthusiasm is the assumption that a stronger father presence is generally beneficial. Largely absent from the lobby for father-oriented initiatives, however, are the women who have been involved with these men. What can they tell us about the roles that fathers play in the lives of their children, and how do the women view the prospect of increased father involvement? In exploring this issue, this chapter reports on in-depth interviews with 41 current and recent TANF recipients. In these interviews, the women discuss the various contributions that fathers make to their children, their strengths and limitations as fathers, and the benefits and challenges of their varying levels of participation in family life.

Dads and Welfare-Reliant Moms

A combination of time, money, and emotional support have been identified by some family advocates and researchers as among the contributions that fathers make to their children (Black et al., 1999; England and Folbe, 2002; Graham and Beller, 2002; Lamb, 1997). For nonresident fathers, higher levels of social and emotional involvement are correlated with the payment of child support (McLanahan et al., 1994; U.S. Census Bureau, 1997). Although numerous studies have found positive associations between fathers' economic and social involvement and positive child outcomes, other researchers report that the results are mixed and difficult to interpret because the definitions of involvement are so varied, as are family contexts (Black et al., 1999; Jackson, 1999; Lamb, 1997, 2002a; Yogman et al., 1995).

Much of the research on father involvement and the roles of fathers in child development has been conducted with middle-class, married, or divorced families (Hernandez and Brandon, 2002; Lamb, 1997; Seltzer et al., 1989; Tamis-LeMonda and Cabrera, 2002). Many of the current policy initiatives directed toward low-income and unwed fathers have been built on assumptions gleaned from this research. But the family networks and social contexts of many low-income and unwed mothers and fathers raise questions about the appropriateness of generalized applications of these findings, and the risks of oversimplifying the problem as related to welfare-reliant households (Carlson and McLanahan, 2002). Increasingly research efforts are being directed toward gaining a better understanding of the characteristics and social roles of fathers. What are the circumstances of the men who are the targets of ambitious legislative efforts?

Until recently, little demographic information has been available on low-income nonresident fathers, in part because they are not easy to identify and locate, and because most policy was focused on unwed and welfare-reliant mothers. Now several projects designed to develop more detailed portraits of the individual attributes and social worlds of these men are underway.[1] Although most welfare recipients are not married and not living with a father of their children, studies have indicated that most fathers of children born to unwed women are romantically involved with the mother at the time of the child's birth, visit the mother and child at the hospital, and are optimistic about their future relationship with the mother (Carlson and McLanahan, 2002; Johnson, 2001). These fathers often are eager to express their commitment to the family through child support payments, involvement in family life, and parental decision making (Lin and McLanahan, 2001). As romances and relationships break off, typically within two years of the birth, involvement with the children usually decreases (Johnson, 2001; Lerman and Sorenson, 2000; Nord and Zill, 1996).

Though many nonresidential fathers of welfare recipients have long been labeled "absent," a growing body of research indicates that a majority are in fact present either as cohabiters, or steady or occasional visitors (Bumpass and Lu, 2000; Danziger and Radin, 1990; McLanahan and Carlson, 2002; Roy, 1999). Focus group and in-person interviews with low-income nonresidential fathers indicate a wide variety of reactions to parenting ranging from strong commitment to disinterest (Anderson et al., 2002; Nelson et al., 2002; Roy, 1999). In recent years, more aggressive child support enforcement resulted in increases in child support among this population, though participation rates and payment levels remain low (Graham and Beller, 2002). Other studies indicate that many fathers of current and former TANF recipients prefer to *informally* provide various levels of cash, in-kind, and child care assistance either consistently or irregularly (Edin and Lein, 1997; Furstenberg, 1995; Roy, 1999; Waller and Plotnick, 2000), and that these contributions are important sources of assistance and "income packaging" among many TANF recipients (Edin and Lein, 1997; Jarrett et al., 2002; Nelson et al., 2002).

Compared to the general population, the fathers of welfare children are more likely to be younger, never married, low-income, not working, less educated, incarcerated, and/or involved with substance abuse (Cabrera, et al., 2002; Garfinkel et al., 1998; McLanahan and Carlson, 2002; Rodriguez et al., 2001; Sorensen, 1995; Wilson and Brooks-Gunn, 2001). Incidences of domestic violence among welfare caseloads are high, with several studies indicating that between 40 and 75 percent of female public assistance recipients report that they have experienced severe domestic violence as adults (Barush et al., 1999; Pearson and Griswold, 1999; Tolman and Raphael, 2000).

Although many policy makers have advocated initiatives that encourage marriage and the increased social presence of nonresident fathers in the lives of their children, the growing literature on the social, economic, and personal attributes of these men suggests that the effects on families may be mixed. Many researchers qualify their support of such efforts to those facilitating involvement of "positive" fathering (Lamb, 2002a). Although many TANF recipients appear to approve of an increase in fathers' economic support of their families, there is some evidence that many would not welcome their larger role in household decision making (Lin and McLanahan, 2001). Overall there is a paucity of information originating from these women regarding their views of the roles fathers play in the lives of their children. What can they tell us about the kinds of social and emotional contributions that fathers make? What determines the quality of their parenting, and how do the women regard the possibility of increased interaction?

The New Jersey Qualitative Study

Our qualitative interviews were conducted as a component of a larger study of the long-term effects of Work First New Jersey (WFNJ), a welfare initiative implemented in 1997, which followed the 1996 federal reforms and enacted work requirements for most welfare recipients, a five-year time limit, and expanded support services. The larger study included telephone interviews with about 2,000 individuals who participated in WFNJ in its first 18 months. These respondents were interviewed five times at 9- to 12-month intervals between 1999 and 2003 to collect quantitative information on a wide range of variables including employment and income status (Zippay and Rangarajan, 2004). To obtain in-depth and contextual information on the work and life experiences of participants in the WFNJ program, interviews were conducted with a subsample of respondents who were visited once annually in 2000, 2001, and 2003.

The qualitative sample was drawn to include respondents from a variety of geographic locales. Counties were stratified into high, medium, and low density based on population counts. The high-density counties of Camden, Essex, and Middlesex were purposefully included because they contained the largest portions of the state's welfare caseload, and another four counties were selected at random (Atlantic, Burlington, Mercer, and Union). A purposeful sampling method was used to select respondents from these counties based on their employment and welfare status at the time of the first telephone survey. Equal numbers of respondents were selected from each of the following categories: Those who were receiving TANF; those who were working and not receiving TANF; and those who were not working and not receiving TANF. The sample for the qualitative study purposefully contained more respondents who were not working than the full sample of 2,000 respondents participating in the quantitative survey since we focused on challenges to employment faced by some respondents.

Most of the qualitative interviews were conducted in the homes of the respondents, and a few took place in local restaurants or other community settings at the request of the respondent. The interviews were conducted by members of the WFNJ evaluation team, and by graduate students from Rutgers University. The interviews averaged 90 minutes in length. Most were done in two-person teams. All of the interviews were tape-recorded and later transcribed.

The research protocols were semi-structured and questions were open-ended. Each of the three waves of in-depth interviews contained common questions regarding employment, income, and job-related issues. Each round also included a distinct set of questions concerning a variety of family and life experiences. The mothers were asked to describe the types of interactions they and their children had with fathers, the types of assistance that the fathers provided to the family, and whether or not they were a "good father."

Data Analysis

The results reported here are from information collected during the second round of in-depth interviews conducted in May and June 2001. Information on fathers was provided by 41 of the women interviewed.

The data were analyzed using case and cross-case analyses (Patton, 2001). The transcript for each respondent was read and coded according to the sensitizing concepts represented by the topics covered in the survey. The answers for all of the cases were then grouped according to these sensitizing concepts and analyzed across all of the cases (Berg, 2001). The data were again sorted and analyzed according to axial codes such as employment status and TANF receipt. Subsequent readings focused on the identification of indigenous themes, which emerged from the respondents' comments and observations. Some of the responses were made numeric and reported as frequencies. Responses to the quantitative telephone survey were used as a source of data and method triangulation to affirm some of the patterns identified in the qualitative transcripts (Patton, 2001; Tashakkori and Teddlie, 1998).

Who Are These Mothers?

Of the 41 respondents, 61 percent were African American, 22 percent Latina, and 17 percent White. Fully half had a high school degree or GED, about one-third had less than a high school education, and a minority had some level of post-secondary education. Their average age was 30. About two-thirds of the respondents lived in urban, low-income neighborhoods in Newark, Camden, and Trenton. The rest resided in several less dense communities in New Jersey.

Two of the respondents were married and living with their spouse at the time of the interview, and 5 were living with boyfriends. Most of the respondents ($n = 23$) lived alone with their children; 11 lived in households that included other adult relatives or friends (and 8 of those included the respondent's mother). The mean number of children for the sample was 2.5, and their average age was 9.5. The children ranged in age from 4 weeks to 24 years, with a modal age of 7. Forty percent had children aged 5 or under.

At the time of the second interview (2001), 12 of the respondents were working, and 3 of these were working and also receiving TANF; 16 were collecting TANF and not working; and 13 were neither working nor receiving cash assistance. Of this latter group, 2 had been laid-off and were collecting unemployment insurance, 2 were receiving SSI, and the others were living with adult relatives, friends, or boyfriends who provided them with some support. Most of those who were not working had been employed for various lengths of time during the previous three years. The hourly wages of those who were employed ranged from $5.75 to $15 with a median of $8, and the group included waitresses, construction workers, nurses' aides, restaurant cooks, and administrative assistants.

Who Are These Fathers?

These 41 respondents had a total of 99 children. Twenty-three respondents reported that all of their children had a common father, 12 had children with 2 fathers, 5 said that their children had 3 fathers, and one of them had children by 4 fathers. There were a total of 66 fathers for the 99 children.

Table 6.1 lists the respondents' estimates of the frequency of contact for each of their children's fathers. According to the mothers, a majority of the fathers (75 percent) had some level of contact with their children (3 of the fathers were deceased and that percentage is based on a total of 63 fathers).

Table 6.1 Respondent's estimates of the frequency of father contact with their children

Frequency of contact (n = 66)	Number of fathers
In residence, married	2
Live-in, not married	5
Daily visits	3
Weekly	14
Twice monthly	5
Monthly	2
Child lives with father in summer	1
Several times a year or less	15
No contact	16
Deceased	3

Of the fathers, 38 percent (n = 24) had daily or weekly contact with their children, including 7 who were resident at the time of the interview as either married or living with the mother. About 37 percent were in more sporadic contact with their children, ranging from a few visits a month to a few per year. And one-quarter (n = 16) of the fathers had no contact with their children.

The estimates that the women provided were based on the fathers' visiting patterns at the time of the interview. As many commented, these patterns were often in flux and could be unpredictable. A man who had been in contact weekly might drop to a few visits a month or a year. According to respondents' reports, for example, 11 of the 16 fathers who had no current contact with their children had previously had some level of family involvement. The reasons given for these fluctuations varied: Changes in the relationship with the mother; the father's involvement with drugs or alcohol; incarceration; involvement with other women and other children (often younger); and relocation.

In addition to contact with their children, most of the fathers provided some level of cash or in-kind assistance. According to the mothers, about one-third of the fathers were currently paying child support (including two of the fathers who had no personal contact with their children or the mother). As has been reported in several other studies (Edin and Lein, 1997; Jarrett et al., 2002; Nelson et al., 2002), it was more common for the fathers to provide material assistance that was informal, irregular, and varied in substance and amount: Cash, clothing, entertainment, food, assistance with child care, and others.

Information received from the mothers on the fathers' employment was sketchy. Several of the fathers were reported to hold full- or part-time jobs as computer programmers, chefs, car mechanics, and janitors. Others were said to be working in the underground economy (in some cases, allegedly to avoid paying child support). Some were unemployed or disabled. And there were several women who said they simply didn't know whether or where the fathers were working.

The "Good Father"

The respondents were asked if each father for each child was a good father. About one-quarter of the fathers ($n = 16$) were reported by the women to be "good" and almost three-quarters ($n = 45$) were, often emphatically, described or denounced as "no good," "bad," "terrible," "miserable," and so on. One father was described as "sometimes good, sometimes bad," and one respondent did not provide information.

In describing the characteristics of the good fathers, many of the women focused on what they called "being there" for the children. It was a term that was used often among these respondents, and appeared to embody emotional attachment as well as physical presence. Interestingly this phrase has also been recorded by other researchers as one frequently used by non-resident, unwed fathers to describe the qualities of a good father (Allen and Connor, 1997; Nelson et al., 2002).

As described by the sample respondents:

He's always there, no matter what happens he's always there for his kids. He'll do things like iron [son's] clothes, get him ready for tomorrow and stuff . . . He's a good father, a good provider.

He comes by, he loves his kids. My son will go down to the garage [car repair shop] and work on the car with him. He takes my son all the time fishing with him . . . He gets [the kids] and takes them places. You know he's all right.

He's there—he was always doing things with them. When [kids were younger] he used to play baseball and whatever with them. But now that they're older it's more like they're friends.

Several descriptions made references to personal qualities suggesting generosity or kindness:

He is helpful and hard working and supportive.

He is an excellent father—kind hearted, a nice guy. He visits [the kids] everyday, takes them out to the park and places.

He's loving and caring and appreciative.

He's nice, he's helpful. He feeds [kids], takes our clothes to the laundromat for us . . . He'll take them to the park and give them quality time.

The consistency of interaction was a central component of the favorable ratings of fathers, as were romantic feelings toward them: All but one of the women who had married or had live-in relationships described that father as good. And all but one of the good fathers visited daily or weekly. However frequency alone was not enough to define the fathering as high-quality (since other weekly visitors were described as bad fathers). Rather it was characterized by fathers who interacted consistently with their children and who behaved responsibly; that is, those who were thoughtful about their children's needs, willing to make time for child-centered events, and who built family connections by being in tune with the activities that their children enjoyed.

> He's a good father. I mean, he is the best dad ever. We go out as a family. He plays with the kids. He's a big kid at heart.

> He is responsible . . . takes the kids to the playground, he takes them to the zoo. And he helps me out with money and child care a lot.

> He does the things [son] likes . . . they play video games, eat, go to the movies together.

> He supports them at everything. School, materials, education, and he takes them out to do things.

While most women mentioned the provision of cash or material goods in their descriptions of good fathers, it did not appear to be the most important attribute to all of the women. At least half of the men who were described as good fathers did not pay child support. Most, but not all, contributed varied amounts of cash (large and small) on a regular or irregular basis.

> The financial situation is not that great at all [father does not pay child support and contributes cash on an irregular basis]. That's important, but it is more important that she [daughter] gets to know her father and he gets to know her.

Most fathers also regularly or occasionally purchased a variety of items for the children or the household: Clothes, movie tickets, fast food, or money to pay the cable TV bill. Some provisions were systematic and regular, but most arrangements were ad hoc and resulted from whim, bargaining, arguing, or simple request. Although these contributions were mostly irregular and sometimes meager, many women appeared to regard them as a critical resource supplement, often soliciting the fathers for "extras" or basics.

> Sometimes he'll pay the bills or rent, buy miscellaneous things that I need for the house.

> If I cause enough fuss, he will give me some of what we need.

> He picks [daughter] up, he spends time with her. And he buys her what she wants as far as clothing and toys and stuff.

> He knows when we need something. And if I have to ask him he comes up and just brings it.

He buys clothes and stuff for [son] and keeps it over there [father's house] for him when he visits.

Many fathers provided assistance with child care on a regular or occasional basis. They picked children up from school, babysat at odd hours when mothers worked, or helped out as needed. Many women depended on their availability as part of their "package" of child care providers (Zippay and Rangarajan, 2001) and as part of the package of paternal assistance that contributed to their ability to manage their household:

He's even taken days off when we didn't have a babysitter and kept them. You know, we've taken turns [filling in for the babysitter]. And that is what makes things a lot easier on me, 'cause he's very much involved with them.

Sometimes their child care contributions were especially critical: One non-resident father who was described as a good and loving parent was jailed for failing to pay traffic tickets, and had been caring for his children while the respondent was in a residential drug treatment facility. His incarceration almost led to involvement with protective services until a relative was found to provide child care.

The description of the incarcerated father as good and loving highlights a paradox: Some of the men who were described as good had attributes that others might have used to label them as lacking, including some who were intermittently or chronically unemployed. A few had histories of abuse: Two of the men who were described as good fathers had been physically abusive to the respondent, though they were described as markedly different with their children.

The "Bad Father"

Of the 45 fathers who were described by the respondents as "not good," 29 (64 percent) were involved to varying degrees in the lives of their children, though it was often quite limited. According to the respondents, 2 saw their children daily and 7 visited weekly. Five visited a few times a month, and about 15 visited monthly or sporadically at several times a year or less. In addition, 16 had no contact with their children in the year prior to the interview. At least 8 were paying child support, and about half of those in contact with the children contributed varying levels of cash on a regular or irregular basis.

Mothers articulated a variety of reasons for why fathers were not deemed good. In addition to abandonment or limited involvement, these included drug or alcohol abuse, "fast" living, personal violence, criminal involvement, irresponsible behavior, or limited financial or emotional support. According to the respondents, at least 8 were involved in dealing and/or abusing drugs, 5 were alcoholics, 11 were incarcerated, and 10 had previously been physically abusive to the respondent.

Almost a third of the bad fathers had frequent visits with their children—daily, weekly, several times a week, or a few times a month. Most of the fathers picked up the children and took them out, or brought them to their own homes or those of a girlfriend or relative (usually the child's grandmother). In describing the negative aspects of this fathering, the respondents most often described behaviors that conflicted with their own parenting styles and sense of propriety. Sometimes the behavior was described by the women as irresponsible or inappropriate:

He keeps her up really late to go to restaurants . . . last week he took her to Pennsylvania without telling me.

He took her to see "Halloween 13" and she is only seven. Then they go back to his friend's house and I don't like the people who hang around there.

He is a compulsive liar and mean . . . he is always promising things to [daughter] and then doesn't deliver.

Some of the fathers were involved with drugs or showed criminal behavior, and the mothers were concerned about the negative influences these men were having on their children. For example, each of the fathers described in the following extract pay child support and expect to see their children regularly.

Like last week he took [kids] Tuesday and Wednesday and now he wants them tonight. I don't feel he deserves them because he doesn't do good things . . . he tells them he is on drugs . . . I don't want my kids, my son, to do drugs.

He tries to be there [father comes by weekly], but because of his past history [domestic violence and crime], you know, I don't want my kids to follow into that life.

He gets high and they [kids] know it . . . he lets them know it. I don't want my kids around that.

Of the fathers described as bad, 11 were in jail or in prison at the time of the interview, and several were said to be frequently "in and out" of jail. Again many of the women feared that the father's contact with their children provided a negative role model and would draw the children into an unsavory social world:

[Father] is incarcerated and he gets mad at me and he says, "You can bring my son to see me," and I'm like, "I'm not gonna bring him to see you in there." I don't want [son] to think, well if my dad is in this place it's ok for me to be in that place also. You know?

My daughter's father—I don't even like talking about him [because of criminal behavior]—he was getting out of jail and he came to see her last week. I don't like that.

Many women were also frustrated by fathers whose contact with their children was inconsistent or infrequent. Some fathers visited every few months or several times a year. Some would come by weekly for a while and then stop showing up.

> Sometimes he comes by. And then he could just disappear from their lives for months and not call to see if they are still alive . . . he don't care [and] he lies a lot. He offers gifts that never come.

> Sometimes he does stuff for her and sometimes he doesn't come around.

Some mothers reported that the inconsistency left their children confused and saddened:

> [Son] was going to stay with his father every other weekend, and his grandmother lived there too. But now he hasn't been there for four months—it just stopped. I have no idea why. And [son] feels bad, he doesn't understand.

Some gave examples of fathers who would give a block of time to their children and then assume that they could abandon their fathering role for a while:

> A few years ago he took them to Disney World. Then he called me and said, "You know, I can't do nothing for them now for a year."

Others expressed irritation because they felt that the fathers had no need to be consistent because they, as mothers, were shouldering the bulk of the care. As one mother explained, "He doesn't care. He ain't got no responsibilities, 'cause it is all here on me."

In discussing what was troublesome about some of the fathers who were involved with their children, some women referred to them as "not there," a term which seemed to denote a lack of attentiveness rather than physical presence. They gave examples of what they considered self-centered behavior and that reflected a lack of understanding of the nuances of their children's lives or development:

> He is not really there . . . When I take the kids to visit him he is always lying on the couch. I talk to him on the phone to try to get him to do the father thing, but that is pretty hard.

> He is the one who buys her clothes. He thinks he is a decent father but he don't even know what size she wears. He always calls to ask me. How can he really know his daughter when he don't even know her size?

> He's not there really as a father. He doesn't call to say, "How are you?" or "How is school?" And if [kids] call him he says, "What do you want?"

In some cases, there was a complete absence of contact between fathers and their children. In these cases, the reasons for their departures varied.

At least three of the fathers had abandoned the mother after finding out that she was pregnant. A few women did not know who the father was. Most of the other men had been involved to some degree with the mother and children for varying lengths of time after the child was born. According to the mothers, the relationships and contact ended for various reasons such as incompatibility, drug and alcohol use, domestic violence, other women, or a lack of interest by the father in his family. It appeared that about half of the break-ups were initiated by the women.

It was terrible—he was lying, cheating, running around. I said, that's it.

I left because he was alcoholic and violent. He won't mess with me anymore now.

I had to actually break up the relationship to stay clean. In order to leave drugs I had to leave him.

Wanting More from Bad Fathers

Would they prefer more from these men? While a few of the women reported that they would like more financial support, many of the women seemed puzzled or incredulous that an interviewer would even ask such a question. The behaviors of these men were often difficult or extreme and included drug and physical abuse. One woman said that the absence of their fathers was a "good influence" on her sons:

And I am happy [that they are absent] because I know that my kids will not go down the same road as their fathers did.

Some did not want any intrusions into their self-directed household:

My children are at an age now where a father right now would damage them. To step into their lives at this late period in their life? And they've gone so long without one?

Others, again, did not want the presence of a father who might model a negative life style:

He [father] use the weed a lot. He sees his children on the street and doesn't even acknowledge them. I don't want my children with him.

Because so many women had reservations about the behaviors of the fathers whom they labeled bad, many were conflicted about the contact that the men had with their children. While some tried actively to limit or prevent visits and interaction, others felt strongly that even though they didn't approve of a father's behavior, they should not deny him access to his children or prevent the children from seeing him.

I rather they not be there, but I won't deny him his right to see his children.

I don't like what he is doing . . . But I won't punish the kids by not letting them go see him when they want to.

Although the majority of women interviewed had a variety of reservations regarding the behavior and the parenting of the fathers they labeled as not good, very few women indicated that they initiated discussions with dads about their parenting. On the contrary, many made comments about their purposeful lack of communication. To avoid arguments and conflict, many said, they tried not to be present when the fathers came to pick up the children, and that they avoided conversation. Sometimes they knew little about the lives of the fathers; a few said they didn't know what the father did with the children during his visits.

I don't be around him. I haven't talked to him in years. [Respondent's children visit father every week.]

I'll talk to [father's] mother and she'll tell me some things—but I refuse to talk to him.

He [father] talks to my mother. I wish not to talk to him. [Father had been abusive to respondent].

Women in men's lives played out prominently in mothers' comments. It appeared that the children's visits with their fathers were often (or in some cases primarily) to their paternal grandmother or to other women involved in their father's life. Some of the respondents indicated that these were among the most positive aspects of their children's interactions with their fathers:

I want her [daughter] to spend time with her father and her grandmother, 'cause he lives with his mom, and he has a sister so she'll get a chance to see her, and his other kids.

He goes [to visit father] every other weekend and his grandmother live there too.

The great grandmother lives right around the corner, so it's not bad.

A few respondents indicated that they felt these other women in children's lives took on primary oversight responsibilities during these visits:

He [father] takes them places and buys things they need. But I know it is really his wife who makes sure he does the responsible thing.

He [father] is an alcoholic. So when [children] visit I think his mom and dad take care of the kids more than he does, personally.

Children's Views

The respondents were not asked directly about their children's feelings toward their fathers. But in the course of the conversations, several of the women spoke of their children's love of their fathers, even when the mothers had reservations about them:

> But my daughter loves her daddy. That's something I can't deny her.

> On Christmas day my daughter was very unhappy and sobbing. I asked her what was wrong and she said she missed her daddy. She hardly sees him, but she loves him.

> Don't get me wrong, my kids love their father. But they do understand what he does for them and what he doesn't . . .

Two of the children had fathers who had died in the year preceding the interview, and both fathers had only been in touch with their children occasionally. Both youth were teenagers, and the respondents reported, with some surprise, the intensity of their reactions.

> When my daughter found out [about his death] she "bugged," cried and cried.

> When I go in to wake her up she might have [father's] picture laying next to her on her bed . . . that was her hero. Till this day it is. And I never talk negative about their father in their presence. [The father was involved with drugs.]

Can Mothers' Voices Inform Policy Options?

The findings from this study represent the experiences of a small sample of respondents from primarily urban, high-poverty neighborhoods in New Jersey. Because the original sample was purposefully drawn to include greater numbers of women who were not working, it is likely that this group consists of women—and perhaps fathers—who experience more social, psychological, or economic challenges than the full population of current and recent TANF recipients in New Jersey.

The legislation and programs resulting from the 1996 welfare reform—including stronger paternity establishment, child support enforcement, and initiatives to encourage two-parent households—have attempted to shape both father involvement and family structure. Although policy makers' perspectives on father involvement may assume beneficial impacts, the stories told by the women interviewed for this study underscore how mixed the dynamics and effects of these unions can be, and the importance of gathering context-specific information on their widely varied experiences.

The men described by the respondents represented a heterogeneous group along a continuum that included very caring and devoted fathers, those whose contact and attention was sporadic, those whose interactions with their children were coincident with involvement in drugs, violence, and crime, and those who were completely absent. Although only a handful of the women in the sample were married or living with a boyfriend, a majority of the nonresidential fathers were socially involved at some level with their children. But social involvement alone was not an indication of positive fathering. The men who were labeled good fathers were most often those who had frequent contact with their children, *and* whose behavior included characteristics such as attentiveness and emotional attachment. The fathers labeled not good—including some who visited daily or weekly— were most frequently described as exhibiting varying degrees of negligent, emotionally detached, or problematic behavior.

The numbers of men who were socially involved with their children while also engaged in addictive, abusive, or criminal activity, put many of the women in this sample in a difficult position. TANF policies encourage and/or mandate recipients to work, to foster connections with their children's fathers, and to promote family values, which include the provision of a safe and healthy environment for their children. But for many of the respondents in this sample, maintaining a relationship with some fathers compromised these efforts: Their children were connected to risky or unhealthy physical and social environments (including drugs and crime), and the women could not fully separate themselves from networks and influences that could hinder, rather than support, their transitions to employment.

The issue of communication with nonresidential fathers posed a similar dilemma. To promote healthy two-parent relationships, research suggests a process of open communication and problem solving among mothers and fathers to clarify and resolve parenting roles, responsibilities, and differences (Katz and Gottman, 1993; Lewis and Feiring, 1998; Westerman and Schonholtz, 1993). Research also indicates that parental conflict has a negative effect on children (Emery, 1994; Featherstone, 2001; Stocker and Youngblade, 1999). By avoiding communication with the father, some respondents in this sample purposefully minimized overt conflict. In so doing, however, they also avoided addressing concerns they had regarding the father's parenting behavior, and were not involved in problem solving around these issues.

The complicated nature of father involvement was also underscored by the fact that the respondents' descriptions of good and bad fathers were not always easily categorized or defined according to standard conceptualizations. Among the fathers labeled good, there were several who had attributes that fell outside the norm of what many would regard as positive fathering (including jail terms and chronic unemployment), yet they were appreciated by the mothers and children for their attention and care.

Similarly the cash and in-kind contributions offered by both good and bad fathers were typically nontraditional in form and variously regarded by the mothers as positive or negative, depending on the character and situation of the father. For example, many of the fathers perceived as good did not pay formal child support but gave cash irregularly. Others offered little cash but provided nonfinancial contributions—such as child care—that were highly valued by the mothers. It is unclear to what degree some women have accepted or expressed appreciation for lesser behavior or contributions because their expectations of the men in their lives have been conditioned by a history of male poverty, delinquency, neglect, or abuse.

The information generated by this study also suggests that some of the fathers' contributions (both positive and negative) may come not only from themselves as individuals, but from their broader social networks. For example, reports that children's visits to their fathers often involved interactions with paternal grandmothers, relatives, or other women may be an important mediating factor in associations between father involvement and child behavioral outcomes, and is an area for future research. The fathers' circles of friends represent yet another set of influences on the children, and the positive and negative effects of their networks of both kin and associates is an additional area for exploration.

Among this sample of mothers, the dynamics of paternal involvement were varied, fluid, and multifaceted. While some of the women would welcome a stronger father presence and additional economic or social support, others would shun it to avoid anticipated negative effects. For many of these families, strengthening father involvement would clearly require an array of program responses, which go well beyond paternity establishment and child support enforcement. Data collected from TANF recipients and other members of these low-income communities can provide empirical, context-based information on the meanings, strengths, and weaknesses of patterns of paternal engagement, and a better understanding of why some women prefer to limit or avoid that involvement.

Note

1. These studies include the Fragile Families and Child Well-being Study (McLanahan and Garfinkel, 2000), the Early Head Start Research and Evaluation Project (Brooks-Gunn et al., 2000), the Early Childhood Longitudinal Study (National Center for Education Statistics, 1999), and several smaller ethnographic studies (Anderson et al., 2002; Jackson, 1999; Nelson et al., 2002).

References

Allen. W. and Connor, M. (1997). An African American perspective on generative fathering. In A. J. Hawkins and D. C. Dollahite (eds.), *Generative fathering: Beyond deficit perspectives* (pp. 52–70). Thousand Oaks, CA: Sage.

Anderson, E., Kohler, J., and Letiecq, B. (April 2002). Low-income fathers and "responsible fatherhood" programs: A qualitative investigation of participants' experiences. *Family Relations, 51*(2), 148–156.

Barush, A., Taylor, M. J., and Derr, M. (1999). *Understanding families with multiple barriers to self-sufficiency.* Salt Lake City, Utah: University of Utah, Social Research Institute.

Berg, B. I. (2001). *Qualitative research methods.* Boston, MA: Allyn and Bacon.

Black, M. M., Dubowitz, H., and Starr, R. H., Jr. (July/August 1999). African American fathers in low income, urban families: Development, behavior, and home environment of their 3-year-old children. *Child Development, 70*(4), 967–978.

Brooks-Gunn, J., Berline, L. J., Leventahl, T., and Fuligini, A. (2000). Depending on the kindness of strangers: Current national data initiatives and developmental research. *Child Development, 71,* 257–267.

Bumpass, L. and Lu, H. H. (2000). Trends in cohabitation and implications for children's family contexts. *Population Studies, 54*, 29–41.

Cabrera, N., Brooks-Gunn, J., Moore, K., West, J., Boller, K., and Tamis-LeMonde, C. S. (2002). Bridging research and policy: Including fathers of young children in national studies. In C. S. Tamis-LeMonde and N. Cabrera (eds.), *Handbook of father involvement: Multidisciplinary perspectives* (pp. 489–523). Mahwah, NJ: Lawrence Erlbaum Associates, Publishers.

Carlson, M. J. and McLanahan, S. S. (2002). Fragile families, father involvement, and public policy. In C. S. Tamis-LeMonda and N. Cabrera (eds.), *Handbook of father involvement: Multidisciplinary perspectives* (pp. 461–488). Mahwah, NJ: Lawrence Erlbaum Associates, Publishers.

Danziger, S. and Radin, N. (1990). Absent does not equal uninvolved: Predictors of fathering in teen mother families. *Journal of Marriage and the Family, 52*, 636–642.

Edin, K. and Lein, L. (1997). *Making ends meet.* New York: The Russell Sage Foundation.

Emery, R. E. (1994). Interpersonal conflict and the children of discord and divorce. *Psychological Bulletin, 92*(2), 310–330.

England, P. and Folbe, N. (2002). Involving dads: Parental bargaining and family well-being. In C. S. Tamis-LeMonda and N. Cabrera (eds.), *Handbook of father involvement: Multidisciplinary perspectives* (pp. 387–408). Mahwah, NJ: Lawrence Erlbaum Associates, Publishers.

Featherstone, B. (2001). Putting fathers on the child welfare agenda. *Child and Family Social Work, 6*, 179–186.

Furstenberg, F. (1995). Fathering in the inner city: Paternal participation and public policy. In W. Marsiglio (ed.), *Fatherhood: Contemporary theory, research, and social policy* (pp. 119–147). Thousand Oaks, CA: Sage.

Garfinkel, I., McLanahan, S. S., and Hanson, T. L. (1998). A patchwork portrait of nonresident fathers. In I. Garfinkel, S. S. McLanahan, D. R. Meryer, and J. A. Seltzer (eds.), *Fathers under fire: The revolution in child support enforcement.* New York: The Russell Sage Foundation.

Graham, J. W. and Bellar, A. H. (2002). Nonresident fathers and their children: Child support and visitation from an economic perspective. In C. S. Tamis-LeMonde and N. Cabrera (eds.), *Handbook of father involvement: Multidisciplinary perspectives* (pp. 431–454). Mahwah, NJ: Lawrence Erlbaum Associates, Publishers.

Hernandez, D. J. and Brandon, P. D. (2002). Who are the fathers of today? In C. S. Tamis-LeMonde and N. Cabrera (eds.), *Handbook of father involvement: Multidisciplinary perspectives* (pp. 33–62). Mahwah, NJ: Lawrence Erlbaum Associates, Publishers.

Horn, W. and Bush, A. (Fall 1997). Fathers and welfare reform. *Public Interest, 12*, 38–48.

Jackson, A. P. (March 1999). The effects of nonresident father involvement on single Black mothers and their young children. *Social Work, 44*(2), 156–167.

Jarrett, R. L., Roy, K. M., and Burton, L. M. (2002). Fathers in the "hood": Insights from qualitative research on low-income African American men. In C. S. Tamis-LeMonda and N. Cabrera (eds.), *Handbook of father involvement: Multidisciplinary perspectives* (pp. 211–248). Mahwah, NJ: Lawrence Erlbaum Associates, Publishers.

Johnson, W. E., Jr. (2001). Paternal involvement among unwed fathers. *Children and Youth Services Review, 23*(6/7), 513–536.

Katz, L. F. and Gottman, J. M. (1993). Patterns of marital conflict predict children's internalizing and externalizing behavior. *Developmental Psychology, 29*, 940–950.

Kobell, H. L. and Principe, D. (March 2002). *Do nonresident fathers who pay child support visit their children more?* Number B-44 in Series, New Federalism: National Survey of American's Families. Washington, DC: Urban Institute.

Lamb, M. E. (1997). *The role of the father in child development* (3rd ed.). New York: Wiley.

Lamb, M. E. (2002). Infant–father attachments and their impact on child development. In C. A. Tamis-LeMonda and N. Cabrera (eds.), *Handbook of father involvement: Multidisciplinary perspectives* (pp. 93–117). Mahwah, NJ: Lawrence Erlbaum Associates, Publishers.

Lin, I. F. and McLanahan, S. S. (2001). Norms about nonresident fathers' obligations and rights. *Children and Youth Services Review, 23*(6/7), 485–512.

Lerman, R. (May 2002). *Should government promote healthy marriages?* Urban Institute Studies, Number 5 in Series, Short Takes on Welfare Policy. Washington, DC: Urban Institute.

Lerman, R. and Sorenson, E. (2000). Father involvement with their nonmarital children: Patterns, determinants, and effects on their earnings. *Marriage and Family Review, 29*(2), 137–158.

Lewis, M. and Feiring, C. (eds.) (1998). *Families, risk, and competence.* Mahwah, NJ: Lawrence Erlbaum Associates, Publishers.

McLanahan, S. and Carlson, M. J. (2002). Welfare reform, fertility, and father involvement. *The Future of Children, 12*(1), 147–164.

McLanahan, S. and Garfinkel, I. (2000). *The fragile families and child well-being study: Questions, design, and a few preliminary results.* Discussion Paper No. 1208–00. Madison, WI: Institute for Research on Poverty.

McLanahan, S., Seltzer, J., Hanson, T., and Thomson, E. (1994). Child support enforcement and child well-being: Greater security or greater conflict? In I. Garfinkel, S. McLanahan, and P. Robins (eds.), *Child support and well-being.* Washington, DC: Urban Institute.

Mincy, R. R. and Dupree, A. T. (2001). Welfare, child support, and family formation. *Children and Youth Services Review, 23*(6/7), 577–601.

National Center for Education Statistics. (1999). *Early childhood longitudinal study: Birth cohort 2000.* http://nces.ed.gov.

Nelson, T. J., Clampet-Lundquist, S., and Edin, K. (2002). Father involvement among low-income, noncustodial African American fathers in Philadelphia. In C. A. Tamis-LeMonda and N. Cabrera (eds.), *Handbook of father involvement: Multidisciplinary perspectives* (pp. 525–554). Mahwah, NJ: Lawrence Erlbaum Associates, Publishers.

Nord, C. W. and Zill, N. (1996). *Non-custodial parents' participation in their children's lives: Evidence from the survey of income and program participation, Volume II.* Washington, DC: Office of Assistant Secretary for Planning and Evaluation, U.S. Department of Health and Human Services.

Patton, M. (2001). *Qualitative research and evaluation methods.* Newbury Park, CA: Sage.

Pearson, J. and Griswold, E. A. (1999). Child support and domestic violence: The victims speak out. *Violence Against Women, 5*(4), 427–448.

Personal Responsibility and Work Opportunity Act (1996). Public Law, 104–193, 110 Stat.2105.

Rodriguez, E., Lasch, K. E., Chandra, P., and Lee. J. (2001). Family violence, employment status, welfare benefits, and alcohol drinking in the United States: What is the relation? *Journal of Epidemiogical Community Health, 55,* 172–178.

Roy, K. (July 1999). Low-income single fathers in an African American community and the requirements of welfare reform. *Journal of Family Issues, 20*(4), 432–457.

Seltzer, J. A., Schaeffer, N. C., and Charng, H. W. (1989) Family ties after divorce: The relationship between visiting and paying child support. *Journal of Marriage and the Family, 53,* 79–101.

Sorenson, E. A. (1995). *National profile of noncustodial fathers and their ability to pay child support.* Unpublished paper. Washington, DC: Urban Institute.

Stocker, C. M. and Younglade, L. (1999). Marital conflict and parental hostility: Links with children's siblings and per relationships. *Journal of Family Psychology, 13,* 598–609.

Tamis-LeMonda, C. S. and Cabrera, N. (eds.) (2002). *Handbook of father involvement: Multidisciplinary perspectives.* Mahwah, NJ. Lawrence Erlbaum Associates, Publishers.

Tashakkori, A. and Teddlie, C.(1998). *Mixed methodology.* Thousand Oaks, CA: Sage.

Tolman, R. M. and Raphael, J. (2000). A review of research on welfare and domestic violence. *Journal of Social Issues, 56*(4), 655–682.

U.S. Census Bureau. (1997). *Child support for custodial mothers and fathers*: 197. Report No. P60–212. Washington DC: Author.

Waller, M. and Plotnick, R. (2000). A failed relationship? Low-income families and the child support enforcement system. *Focus, 21,* 12–17.

Wilson, M. and Brooks-Gunn, J. (2001). Health status and behaviors of unwed fathers. *Children and Youth Services Review, 23*(4–5), 377–401.

Westerman, M. A. and Schonholtz, J. (1993). Marital adjustments, joint parental support in a triadic problem-solving task, and child behavior problems. *Journal of Clinical Child Psychology, 22,* 97–106.

Yogman, M. W., Kindlon, D., and Earls, F. (1995). Father involvement and cognitive-behavioral outcomes of preterm infants. *Journal of the American Academy of Child and Adolescent Psychiatry, 34,* 58–66.

Zippay, A. and Rangarajan, A. (2001). *Struggling to make it: Voices of New Jersey work first families.* Princeton, NJ: Mathematica Policy Research, Inc.

Zippay, A. and Rangarajan, A. (2004). *In their own words: WFNJ clients speak about work and welfare.* Princeton, NJ: Mathematica Policy Research, Inc.

CHAPTER SEVEN

Deadbeat Dads or Fatherhood in Poverty?

DAVID J. PATE, JR.

The notion of fatherhood has taken on several connotations in the battles over welfare reform since the 1960s. Fathers who failed to contribute to the family's well-being were first described as absent, then as deadbeat. The latter term recognizes that some of these fathers are simply dead broke, and only infrequently possess the financial capacity to aid their children. Yet despite ongoing, heavily politicized debates over the role of fathers and the importance of marriage in poor communities, we know very little about how these men view their circumstances and responsibilities toward their families.

This chapter examines how some men push to meet the basic financial and even emotional needs of their children, drawing on qualitative data collected as part of the Wisconsin Child Support Demonstration Evaluation (CSDE). Through ongoing interviews with three African American fathers, conducted in the wake of Wisconsin's infamous effort to dramatically reduce the welfare rolls, we come to see how they manage their day-to-day existence and interact with their families and children.[1]

A variety of policy makers and scholars, given rising concern over "family formation" in poor communities, are hopeful that men can be attracted to marriage or reunited with their children within a nuclear family. Much of the debate assumes that most men are irresponsible and that enforcement of child support is the most that can be accomplished. Yet more recently, the Bush Administration has advanced the idea that government intervention might raise marriage rates, presumably without boosting fertility rates, or move men to connect more deeply with their families. Such policy thrusts assume that noncustodial fathers are uninvolved with their children. But recent research has challenged this, showing that many interact often with their children and former partners (Achatz and MacAllum, 1994; Johnson et al., 1999; McLanahan et al., 2001; Waller, 2002).

Child Support Research—A Window
into the Lives of Fathers

Earlier work on fathers—including their financial capacity and personal responsibilities—entered their world through the child support system. This has been both an illuminating and a limiting frame within which to explore men's lives. The initial problem across many states is the issue of how to establish paternity for children born to unmarried parents. Paternity determination rates in the 1980s ranged from a high of 67 percent in Michigan to a low of 14 percent in Louisiana, and 20 percent in New York. Two decades ago, over two-thirds of children born out of wedlock had no legally recognized father (Dowd, 2000). This despite the fact that paternity must be established so that children gain legal access to their father for emotional and financial support.

Policy makers and mothers remain concerned over uneven collection of child support payments from fathers. Only 40 percent of all women eligible for child support actually received payments from noncustodial fathers in 1999 (U.S. Census Bureau, 2000). The problem is even greater among mothers receiving cash aid under TANF—just 28 percent of these women reported receipt of any child support in 1998.

We also know that many unmarried fathers and those whose children receive public assistance exhibit low earnings and high unemployment (Mincy and Sorensen 1998; Meyer 1998). Not surprisingly underemployed men show lower consistency in providing child support (Bartfeld and Meyer, 1994). Research in Wisconsin found that one-third of the fathers awarded formal orders by the courts to pay child support actually paid nothing in the first year (Meyer, 1999).

In this context, the 1996 welfare reforms allowed the states to put in place more stringent practices to establish paternity and enforce child-support orders by the courts. The PRWORA reforms also promoted voluntary paternity acknowledgment. These policy changes have been associated with a rising number of established paternities (U.S. Office of Child Support Enforcement, 2000; Sussman, 2004). The rate of child support payments also has risen significantly in some states.

Still large numbers of mothers continue to rarely benefit from child support. In turn this has moved policy makers to support ever more punitive measures aimed at "deadbeat dads," including revoking fathers' driver's licenses, professional certificates to work in the trades, and pegging child-support levels to imputed, not actual earnings. Yet any gains in child-support payments are often retained by the state and offset cash aid going to the mother (for women who remain within the TANF system). Wisconsin, however, provided a full pass through of child-support payments at the time of our study.

Research around the child support issue also has taught us that nonpaying fathers are a diverse group, including many who continue to lack the economic resources or wherewithal to provide significant support to their families (Cancian and Meyer, 2004; Mincy and Sorenson, 1998; Sorenson and Zibman, 2000). The research reported in this chapter stems from earlier qualitative research, which illuminates the diversity of men for whom this evolving array of policies are targeted. Several scholars have shown that many men remain quite involved with their children and former partners, contributing small amounts of money and significant amounts of emotional and social support (Edin et al., 2001; Johnson et al., 1999; Sorensen and Zibman, 2000; Waller and Plotnick, 2001). In some ways, the policy focus on child support and resulting characterizations of fathers have blinded us to understanding why some fathers do remain involved and the ways in which they continue to support their families.

Defining Fatherhood in Poverty?

While the social construction of fatherhood has taken on multiple meanings, Kost (2001) argues that current concerns about fatherlessness and deadbeat dads in the social and economic arenas reduce the duties and responsibilities of a father to a one-dimensional identity: That of breadwinner. More recent work, however, has delved deeply into the emotional and social facets of family support. African American men, in particular, may face multiple constraints on their capacity to carry out the traditional role of a responsible father.

The challenge of paying child support or financially providing for one's family consistently is especially problematic. Cultural barriers associated with acknowledging paternity, difficulties in the father–mother relationship, and persistent poverty often characterize the African American experience of fatherhood (Liebow, 1967; Stack, 1974). Black fathers in low-income communities have been characterized as nonexistent (Hamer, 2001), as sexual predators, or as noninvolved (Roberts, 1998). Some conservative scholars have used this as a rationale for more punitive policies or more hopeful measures aimed at promoting marriage (Horn and Bush, 1997; Murray, 1984).

Yet several investigators have advanced empirical findings that contradict these stereotypical views (Johnson et al., 1999; Pate, 2002; Waller and Plotnick, 2001). Recent studies suggest that many fathers make informal monetary or in-kind contributions to their children, that they are often frustrated that child support payments do not go directly to their children, and that many live with their children, and are actively engaged in their families' daily lives (Edin et al., 2001; Hamer, 2001; Mincy and Sorenson, 1998). This chapter stems from this line of qualitative research. What's key is trying to understand how these men define themselves as "good fathers," that is, the identity and attributes associated with responsible fatherhood in their daily contexts.

Characteristics of Participating Fathers

This study included 44 African American men who ranged in age from 21 to 57 years. Ten had fathered one child each; 2 had each fathered more than

10 children. Twenty-two of the sampled fathers had children with more than one woman. Thirty-one fathers had lived with their biological children and 21 with children they did not father. Most fathers were currently not living alone: About half lived with a female partner, and several lived with their mothers. The majority of men participating in the study were neither homeowners nor listed on the lease at their current address. Indeed many had no stable address and moved among the homes of kin and friends. Eight of the 16 fathers who had ever been married were currently married but not necessarily living with their wives.

Being part of a wider evaluation study, administrative data pertaining to their earnings, welfare status, and child support payments were available, offering a more complete profile of their circumstances. The fathers had low formal earnings, averaging about $9,600 in 1999, and $8,000 in 2000. All fathers were faced with court-ordered child support obligations at the time of our interviews. In 1999, the average father paid $1,400 in child support. Fathers typically owed substantial amounts to the state for hospital costs associated with childbirths, interest on child support arrears, and public assistance reimbursements.

Three Fathers, Eight Mothers, and Ten Children

Three of the fathers who participated in the study are described here. This analysis delved into how these men defined and what they felt about their responsibilities to their children and families. The 1996 reforms were founded in part on the premise that the promotion of responsible fatherhood was integral to child well-being. But how did these men actually understand these moral obligations and reflect on their ability to deliver the support they owed their family?

All three were employed. Each man had fathered a child before reaching age 21. Most of their children were born before the 1996 welfare reforms, holding implications for the changing rules of legally sanctioned child support. I begin with a description of each father, then bring forward their own voices to illuminate their conceptions of responsibility and moral obligation toward their children and former partner.

Jimmy is a 23-year-old father of a little girl, aged 3. He attained a high school diploma and worked as a third-shift security guard earning $9.00 an hour (figure 7.1). He lived with his biological mother at the time of our interviews. His biological father and sister assist with child care responsibilities. Jimmy's daughter, Sonja, stayed with him five–six days a week. He shares joint custody of the daughter on an informal basis, even though the mother had legal custody under their divorce arrangement. They have neither the time nor money to hire a lawyer to alter the official order.

Neither are they inclined to change the legal custody arrangement as Sonja's mother still draws TANF aid as a family unit, on behalf of herself and Sonja. Jimmy therefore is required to pay child support. At the time of

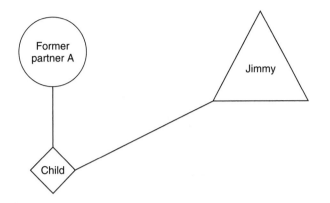

Figure 7.1 Jimmy and his child. —Indicates the biological relationship of the parents with the child.

the interviews, he had just received an active child support order including the cost of the "lying-in fee" (the birthing costs covered by Medicaid). In Wisconsin and other states, birth costs of children who receive Medicaid services are charged to noncustodial fathers and collected by the child support agency. He faces a bimonthly child support payment of $97.50.

RJ is a 32-year-old father of six children by five women. He also served as stepfather to one child of his fiancée (figure 7.2). His children ranged in age, at the time of the interview, from 4 to 14. He was living with his fiancée of four years in a rental house where his share of the rent was $375 a month. Involved in drug trafficking between ages 14 and 22, he later attended technical college to obtain a cosmetology degree. During our interviews, RJ worked as a barber. Due to his dependence on clients for daily work, his wages fluctuated. Four of the mothers of his children had received welfare assistance in the past. He therefore has four separate child-support orders. After failing to pay the level of child support required by court order, RJ was charged with four felonies and imprisoned. Upon release, he was on probation for five years. His child support order for all four children amounted to about $700 a month.

Steven, a 44-year-old father of three children, lived with his wife of 10 years during our interviews (figure 7.3). They reside in Section 8 supported housing, paying $375 per month. Since Steven is not listed on the lease, his residence at the home is illegal. His 3 children, ages 13, 21, and 27, have two different mothers. Both mothers were long-term welfare users, and Steven had a long history with child support and cash aid systems much before we met.

His current child support debt amounts to $63,064, with a court order of $50 monthly. Steven also owes the state $37,673 in past AFDC arrears, including $19,048 interest (set in Wisconsin at 17 percent per annum), $4,117 in birth cost fees, and $349 in administrative costs. The remaining

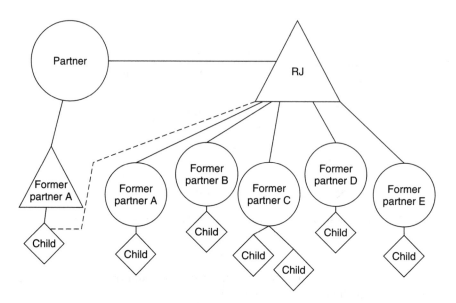

Figure 7.2 RJ and his children.---Indicates the nonbiological relationship of RJ with the children in the household.—Indicates the biological relationship of the parents with their children.

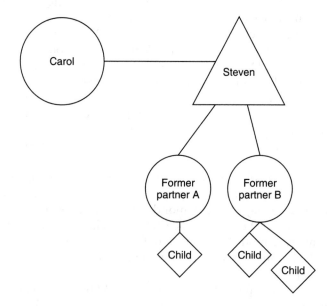

Figure 7.3 Steven and his children.—Indicates the biological relationship of the parents with their children.

amount of $906 is arrears owed and $843 in interest from the welfare system. His current child support order of $50 was calculated by multiplying his current weekly salary by 17 percent (the amount for a child under the age of 18). Steven earned $7 per hour during our interviews as a part-time health care worker, assisting adults in their homes. He also worked off the books as a tenant manager, earning another $100 per week. His wife suffered from severe asthma while Steven participated in the study. She died soon after our second interview with Steven. Since his tenancy was illegal, he was forced to leave his home and move into a shelter.

Conceptions of Personal Responsibility

All three men provided some financial support for their children prior to the 1996 welfare reforms. In fact each was employed when our interviews began in 1999 and set aside a portion of their earnings for their children. These men discussed job opportunities in the suburbs, as opposed to staying in the central city. But obstacles in finding and getting to jobs were great: The lack of reliable transportation, occasional police harassment, and discomfort in entering better-off communities where they felt unwelcome.

Before welfare reform, paternity establishment and child support collection was relatively weak. Previously the low-income noncustodial parent had a moral responsibility to provide for his children, but his legal responsibilities were not enforced by law. With less aggressive child support enforcement, fathers could use their limited resources and devote them entirely to the child and her/his well-being. Fathers could risk not repaying the state for their children's TANF support and instead make informal arrangements with the mother to pay something—in kind or in cash—when they were able to. Now these men faced stiff child support obligations and a mountain of debt to the state, pressure that could result in jail if ignored. Yet these men asked why they should work hard to simply see their cash going back to the state, rather than actually aiding their family (also see, Garfinkel et al., 1998). Nor was credit granted by the system if fathers were present, offering emotional and social support.

Jimmy reflects on his initial reaction to the birth of his child in the following passage. He remembers that he had to change his personal plans and attend to his new responsibilities as a father.

> *Jimmy:* See, I was going to school 'til I had my daughter and that just sidetracked me, cause you know, that was a big thing . . . I didn't think I could handle it, all of that pressure [with school assignments, new baby, relationship] . . . [However, I] realize that I [need to] go back to school to catch that degree cause it's better . . . for me . . . And the next thing I know, you know, I had to get a job. You know what I'm saying. I wouldn't make no money, going to school, you know what I'm saying, I had to buy Pampers and all of that,

so . . . And I was still working part time, but you know, I had to get a full time to get all of [the baby stuff].

Interviewer: So you really took on the responsibility. You're saying that you had a responsibility . . .

Jimmy: This is my child, you know what I'm saying. I do everything for my child; I don't expect nobody else to.

Jimmy also discussed his current arrangement with the mother of his child. He agreed to be responsible for the child while the mother was at her second job. He apparently took on this role, supporting the mother's income, without any coercion or demands from the mother or the state. He felt it was his responsibility to assist in the caretaking of his child.

Interviewer: How did you decide to have so much involvement with your daughter five days a week? . . .

Jimmy: Because I work third shift, and she works . . . during the day . . . I get my daughter every day at two o'clock from day care. [I] have her until nine o'clock, . . . So that's just how our schedules fit, you know what I'm saying. It would be better for us, you know what I'm saying, so that's not even the half of it.

Interviewer: How is that [schedule] working out for you?

Jimmy: Oh it works [out] fine, you know what I'm saying. I love it, . . . sister stays next door with my little nephew and he's three years old, about to turn four. My daughter just turned three . . . and they both be over here doing they thing, you know what I'm saying, just doing . . . [whatever]. So I like it, you know what I'm saying, it's nice, you know? . . .

Everyone is amazed [that I am able to have my daughter so often] . . . because [even though] . . . my daughter [is not living] with me, [it] is basically like she is staying with me—because she is with me . . . I'd say eighty percent of the day, you know what I'm saying, [be]cause she don't go home until nine o'clock [at night] . . . She spend[s] more time with me than her mother, you know what I'm saying, to be honest, but . . . Since the summer months have started, her schedule had just switched around a little bit more. I only have my daughter like four days a week now, you know what I'm saying. But sometimes, five, six, you know what I'm saying. It all depends on how the, how the week falls, you know what I'm saying, but, but then it might start back up, you know it's going to be five, six days a week, like that again, but for right now, you know, . . . It's cool— . . . I don't have a problem watching my daughter every day. That's not a problem at all. Cause if it was a problem, I would've never had my daughter . . . you know what I'm saying.

Jimmy went on to further reiterate his philosophy on his responsibility to his child.

Jimmy: I got a couple of friends that just don't take care of their kids at all. And it's just like, well, why do you have a kid? . . . , if you're not even going to take full responsibility of it—I know it's hard, don't get me wrong. It's hard when you're not with your baby mother, you know what I'm saying . . . I just feel do the best that you can, you know what I'm saying, to know, for your daughter or your son to [see] that, . . . you're there—It's not always giving them things, it's just, it's being there . . . This is my everything. My baby's my world, you know?

Yet when Jimmy turned to his current responsibility to pay formal child support, he expresses frustration and bewilderment at the state's request. He initially paid the birthing cost to the child support agency. Then he was instructed to pay child support for his child that is in his care for the majority of the week.

Interviewer: How did you pay the lying-in fees? Did you pay them straight out, or was [it] over an extended period of time?

Jimmy: There was a payment [plan overtime] . . . I don't know how much they end up taking out of my check every two weeks . . . [all I know] they took a lot . . . [In fact] they (child support) took out actually, like a thousand, almost twelve hundred extra dollars and sent me a [refund check].

Four months after paying off the birthing cost fee, he received a letter from the child support enforcement agency stating that he had to appear in court.

Interviewer: When you were summoned to court by the child support agency . . . Did you have, did you have any fear, any trepidation?

Jimmy: Well, only fear I had was I knew when I was going down to court, they were going to stick me with child support . . . And I just knew that, and I just had the thing [coming] cause . . . he was, . . . commissioner for I would say two months. And I just knew that . . . 'cause that's how they always do. 'Cause I was getting [from the commissioner] "the fathers don't do anything speech," . . . at the time our child couldn't get um, insurance under my job, you know what I'm saying . . . I actually have insurance under my mom's right now. I don't have insurance under my job; I can, but I didn't, you know what I'm saying . . .

After the court hearing, Jimmy was ordered to pay child support despite his intensive involvement with his child. He complained: "I take care of my child." During the conversation, he questioned the rationale for child support. "When you have your child everyday, Why you gotta pay child support? I just do not understand it."

RJ also had considerable experience with the child support system. His children had received cash aid under AFDC and continued after 1996 under Wisconsin's TANF program. RJ discussed the delicate balance between paying formal child support versus continuing to provide informal support. He had been charged with four felony counts for nonpayment of child support. By the time we met RJ, his debt to the state far exceeded what he owed in child support to the mother.

> *RJ:* Far as child support . . . I always have took care of my kids but I never knew that I had to take care of them in the system [government]. You know, I thought W-2 [TANF] was just a program to help mothers out but come to find out the fathers really got to pay it back [to the state]. You know, so far as W-2 now, like I talked to all my baby mothers now, [and if there is some way], that I can get them [off the government rolls] and make a better life for my kids then I [will] . . . I been in the system now for sixteen years. They caught up with me approximately two years ago (since welfare reform) and ever since then—I been taking care of everything— I need to take care of. So far, I'm trying to do the best that I can with the type of income I have and with the amount of kids that I have.

In Wisconsin, an arrest warrant is issued for a noncustodial parent if child support is 120 days past due. RJ discussed how, despite the testimony of one of his children's mother in his defense, he was convicted and served time.

> *RJ:* I [was picked up] for a felony warrant . . . for child support . . .
> *Interviewer:* You have a felony record for delinquent child support?
> *RJ:* Yes, they turn me into a felon because I didn't take care of it [the payment] through the [formal] system. They wanted me to pay back the mother of my child $5,000 and instead of [listening to her at court]—they did not listen to her at all. She was telling the world, he . . . take[s] care of his [financial responsibilities] . . . to his daughter. They didn't hear me out—. They didn't say anything to me.
> *Interviewer:* So the mother intervened on your behalf?
> *RJ:* The mother was . . . there on my behalf, but they wouldn't even listen to her testimony. They said, far as they concerned, I'm a felon . . . [They said] I'm a dead-beat dad. A dead-beat dad is when a dad don't take care of they child, and I take care of my kids as far as clothes, schooling, medical, food on the table, clothes on they back, shoes on they feet. I mean, I even take time out to do my girls' hair, so, I mean, most fathers don't do that much.

RJ discussed how he defined his responsibilities for his children under the new, post-1996 welfare rules. He believed that the state was pressing a stronger obligation to help get his children off the cash aid system. RJ said,

"I think the fathers' obligation should [be] to keep these mothers up off the system period, and let us be a father and take care of our kids." But he also complained that his chances of steady employment had been undercut after becoming a convicted felon.

>*RJ:* They won't even give me a good job being a job coach, or even a person to talk to people because I'm a felon.
>
>*Interviewer:* How does [the felony] prevent you from getting a [better] job?
>
>*RJ:* This prevents me from getting a job. This prevents me from doing anything I wanted to do. I wanted to go work with kids in the group home. They told me, we can't hire you because you [have] a felony [on your record]. I don't mind going to a half-way house where there are dead-beat dads, they want to call us, and let them know this kind of information but they want them to say, well, you got to make this much amount of money a month to be out of the system [government] . . . you got to have a good-paying job, you got to at least be doing forty hours a week [to take care of your kids and pay child support].

The third father, Steven, had been enmeshed with the old AFDC system for over 20 years when we met him. Yet his links to the child support system differed from RJ and Jimmy. An older man, Steven was 44 years old and expressed a differing view of the father's responsibilities in the post-1996 world of welfare.

>*Interviewer:* How did you learn that you had child support payments?
>
>*Steven:* I went to court for my daughters, and I was working for the city. I had to sign a court waiver for them.
>
>*Interviewer:* Can you explain it?
>
>*Steven:* Well, back then you sign a piece of paper. You know, when you go to court the judge gives you so much an amount to pay. Okay, then you sign this waiver for this amount to come out of your check. Just like your income tax . . . You don't sign nothing. You work a job over thirty day—they automatically take out child support. Any job over thirty days.
>
>*Interviewer:* What do you think of the father's obligation under the new rules of welfare?
>
>*Steven:* Pay child support.
>
>*Interviewer:* How long have you owed child support? How long have you been paying it?
>
>*Steven:* Almost about 20 years.
>
>*Interviewer:* So the father's obligation in your opinion is to pay child support. Anything else?
>
>*Steven:* Yeah, and to take time out with their kids.

Steven maintained that the new system demanded that he shift his responsibility as a father to paying formal child support. For Steven, the policy shifts in Wisconsin were relatively positive as he now saw a direct link between his child support payments and his child's well-being:

> *Steven:* My kid's mother is getting child support checks now. I called her about a month [ago], she told my daughter to tell daddy "thank you." I said thank you for what? She said, "I'm getting child support checks now." Now I'm seeing where my money is going.
> *Interviewer:* She's getting all of the money that's coming out of your check?
> *Steven:* Yeah, I was sad about that . . . I used to couldn't see what was taking my money. She wasn't getting no checks. Now she gets them.
> *Interviewer:* Does that make a difference in the way she talks to you?
> *Steven:* Oh yeah! Lots of difference, because she's getting some money now. She's getting child support now. I mean, the time I've been paying child support, I've never heard [about] none of the mothers getting any money.

In the case of Jimmy, who provided almost full-time child care for his daughter, his role as a responsible parent was clearly apparent. Indeed he was paying the day-to-day expenses of raising his child, so when he was called upon to pay for his daughter's birthing fee and the child's TANF cash payments, this came as a surprise.

> *Jimmy:* I paid the hospital fee.
> *Interviewer:* Oh, you did.
> *Jimmy:* I paid that off. They take that out of my check. I paid that back . . . eleven hundred thirty dollars. I paid that back like in a year and a half time, there. I forgot how much they were actually taking out of my check. But I paid that back. You know what I'm saying, I thought that was the only thing I was going to have to pay.

Eventually Jimmy paid off the birth cost fees, but was ordered to make biweekly child support payments.

> *Jimmy:* This guy [lawyer] from the state [said] when I was on the stand; I got to pay all that money [cash assistance] back. See, and it doesn't, . . . it doesn't go to the state, it goes to my daughter's mother. I'm giving her money?—Why [am] I [giving] her money and I have my daughter [everyday]? She ought to . . . be giving me money to be honest, but you know what I'm saying, I just think I'm getting [screwed] in the game big time.
> *Interviewer:* So, when they said you were paying child support did they [tell] you about some kind of program the money goes through to the mother directly?

Jimmy: Yeah, it goes directly to the mother. Directly, all of it. All. They take out, what, what is it? I don't know, got a check stub in my wallet. Basically like ninety seven fifty to be exact, and she's getting it, all the ninety seven fifty.

In general, these fathers wanted to be viewed as responsible parents who financially helped to support their families. These men paid their child support consistently, either because their employers garnished their wages or because they voluntarily made monthly payments. Yet the formal child support system left them feeling powerless because their informal contributions were never recognized by caseworkers or the courts. RJ talked of these legal disincentives to be close to one's family and provide informal support.

RJ: They could call us dead-beat dads, say what they want to say about us, put us in this system (child support enforcement program) and play with us like they been doing, and [not allow] us, . . . to get more into doing more for our kids, the system is what make a man run. The system . . . puts a warrant out for somebody [to] arrest them, suspend their driver's license, because they ain't paying child support? [It's frustrating].

Importantly these men sometimes linked their manhood and identity with their capacity to be involved in their children's lives. As Steven put it:

Steven: Manhood is not the number of babies you make. A man to me is [someone] who is out there taking care of his responsibilities, doing whatever he can do. If I got to go without a piece of clothing on my back for my kids, I'm going without because my kids come first. That's a man. A man is when your kids ain't out here starving, looking like a bum, out here in the cold. You know, a man is going to take care of his domain. You ain't got to be with the mother to take care of your kids.

Implications—How We Portray Fathers, How to Form Stronger Families

This chapter began by highlighting the simple portraits of fathers sketched by politicians and welfare reformers—so eager to inflict tough love on a rather faceless mass of deadbeat dads. We have seen how three fathers had indeed reneged on their moral and financial commitments to their families—both their children and their former partners.

But the voices of these men also display a certain amount of caring—at least in how they reflect on their responsibilities to family and how they are viewed by others. Even this brief exploration of these men's beliefs and intentions suggests that gross generalities about the fathers of welfare children don't always hold water. Within stiff economic, legal, and social constraints, these men are attending to family obligations in different ways.

The second major finding, stemming from this qualitative study, is that policies aimed at extracting resources from these fathers lead to unintended consequences and distorted incentives. Two of these fathers spoke of how caseworkers and the courts never recognize the informal ways they support and connect with their children over long periods of time. They are certainly not ideal fathers, but these men clearly care about their families and already feel the obligations that policy makers try to hammer into their heads and hearts. The levels of arrears, stemming from child support and required reimbursements to the state for TANF supports, are almost comical when put up against the minimum wage jobs held by these men. Does the state really expect to collect on these debts? Meanwhile these fathers ask why they should work, sometimes at menial low-wage jobs, when earnings go back to the state, not to their children. Somehow policy makers must reassess the kinds of incentives and disincentives they create, often in the name of cracking down on deadbeat dads. The post-1996 crackdown, in some cases, is neither strengthening family formation nor bringing new sources of cash to mothers and children.

Federal and state policy makers might consider specific ways of getting these incentives right, offering meaningful supports and sanctions for fathers—aiming to truly strengthen families and provide more adequate support for children. For instance, future reforms might consider: (1) Forgiving arrears owed to the state; (2) more emphasis on assistance to custodial parents in the collection of child support arrears owed to them from noncustodial parents who have the ability to pay; (3) reconsider the use of incarceration as an enforcement tool if the noncustodial parent presents an inability to pay; and (4) the implementation of a full pass-through and disregard in all states.

This chapter has explored the role of responsibility for low-income, noncustodial fathers and their children in the era of welfare reform. Each of these fathers provided insight on the monetary and nonmonetary contributions that they made to their children on a day-to-day basis. Child support enforcement was a source of frustration and pain for these men in various ways. For example, Steven's children and grandchildren might benefit from his financial support, but his income is currently diverted to paying off the mothers' past welfare debts and he lives under the constant threat of imprisonment if he does not cooperate with the child support enforcement system. Devolution did not change much for these fathers in terms of social services, but the new tools of child support enforcement provided them with additional loss of control over their lives. The new welfare legislation brought with it an increased number of enforcement tools for the collection of child support along with tougher sanctions and immediate wage garnishment.

One of the goals of the child support enforcement system is to benefit the families of poor fathers. This research has shown that the effects of the child support enforcement mechanisms used, including imprisonment and tax interceptions, generally caused anxiety and frustration for these fathers, who were already emotionally and financially involved with their children. It could also be hypothesized that the new welfare reform laws have made these fathers less responsible because they have had to manage the ability to pay child support and take care of their children, which is nearly impossible on their limited incomes. It was in their engagement in the child support system that these men believed they had no real agency, no ability to act and have direct, positive impact on their lives or on their children's lives.

Notes

The Institute for Research on Poverty, University of Wisconsin, Madison, supported this research. Additional assistance was provided by Jacquelyn Boggess of the Center for Family Policy and Practice and Dawn Duren of the Institute for Research on Poverty.

1. These findings stem from a larger evaluation of the child support component of Wisconsin's welfare reform initiative—Wisconsin Works—W2, conducted by the Institute for Research on Poverty (IRP), and funded by the state of Wisconsin. This chapter presents findings from a subsample of a qualitative study of African American fathers in Milwaukee, whose children were receiving TANF cash aid and support services. The overall project included a random-assignment experimental evaluation, a survey of participating mothers and fathers, and an ethnographic component (detailed in Cancian et al., 2001).

References

Achatz, M. and MacAllum, C. A. (1994). *Young unwed fathers: Report from the field*. Philadelphia: Public/Private Ventures.

Bartfeld, J. and Meyer, D. R. (1994). Are there really dead-beat dads? The relationship between enforcement, ability to pay, and compliance in nonmarital child support cases. *Social Service Review, 68*(2), 219–235.

Cancian, M. and Meyer, D. R. (2004). Fathers of children receiving welfare: Can they provide more child support? *Social Service Review, 78*(2), 179–206.

Cancian, M., Caspar, E., and Meyer, D. R. (2001). Experimental design. Technical Report 1. In D. R. Meyer and M. Cancian (eds.), *W-2 Child support demonstration evaluation, phase 1: Final report. Volume III: Technical reports*. April. Report to the Department of Workforce Development, Institute for Research on Poverty, University of Wisconsin, Madison.

Dowd, N. E. (2000). *Redefining fatherhood*. New York: New York University Press.

Edin, K., Lein, L., Nelson, T., and Clampet-Lundquist, S. (2001). Talking with low-income fathers. *Poverty Research News, 4*(2), 10–12.

Garfinkel, I., Meyer, D., and McLanahan, S. (1998). A Patchwork Portrait of Nonresident Fathers. In I. Garfinkel, S. McLanahan, J. A. Seltzer, and D. R. Meyer (eds.), *Fathers under Fire: The Revolution in Child Support Enforcement*. New York: Russell Sage Foundation.

Hamer, J. (2001) *What it means to be daddy: Fatherhood for Black men living away from their children*. New York: Columbia University Press.

Horn, W. and Bush, A. (1997). *Fathers, Marriages and Welfare Reform*. Indianapolis, IN: Hudson Institute.

Johnson, E., Levine, A., and Doolittle, F. C. (1999). *Fathers' Fair Share: Helping Poor Fathers Manage Child Support and Fatherhood*. New York: Russell Sage Foundation.

Kost, K. A. (2001). The function of fathers: What poor men say about fatherhood. *Families in Society: Journal of Contemporary Human Services, 82*(5), 499–507.

Liebow, E. (1967). *Tally's corner: A study of negro streetcorner men*. Boston: Little, Brown.

McLanahan, S., Garfinkel, I., and Audigier, C. N. (2001). *The fragile families and child wellbeing baseline city report: Milwaukee.* Princeton, NJ: The Center for Research on Child Wellbeing (Princeton University).

Meyer, D. R. (1998). The effects of child support on the economic status of nonresident fathers. In I. Garfinkel, S. McLanahan, J. A. Seltzer, and D. R. Meyer (eds.), *Fathers under fire: The revolution in child support enforcement.* New York: The Russell Sage Foundation.

Meyer, D. R. (1999). Compliance with child support orders in paternity and divorce cases. In R. A. Thompson and P. R. Amato (eds.), *The Postdivorce Family.* Thousand Oaks, CA: Sage Foundation.

Mincy, R. B. and Sorensen, E. (1998). Deadbeats and turnips in child support reform. *Journal of Policy Analysis and Management, 17*(1), 44–51.

Murray, C. (1984). *Losing ground: American social policy.* (10th anniversary ed.) New York: Basic Books.

Pate, D. (2002). An ethnographic inquiry into the life experiences of African American fathers with children on W-2. In D. R. Meyer and M. Cancian (eds.), *W-2 child support demonstration evaluation, report on nonexperimental analyses, fathers of children in W-2 families, volume II.* Report to the Department of Workforce Development. Madison, WI: Institute for Research on Poverty, University of Wisconsin, Madison.

Roberts, D. (1998). Welfare's ban on poor motherhood. In Gwendolyn Mink (ed.), *Whose welfare?* New York: Cornell University Press.

Sorensen, E. and Zibman, C. (2000). *To what extent do children benefit from child support?* Washington, DC: Urban Institute.

Stack, C. (1974). *All our kin: Strategies for survival in a Black community.* New York: Harper.

Sussman, S., welfare rights attorney, personal communication, June 16, 2004.

U.S. Bureau of the Census. (2000). *Child Support for Custodial Mothers and Fathers: 1997. Current Population Reports, Series P60–187.* Washington, DC: U.S. Government Printing Office.

U.S. Office of Child Support Enforcement. (2000). *Child support enforcement, FY 1999, preliminary examination.* Available at http://www.acf.dhhs.gov/programs/cse/rpt/annrpt23/98artext.html.

Waller, M. R. (2002). *My baby's father: unmarried parents and paternal responsibility.* Ithaca, NY: Cornell University Press.

Waller, M. R. and Plotnick, R. (2001). Effective child support policy for low-income families: Evidence from street-level research. *Journal of Policy Analysis and Management, 20,* 89–110.

CHAPTER EIGHT

Implications for Families, Children, and Policy Makers

Jill Duerr Berrick and Bruce Fuller

Public policies in democratic societies necessarily stem from the moral values of citizens, often rooted in the cultural or economic interests of particular social classes. When the political left pushes to boost the minimum wage, expand preschool programs, or keep religion out of public schools, a particular set of social values predominates. When conservatives trust the market to provide livable wages, push marriage as a sacred activity, or allocate public dollars to aunts and boyfriends to provide child care, here too, fundamental values are being expressed through policy.

One crucial finding from the studies presented in this volume is that many low-income parents also hold and try to live by basic American values. Many mothers are eager to work, to become economically self-sufficient, to find affordable and safe child care. Yet this echo of social commitments and individual aspirations reveals that the problem is not necessarily a lack of moral fiber, as some welfare reformers would have it. Instead parents face terrible trade-offs: Take a minimum-wage job but depend on low-quality child care; rely on earned income rather than public assistance but risk health care coverage for them and their children; work 40 or more hours a week but lose time with their children.

The steady toughening of work requirements and signaling of "personal responsibility" has been a huge political success. But shrinkage of the welfare rolls has not led to significant reductions in child poverty or strong gains in parents' quality of life. Indeed since 2002, more than 1.6 million more children have sunk beneath the poverty line (U.S. Census Bureau, 2003). This volume helps us understand why families remain poor, by presenting the context and daily realities of what life is like for low-income women.

A significant departure from only a few decades ago, women are now called to work while leaving their children in the care of others. For some, we have seen how new opportunities to work are greeted with enthusiasm. Indeed work that is inherently interesting, offers flexibility, and is personally satisfying may yield a valued trade-off to women who might otherwise spend their days in full-time parenting.

But the daily lives of many poor families have not significantly improved, as the previous chapters so vividly detail. For many women in the workplace, and particularly low-income women, we have seen how employment prospects remain rather dim. For poor women, the new policy demands to work outside the home—in addition to managing the "second shift" of work inside the home—are intensifying the already stiff challenges of parenting (Hochschild, 2003). The job these mothers face is daunting: Raising children who attend substandard schools, contending with high rates of crime and victimization, living in low-quality housing (Brooks-Gunn et al., 1997), dealing with poor or chronic family health problems (Epstein, 2003), and relying on public transport and numerous public and private agencies (chapter 1). The challenges of daily life become even more difficult when the demands of low-wage workplaces are factored in.

In this final chapter, we briefly review major findings, looking across these fine qualitative studies of low-income families facing the new policy environment. We emphasize that policy makers—as they continue to reform welfare—might squarely face the contradictions and trade-offs manifest in federal and state efforts aimed at supporting poor families. First and foremost, *as work hours increase, motherhood is squeezed.* When the government tells women to spend more time in the labor market, they must spend less time with their children (Fuller et al., 2002a). How could it be otherwise? In the early years of welfare reform, women were required to work part-time. With each passing year, work participation rates and weekly work hours have increased. Today low-income single women are required to work 30 hours per week simply to maintain eligibility for cash aid.

The latest debates in Congress center on increasing work hours to 40 per week for parents on welfare. While the 40-hour work-week may be perceived as the standard in the United States, recent data suggest otherwise. In 2001, 39 percent of women with children worked full time, full-year; another 37 percent worked either part-time or part-year (Lyter et al., 2002). In addition, a recent study by the Urban Institute indicated that raising work requirements to 40 hours per week would create serious hardships for some families (Weil, 2002) and ultimately postpone women's economic self-sufficiency. No doubt, adding another 10 hours to an already hectic work-week would further reduce women's time with their children. And up to 40 percent of women moving off welfare labor during odd hours, including swing-shifts and weekends when older children are not in school (Fuller et al., 2002b).

The second finding illuminated by our contributors shows that although women's time with children may be compromised, *women continue to put their children's needs above paid employment.* The accounting sheet in middle-class family life is difficult to balance at best, but for the low-income parents we visited in previous chapters, work and children are not equal: Children's needs predominate. Women often take special measures to locate good and then better child care, safer schools, and more trustworthy caregivers—all in an effort to promote their children's safety and secure a more promising future.

Their search for safe, quality child care is particularly noteworthy. It's a new and daunting task for many women who may not have worked steadily since giving birth. Whereas middle-class mothers have the luxury of seeking out child care for their youngster months in advance, low-income women facing immediate work requirements are only given a few days to locate a reliable caregiver (Knox et al., 2003). To make informed decisions about stable quality care while constrained by insufficient lead time, calls into question the kinds of choices low-income women are given. The rushed search for a caregiver also increases mothers' anxiety over child care and heightens their ambivalence about having to leave their children in order to work.

As women respond to the new moral messages encouraging work, new demands are placed on family budgets (e.g., transportation, clothing, and food costs), and *few women experience real economic gains.* As Morris, Scott, and London show (chapter 4), increased work participation brings psychological rewards to some women. But without gains in income, women's employment may be neutral or worse—more harmful than helpful for low-income children. Employment that offers earned income may bring social and developmental benefits to children. But this is highly dependent upon gaining steady livable wages—a goal that remains elusive in the low-wage labor market (Fuller et al., 2002b).

So what are the odds of reaping wage gains big enough to discernibly advance the well-being of parents and their children? Various studies suggest that somewhere between one-half and two-thirds of welfare leavers work following their exit from TANF. Of those working full time, most are making between $6 and 8 per hour, leaving family income well below the poverty line (Acs and Loprest, 2001; Devere, 2001). Real economic gains for welfare leavers are less the norm than the exception. Tracking studies show that two–three years after entering work-first programs, the average mother is earning under $14,000 annually (Fuller et al., 2002b; Weil and Finegold, 2002).

Children's well-being appears to be buffered and advanced by mothers' well-being, mothers' social support, and parenting quality. Mothers who lack such resources may find their job as a parent especially challenging and their children's well-being compromised; resourcefulness in these areas advances positive outcomes for their children. Current welfare reforms are silent on their support for parents in their parenting role. Research included in this volume (chapters 4 and 5) and elsewhere continues to illuminate the powerful effects of parenting on the development of low-income children (Duncan and Brooks-Gunn, 1997; McLoyd et al., 1997; National Research Council, 2001). The 1996 reforms substantially increased funding for child care outside the home. But even conservative reformers have thought little about how family policy could advance mothers' and fathers' capacity to be effective parents.

For the women who don't make it—whose poverty is severe or long-lasting—the consequences may be hazardous for them and for their children. For some, *living in poverty can steadily erode women's capacity to parent effectively*. These are the families who are most likely to maltreat their children and to come in contact with the child welfare system. Although studies to date have not suggested especially large effects on the child welfare caseload as a result of welfare reform (Shook, 1999; Wells et al., 2003), some reform elements display quite destabilizing effects on some of the most disadvantaged families in the United States (see chapter 3). For these women, policies promoting work and marriage may be misguided, whereas programs designed to support parenting quality could better serve children's needs and be more motivating for mothers.

If the trade-offs between work and parenting are manageable, how do low-income women, *not* incapacitated by poverty's effects, make it? How can we learn from their successes? Clearly they rely on both formal and informal supports to raise their children. Among these, *children's fathers often play an influential role*. How families shape the role of nonresidential fathers appears to play out individually, depending upon a variety of factors (see chapter 6). Those fathers who have frequent contact with their children, who show both emotional attachment and attentiveness, are often welcome in single-mother households. Still relationships can be far from smooth. Many women recognize the importance of fathers for their children, yet they also talk of buffering children from disappointment, sheltering them from harm, or filling in when plans fall through. Importantly while fathers' financial contributions are important, just "being there" may be enough for some families.

Finally *dads are feeling the pinch, too*. Increased child support obligations are not only stretching fathers financially, but they also place strains on men's identities as "good fathers" (see chapter 7). Those who attempt to fashion a role of fatherhood based foremost upon love and care may walk a lonely path, as the din of societal pressures focuses increasingly on the centrality of cash support in defining their parental role.

Overall these important findings from qualitative studies converge with a number of quantitative studies (see, e.g., Besharov, 2003; Blank and Haskins, 2002; Loeb et al., 2004; Weil and Finegold, 2002). Both lines of work point to the limitations of current policy thrusts. So what have we learned from this volume that informs fresh policy options to better support and motivate low-income parents?

Policy Opportunities for Improved Child and Family Well-Being

One long-term question is whether the morally charged emphasis on welfare-to-(low-wage) work and personal responsibility is the best strategy for motivating poor parents and raising family income. As women embrace their new role as worker, they do not shed or devalue their role as parent.

Indeed data from the studies presented here suggest just the opposite. Therefore if women must combine their new role in the labor market with their familiar role as parent, public policies could be designed to advance both roles.

Welfare offices and caseworkers are the point of first contact for many low-income women considering employment (Martinson and Holcomb, 2002; Meyers, 1998). As we have seen, caseworkers are rewarded to keep clients in "work activities," often with little regard for parents' worries about their children and home dynamics. But caseworkers can play a major role in communicating a message to parents that acknowledges and celebrates the importance of children and families, while also encouraging the transition to work.

The many requirements associated with welfare reform are daunting for many women. A policy approach that validates women's roles as parents, first, may help to ease the transition. A renewed focus on child care support along with work mandates may also be beneficial to families in the long run. Recent research suggests that strong child care subsidies encourage employment and raise family income among single mothers (Cleveland and Hyatt, 2003; Connelly and Kimmel, 2001). Public policies that support the further development of quality child care options for low-income parents, including greater access to center-based care, would go far in supporting and strengthening children's well-being (Loeb et al., 2004). Given parents' varying child care preferences and irregular work schedules, many rely on kith and kin for child care, now subsidized via vouchers. Efforts to monitor and support improved quality of these informal care providers (Coley et al., 2001) will be essential if we hope to see developmental and cognitive gains in the large majority of children whose parents are transitioning from welfare to work. Without improvements in child care, no one should be surprised when they see little progress in breaking the reproduction of family poverty from one generation to the next.

Other work and family supports, such as health insurance, not only make the transition to work easier, but indeed make caring for children manageable and humane. All children need access to preventive and treatment services; parents who can't access such services indeed compromise their children's well-being, and cannot meet their full obligations as parents. Although health insurance has expanded dramatically in recent years through Medicaid and the Children's Health Insurance Program, 8.5 million children in the United States still go without health coverage (Mills and Bhandari, 2002).

Given that employer-provided health insurance has declined measurably in recent years (Mills and Bhandari, 2002), greater participation in the labor market among low-income families is unlikely to have an appreciable effect on children's health care coverage. Continued expansion of government-supported health insurance, or increased incentives to private employers to expand coverage will be required to reverse current trends.

Once work supports are in place, more needs to be done to make the workplace family friendly. Working 30–40 hours per week in minimum-wage jobs may push the limits and human capacities of many low-income parents (Lovell, 2003). These parents, who also juggle public transportation and a myriad of other public and private service providers (see chapter 1), will be hard-pressed to meet stiffer work requirements. How many middle-class mothers would go down this pathway, further reducing their time at home with their young children? Allowing more flexible work schedules to accommodate the care of children, commute time, and other obligations will bring parents to their jobs in a more motivated state (Fried, 1998).

While voters strongly support employment for women otherwise receiving welfare, policy makers need to take issues of the life cycle back into consideration and give babies back to their mothers. Current welfare reform provisions allow states to exempt mothers from work if they have a young child in the home. Previous federal policy had exempted parents from work if their child was under age 3 (Weil, 2002). Under PRWORA, most states have narrowed the exemption to children under the age of 1 year, while 14 states only provide exemptions to parents whose infants are 13–16 weeks old, and another 6 states offer no exemption at all (Rowe, 2000).

Such policies—beyond discounting the importance of motherhood—place infants in jeopardy in ways that middle-class parents would never risk and, in the long run, are likely to do more damage to young children than their parents' employment gains would provide. If the care these infants and young children receive is of poor quality and their child care providers change frequently, we can be assured that their start in life will indeed be hazardous.

A significant body of literature now exists that documents the importance of the first year of life, both for social–emotional and cognitive development (National Research Council, 2001). Allowing babies to spend at least the first six months with their mothers would demonstrate significant policy support for families and for child well-being, even in the context of a work-first policy environment.

If babies matter, then the most egregious policy of the 1990s—the family cap—should be reconsidered by the states. Although the intent of the family cap may be to discourage additional child-bearing among low-income women, the effect is to deepen poverty significantly for our youngest citizens. Presently 19 states have passed laws affirming the family cap (Rowe, 2000) and thereby reducing family income—in most states by about 30 percent (Berrick, 2005). When no TANF grant in the nation raises a family above the poverty line, the accumulated insult of an additional 30 percent cut places a family in a state of extreme destitution. Given significant evidence suggesting that poverty's negative influence is most pronounced for the youngest children and in the most impoverished families (Duncan and Brooks-Gunn, 1997), the family cap flies in the face of research and imposes the harshest penalties on those least able to tolerate them.

Other efforts to support low-income children and families could include boosting the minimum wage and the earned income tax credit (EITC), both aimed at increasing family income for working parents. Indeed mounting evidence suggests that family income is pivotal in its impact on children and families. Work alone does not necessarily translate into improved outcomes for children (Chase-Lansdale et al., 2003), but work that results in significantly increased income can have important, positive effects (see chapter 4).

If the Congress decides to again raise work requirements, then increases to family income can only come from the market or from government subsidies. Although the EITC expanded dramatically in the 1990s, more headway in this area could ensure a higher standard of living and greater child well-being for a larger proportion of children. Other government subsidies to consider might include child allowances (Lindsey, 2003). However these too would probably be linked to work requirements given that, as this volume suggests, the emphasis on work-based policies for low-income families, which has been so prominent in recent years, is likely to continue. As parents' own voices have so clearly expressed, what they need are not additional morality messages from government, but rather decent paying jobs and the work supports that middle-class Americans take for granted.

Because child well-being depends principally on the caregiving capacities and actions of the parent, stronger support for parenting—not just for marriage—is warranted in both welfare and child care programs. Although we are reluctant to suggest that the welfare state take on a larger monitoring function with low-income families, we see the potential benefits that could result from extending more active support to parents. Policy that builds from the motivating dynamics of parenting may prove more effective than simply banking on moral signals and low-wage jobs.

For those families struggling with their parenting in the context of powerful socioeconomic forces, there may be a role for social services agencies to play. It would involve assisting parents, both with the material aspects of their hardship and with the qualitative aspects of their parenting, in order to improve family functioning and stave off future child welfare involvement (Frame, 1999). Initial findings from the Early Head Start initiative also show that quality home visiting efforts, linked to center-based child care, can yield significant benefits for mothers and children alike (Love, 2002).

Mothers *and* fathers could benefit in this regard. Rather than encouraging mothers to marry absent fathers (as currently advocated in Washington), efforts to support dads in their roles vis-à-vis children could have developmental impacts over the long haul. These services would not only support fathers' active engagement with their children, but their employment prospects as well. Significant evidence suggests that men's employment is likely to have positive effects on families, offering both material and psychological benefits to partners and children (Mincy and Huang, 2001). Therefore the policies earlier proposed—to increase the minimum wage, the EITC, and expand health care coverage—would have beneficial effects for low-income women *and* men and could well improve outcomes for children.

The policy options offered so far are modest adjustments to the status quo. Child care subsidies currently exist, as do health insurance opportunities; we have a federal minimum wage, and a well-established EITC program. A bold policy initiative fully breaking with past tradition would include focused attention on dramatically reducing child poverty in the United States (Rank, 2004). The United Kingdom has taken steps in this direction, with policy prescriptions to end child poverty within the next two decades (Lewis et al., 2003). Today's policy makers only need look across the Atlantic to see leadership in this area. A more modest step would be to build policy and local programs on the basic tenet that most mothers want to advance their children's well-being. Strengthening motherhood first—in part by raising earned income—would be a fundamentally different starting point.

Finally policy makers and local agencies pushing in good faith to implement family and children's programs might acknowledge what they don't know. This volume has documented the daily lives and tough challenges facing low-income parents. As government metes out doses of tough love and personal responsibility, we all have an obligation to listen carefully and learn from those at the receiving end.

If the rhetoric from Washington and various state capitals continues to express concern for advancing children's well-being and it is going to be matched by effective measures, fresh policy options must be considered. The aggressive stance taken toward low-income families, in particular, must be redirected within a new philosophical framework. The moral emphasis on paid employment and personal responsibility, now dominant in America's political culture (Kaus, 1995), is not likely to recede in the near future. Yet rather than government drawing parents into the marketplace with tangential concern for child well-being, new policy options could significantly raise income and better support parents' divided roles and responsibilities to work and to their children.

References

Acs, G. and Loprest, P. (2001). *Final synthesis report of findings from ASPE's "Leavers" Grants.* Washington, DC: Urban Institute.

Besharov, D. J. (ed.) (2003). *Family and child well-being after welfare reform.* New Brunswick, NJ: Transaction Publishers.

Berrick, J. D. (April, 2005). Marriage, motherhood, and welfare reform. *Social Policy and Society.*

Blank, R. and Haskins, R. (eds.) (2002). *The new world of welfare.* Washington, DC: The Brookings Institute.

Brooks-Gunn, J., Duncan, G. J., and Aber, J. L. (Eds) (1997). *Neighborhood poverty: Context and consequences for children. Vol. I and II.* New York, NY: Russell Sage Foundation.

Chase-Lansdale, P. L., Moffitt, R. A., Lohman, B. J., Cherlin, A. J., Coley, R. L., Pittman, L. D., Roff, J., and Votruba-Drzal, E. (2003). Mothers' transitions from welfare to work and the well-being of preschoolers and adolescents. *Science, 299,* 1548–1552.

Cleveland, G. and Hyatt, D. (2003). Child care subsidies, welfare reforms, and lone mothers. *Industrial Relations, 42,* 251–269.

Coley, R. L., Chase-Lansdale, L. P., and Li-Grining, C. P. (2001). *Child care in the era of welfare reform: Quality, choices, and preferences.* Policy brief 01-4. Northwestern University, Johns Hopkins University: Welfare, Children, and Families: A three-city study.

Connelly, R. and Kimmel, J. (2001). *The effect of child care costs on the labor force participation and welfare recipiency of single mothers.* Working Paper #01-69. Kalamazoo, MI: Upjohn Institute for Employment Research.

Devere, C. (2001). *Welfare reform research: What do we know about those who leave welfare?* Washington, DC: Congressional Research Service.

Duncan, G. J. and Brooks-Gunn, J. (ed.) (1997). *Consequences of growing up poor.* New York, NY: The Russell Sage Foundation.

Epstein, H. (October 12, 2003). Enough to make you sick. *The New York Times.*

Frame, L. (1999). Suitable homes revisited. *Children and Youth Services Review, 21*(9–10), 719–754.

Fried, M. (1998). *Taking time: Parental leave policy and corporate culture.* PA: Temple University Press.

Fuller, B., Kagan, S. L., Capary, G. L., and Gauthier, C. A. (2002a). Welfare reform and child care options for low-income families. *The Future of Children, 12*(1), 97–119.

Fuller, B., Kagan, S.L., and Loeb, S. (2002b). *New lives for poor families?* Berkeley, CA: University of California.

Hochschild, A. (2003). *The second shift.* New York, NY: Penguin Books.

Kaus, M. (1995). *The end of equality.* New York, NY: Basic Books.

Knox, V. W., London, A. S., Scott, E. K., and Blank, S. (2003). *Welfare reform, work, and child care: The role of informal care in the lives of low-income women and children.* New York, NY: MDRC.

Lewis, J., Listar, R., and Millar, J. (2003). *Ending child poverty: What is happening in the U.K.?* http://www.impactresearch.org/documents/endingchild.pdf. Retrieved February 11, 2004.

Lindsey, D. (2003). *The welfare of children.* New York, NY: Oxford University Press.

Loeb, S., Fuller, B., Kagan, S., and Carrol, B. (2004). Child care in poor communities: Early learning effects of type, quality, and stability. *Child Development, 75,* 47–65.

Loprest, P. (1999). *Families who left welfare: Who are they and how are they doing?* Washington, DC: Urban Institute.

Love, J. M. (2002). *Making a difference in the lives of infants and toddlers and their families: The impacts of early head start* (Revised, 2004, Technical Report Vol. 1). Washington DC: United States Department of Health and Human Services.

Lovell, V. (2003). *40-hour work proposal significantly raises mothers' employment standard.* IWPR Publication #D457. Washington, DC: Institute for Women's Policy Research.

Lyter, D. M., Oh, G.-T., and Lovell, V. (2002). *New welfare proposals would require mothers receiving assistance to work more than the average American mom; Child care inadequate.* D445. Washington, DC: Institute for Women's Policy Research.

Martinston, K. and Holcomb, P. A. (2002). *Reforming welfare: Institutional change and challenges.* Occasional Paper. Washington, DC: The Urban Institutive.

McLoyd, V. C., Ceballo, R., and Mangelsdorf, S. C. (1997). The effects of poverty on children's socioemotional development. In S. Greenspan, S. Wieder, and J. Osofsky (eds.), *Handbook of child and adolescent psychiatry, Vol. 1.* New York: J. Wiley and Sons.

Meyers, M. (1998). *Gaining cooperation at the front lines of service delivery: Issues for the implementation of welfare reform.* Albany, NY: Nelson Rockefeller Institute for Government.

Mills, R. J. and Bhandari, S. (September 2002). *Health insurance coverage in the United States: 2002.* Washington, DC: U.S. Census.

Mincy, R. B. and Huang, C.-C. (2001). *"Just get me to the church . . . ": Assessing policies to promote marriage among fragile families.* Working paper #02-02-FF. Princeton University, NJ: Center for Research on Child Well-being.

National Research Council. (2001). *From neurons to neighborhoods: The science of early childhood development.* Washington, DC: National Research Council, Institute of Medicine.

Rank, M. (2004). *One nation, underprivileged.* New York, NY: Oxford University Press.

Rowe, G. (2000). *Welfare rules databook: State TANF policies as of July 1999.* Washington, DC: The Urban Institute.

Shook, K. (1999). Does the loss of welfare income increase the risk of involvement with the child welfare system? *Children and Youth Services Review, 21*(8/9), 693–724.

U.S. Census Bureau. (2003). *Income, poverty, and health insurance coverage in the United States.* http://www.census.gov/hhes.www/income.html.

Weil, A. (2002). *Rethinking work requirements.* Washington, DC: The Urban Institute.

Weil, A. and Finegold, K. (2002). *Welfare reform: The next act.* Washington, DC: The Urban Institute Press.

Wells, K., Guo, S., Shafran, R. D., and Pearlmutter, S. (2003). *Deterioration of child welfare families under conditions of welfare reform.* Paper presented at the Joint Center for Poverty Research Conference: Child Welfare Services Research and Its Policy Implications. Washington, DC.

INDEX